THE ROAD TO MINGULAY

By the same author

The Bad Food Guide
The Beverage Report
The Gullibility Gap

Skye
Hebridean Connection: A View of the Highlands and Islands
Road to the Isles: Travellers in the Hebrides

THE ROAD TO MINGULAY

A VIEW OF THE WESTERN ISLES

DEREK COOPER

WITH PHOTOGRAPHS BY
GUS WYLIE

ROUTLEDGE & KEGAN PAUL
LONDON, BOSTON, MELBOURNE AND HENLEY

First published in 1985
by Routledge & Kegan Paul plc

14 Leicester Square, London WC2H 7PH, England

9 Park Street, Boston, Mass. 02108, USA

464 St Kilda Road, Melbourne,
Victoria 3004, Australia and

Broadway House, Newtown Road,
Henley on Thames, Oxon RG9 1EN, England

Set in Ehrhardt, 10 on 13 point
by Fontwise
and printed in Great Britain
by The Thetford Press Ltd
Thetford, Norfolk

Library of Congress Cataloging in Publication Data

Cooper, Derek.

The road to Mingulay
Includes index.
1. Hebrides (Scotland)--Description and travel.
2. Cooper, Derek. I. Title.
DA880.H4C668   1985   914.11'404858   85–2253
British Library CIP data also available
ISBN 0–7102–0178–8

CONTENTS

CONTENTS

PHOTOGRAPHS BY GUS WYLIE

MUSIC IN THE WIND AND MUSIC IN THE SEA

ULLAPOOL AND STORNOWAY

You have to begin a journey somewhere. This one begins on a scorching hot August day in 1983. The place: Ullapool on the north-west coast of Scotland where the car ferry sails for Stornoway.

To be accurate this journey really began in my mind fifty years ago when I first heard my mother and her aunt talking about the Isle of Lewis and in particular a township called Leurbost where my maternal grandmother Seonaid Maclean was born.

I grew up with a very strange idea of Leurbost. It was where people came from: my grandmother had left it to go into service with a family from the mainland called the Moncrieffs. Major Moncrieff was posted to India and they took Seonaid Maclean with them to look after their young family. On the troopship going to Bombay my grandmother met a soldier in the Gordon Highlanders. In India they married and in India my mother and her brother and sister were born. That was at the end of the 1880s, the decade of the Hebridean crofters' revolt when the hunger for land erupted into civil disobedience.

By the time my grandmother sailed for home with her three children, leaving her husband buried in Murree, her sister, Peggy, had also married and was living in Portree in Skye. It was to Skye that Seonaid went and it was to Skye in the house of her aunt Peggy that my mother was brought up. Aunt Peggy used to go home to Leurbost for a holiday once a year but for my mother home was Portree and she never set foot in Lewis.

My curiosity was certainly not inherited from her. Skye she loved: Lewis she didn't care about at all. Every summer after she married and moved to London she took my brother and myself home to Portree and although you can see Lewis from Skye we never went there.

It seemed to me, lying on the grassy cliffs of Kilmuir looking at this hazy blue ancestral land on the horizon, to be a marvellously romantic place. By this time I had begun to explore the inside of my great aunt's glass-fronted bookcase. It contained, besides the Gaelic Bible, a book by someone called Alasdair Alpin Macgregor MA which had an astonishing effect upon me. *Summer Days Among the Western Isles* it was called. The frontispiece, in colour, was a seascape, misty, evocative – although evocative was not a word which had swum into my twelve-year-old ken.

The painting was by W. M. Frazer RSA and that didn't mean much to me either, but the caption seemed highly poetic. 'Oh, there's music in the wind', it ran, 'and there's music in the sea; And the rapture of the tide is putting love on me.' I looked rapture up in my aunt's dictionary. 'Transport of mind, ecstasy.' My mind was transported all right, to islands which seemed to promise all sorts of delights which had not yet materialised in Skye.

I read on about what the author described as the mystical Isle of Lewis, Blue Barra of the Waves, Vatersay, Eriskay, Pabbay – the names rolled round my tongue and reverberated. Above all others I was deeply impressed with Mingulay – Mingulay of the Birds as the author christened it. 'Words fail utterly', wrote Mr Macgregor, a master of words in my view comparable only with the anonymous literati who wrote the yarns for the *Hotspur* and *Wizard*, 'words fail utterly, when an attempt is made to describe to the reader the grandeur and magnitude of the stupendous mural cliffs of Mingulay and the numberlessness of sea-birds that have their dwelling-place among them.'

Mingulay from that day on had a fascination for me rivalled in later years only by Xanadu and Samarkand and even when I discovered that golden Samarkand had been diminished into an industrial cotton-spinning centre where tungsten and molybdenum were mined, Mingulay retained its three syllables of magic, rolling off my tongue like a breaker foaming on the shore or hands plucking on a harp.

A frequent summer visitor to my great aunt's house was that life-long pacifist Hugh Roberton who had founded the Glasgow Orpheus Choir in 1906. Their version of the *Mingulay Boat Song* stirred all the island blood in my veins.

One day, I thought, Mingulay! And one day too I would go to Leurbost and see if I could trace the house in which my grandmother was born. And so on a bright August morning I am making my way up the west coast to Ullapool bound for Mingulay.

Up in this corner of Scotland there's over a million acres of wilderness with a resident population half that of Potters Bar. Glen after glen without a chimney, miles of coastline without even a fisherman's bothy on the beach, vast moors lying in deafening silence.

Patrick Sellars with his dogs and burning torches turned out men to make way for sheep. The potato famine of the 1840s cleared more families, and for the ambitious youngster getting on today almost inevitably means getting out. There aren't many roads and even in the height of August the peace is hardly disturbed.

I find this one of the most beautiful coastlines in the world. For a lot of the way the road winds and twists past lochans clad with lilies, their shores covered in dog roses, foxgloves and wild irises. The sea fingers into the hills in a Norwegian way and at the head of each fjord there's a small settlement – Gairloch for Loch Gairloch, Poolewe in Loch Ewe and, the hub of the west coast, Ullapool on Loch Broom.

Going north I pass Gruinard Bay, with its sandy beach backed by an imposing range of mountains. The day I drove by, Gruinard Island was receiving its annual inspection. It is now over forty years since a team of Porton Down scientists released billions of anthrax spores on the tiny island. When they came to Gruinard in 1941 their mission was so horrifying and so secret that not a soul living nearby knew what they were about. They brought with them a canister of thick brown liquid containing the acutely infectious *Bacillus anthracis*. Sixty sheep had been ferried across to the uninhabited island barely one mile by one-and-a-half wide. The anthrax bomb was exploded. Predictably the sheep began to die within a week of this first experiment.

More anthrax bombs were exploded, six of them in all; a further deadly canister was dropped from the air. Gruinard has been out of bounds to the public ever since. Some think it will be a hundred years before it is free of contamination; others believe it will take a thousand years for the spores to die.

I stop off to have a coffee with some friends at Mellon Udrigle on the promontory facing the island. They tell me what they feel about this blight which they wake up to see across the bay every morning. A lot of the livestock on the mainland took ill and died. Coincidence, or was it anthrax blowing inland?

There have been no cases recently but once a year the scientists, clad in protective space suits, come to take measurements and year after year the warning notices are repainted. Looking out over the sandy beach to Gruinard one of the villagers shook his head. 'It was a desperate thing to do. Imagine doing that!'

3

It is of course part of the price you have to pay for living in so remote a place. 'Whenever they want a rocket range or somewhere to test their torpedoes or fire their shells they come up here. Getting ready for the Russians!' The old man laughs. Down on the beach the children run and play; the cold war seems a long way off.

Descending down the hillside to Loch Broom, Ullapool lies whitewashed and glinting beside the blue of the sea. Designed by a pupil of the great canal, road and bridge builder Thomas Telford it has wide streets and a style all its own. It's not every town that has a known birthday but Ullapool certainly has. It came about in October 1776 when John Knox, acting on behalf of the British Society for Extending the Fisheries, reached a place which he spelt as Ulapule. 'Whatever be the cause,' wrote Knox, 'the arrival of the herrings is more certain here than in any part of the kingdom and it may be fairly conjectured that a million sterling has in the last fifty years been realised from the water of only seven miles in length.'

As a result of Knox's report a fishing station was built on the shores of Loch Broom two years later. Its function was to pickle this limitless supply of fish in brine but a quirk of nature rendered it a short-term investment. In the early years of the nineteenth century the herring forsook the loch and Ullapool lost its importance.

Sailing packets still ran across the Minch to Stornoway but even that residual importance trickled away when the railways came to the west coast. The line from Glasgow was driven through to Fort William and then along the sound of Arisaig to Mallaig which overnight became the most important mainland fishing port north of Oban. Then to compound Ullapool's backwatered isolation the Dingwall & Skye Railway from the Highland capital of Inverness snaked not north to the shores of Loch Broom but west through Garve and Achnasheen to Loch Carron, Strome Ferry and finally to Kyle of Lochalsh. It was from Mallaig and Kyle that the steamers left for Lewis.

In the 1970s the whole scene changed. The road was improved from Inverness to Ullapool and a new roll-on roll-off ferry was built to run back and forth to Stornoway. That wasn't the only bonus; the second shot in the arm was created by our national contempt for mackerel.

Nobody in the Hebrides ever knowingly ate a mackerel; it was looked upon as a scavenger and when the seas were full of herring and haddock and ling there was no need for mackerel anyway. Mackerel has never been popular in the rest of Britain either and the invention of the fish finger created a whole generation who believe that fish is only fish if it is covered with tartrazine-dyed breadcrumbs the colour of orange football jerseys, and comes in a rock-hard frozen stick.

Elsewhere the mackerel is regarded with greater enthusiasm. For some years now every summer a fleet of Eastern bloc vessels has gathered in Loch Broom to take away the mackerel we still refuse to eat – half a million tons of rusty shipping which will load and process 100,000 tons of mackerel before the season is out. They turn Loch Broom into an annex of the Baltic. The factory ships are fed with mackerel by Scottish purse-seiners which can scoop up a thousand tons of mackerel at a time. There are tales in the Ullapool bars of boats earning up to £50,000 a week.

'We had fished our quota,' an east coast skipper tells me, 'and we'd had a good week. But we still had a hold full of mackerel. When it's there it's hard not to take it. Our skipper went alongside one of the Klondykers to see what he could negotiate. He sold them the lot and he came down the gangway clutching two plastic bags full of notes. £8,000 we got for that catch.'

In a shop I meet an old man who'd once sailed with the Holt line. 'If the fishing goes on like this,' he says, 'by the end of the eighties there won't be any mackerel left at all. They have no thought, no thought at all. Six hundred thousand tons they must have caught last year, if you can believe what they say.'

Paradoxically the lucrative Klondyking trade which now boosts Soviet coffers was started by the Scottish Office. Some thirty years ago the government's Herring Industry Board, which undertook to purchase any fish which couldn't be sold for human consumption, decided that transporting surplus herring to Fraserburgh and Grimsby for reduction into oil and meal was uneconomic. They chartered the *Bras*, a Norwegian factory ship, and stationed it at Ullapool. 'We are often criticised', a senior civil servant wrote, 'for being behind other countries and particularly Norway in our techniques. The chartering of a Norwegian factory ship to show us how should be welcomed.'

The government hoped that when the British fishing industry saw the potential of on-the-spot processing local Klondykers would be built in the best spirit of private enterprise. But there was no interest. By default the initiative passed to the USSR and her satellites.

Bulgarians roll ashore to buy tweed; Russians grab soap and Nescafé. In the Fishermen's Mission on Shore Street there are Bibles in Russian and Bulgarian; next door the Soviet crewmen finger the girlie magazines. The shopkeepers of Ullapool haven't seen such a fistful of money since the herring went away.

Nor perhaps a hotter day than this mid-summer Saturday on which I'm beginning my journey to Mingulay of the Sea Birds and Leurbost of the Uncles and Aunties. On the sea wall holidaymakers loll and bake, licking ice creams; old men cover bald heads with handkerchiefs and roll up their flannels to paddle. The thermometer soars into the eighties; Ullapool is transformed into the San Remo of Ross and Cromarty. Along the harbour front the white-harled, granite-stoned and blue-slated houses dazzle the eye.

An odour of heavy duty cooking oil wafts along the sea front. In Ladysmith Street at Sraid Bean a' Ghobha there's a pall of blue smoke and on the Quay Street Gordon's Fish and Chip Bar is frying frantically. But Ullapool has more to offer than greasy chips. In the Ceilidh Place run by the actor Robert Urquhart and his wife, both devout vegetarians, there are salads to go with the sole, scallops, lobster and haddock.

In the Royal Hotel you can have hot Ullapool prawns in garlic butter, smoked wild salmon and Achiltibuie venison pâté. The Harbour Lights Motel offers agneau grillé and Inchbue Lodge features local oak-smoked chicken. At Morefield Hotel you can have fresh local half lobster coated with seafood, or local smoked mussels skewered on kebabs with green salad and spicy dip.

In August Ullapool surrenders to the visitors. Upstairs in the Tourist Information Office they have a wall of coloured snaps of the houses offering accommodation. B & B is £5.75 this year at Oakworth, Roselea, Sunnybank, Hillview, Seaview, Mo Dachaidh and Scionaiscaig. A dyslexic over-apostrophe'd message on the notice board invites tourists to 'Call in at Macdonald's Supermarket, West Argyle Street for your Groceries, Butcher Meet, Ciggarettes, Slush Drinks, Popcorn, Souvenir's.'

Tied up at the pier are the fishing boats – *Morning Star, Vision, Courage.* Just coming alongside with a catch is *Convallaria V*, an east coast boat based at Banff. There's the *Orcades Viking* from Stromness. Fifteen boats altogether, anchored in rows, most of their crews already ashore and driving home in their Renaults and Passats to Buckie and Peterhead for the weekend. From the pier you can't see all the factory ships, but a fisherman tells me that this year there must be up to thirty of these Klondykers lying at anchor gradually filling their holds with the mackerel we don't want.

I bet they serve mackerel across the loch at the Altnaharrie Inn. I tried to time my arrival in Ullapool so that I could go across there and have some of Gunn Eriksen's smörrebrod for lunch but I was late in leaving Inverness. Dinner, says *The Good Food Guide*, might start with nettle or fennel soup, then succulent Loch Broom crawfish, or baked tomatoes followed by salmon in sour cream, roast pheasant with Norwegian game sauce or roast beef in Madeira.

Maybe I'll get something like that on the *Suilven* tonight. Meanwhile the queue is long at Shiners Diner for beefburger and chips and the evening shadows lengthen on the hills behind the town. The *Suilven* is late arriving and by the time all the cars and lorries are off and ours have been loaded on it's 6.15 when we leave, not the scheduled 5.30.

There's a cool nip to the wind up on deck as the *Suilven* threads her way past the Soviet ships. Most of them have a Rostov registration. Alongside the *Rolf Leonhar* a fishing boat from Peterhead is unloading a catch. Will it be pickled, marinated in wine, tinned in oil, flavoured with dill and pepper-corns? One thing for sure, it won't be battered or breadcrumbed and served with chips.

As we sail up Loch Broom and past Altnaharrie visions of Gunn slicing gravlax, stirring the sorrel soup and perfecting her pavlova with Norse cloudberries make me feel peckish. I descend the companionway to the cafeteria. An unrewarding word that, 'cafeteria', with its image of plastic trays and polystyrene cups.

In the heyday of MacBrayne's each of the steamers that plied in Hebridean waters had a dining saloon. At the appointed hour a steward stalked the decks with a big brass bell, summoning the passengers to tables of starched white linen, highly polished cruets and heavy cutlery. Even in the 1930s none of the food that I remember came out of packets or tins. There always seemed to be Mallaig or Stornoway kippers for high tea and at midday there would be piping hot broth, roast mutton and some substantial pudding.

Today the *Suilven* is a floating extension of Ullapool's chip-strewn littoral. I pick up my tray and join the queue. A choice of pie, beans and chips; fried fish served with canned mixed vegetables and chips; beefburger and chips; cold meat and salad. On the counter are buns, pancakes, shortbread and assorted biscuits. A cuisine rich not in imagination but in carbohydrates.

I settle for the fish and chips. Considering we are on the Minch in waters full of fresh fish it seems a sensible choice. They come from the galley covered with breadcrumbs. Maybe if they weren't I would get more taste of the sea and less of the fat in which the fish was fried.

At the next table a party of French people are toying with sausage, egg, beans and chips. What a lost opportunity here to introduce visitors crossing to the Outer Isles for the first time to a real taste of Scotland, not this sub-standard stuff out of the deep-freeze and catering packs. There's no herring on the menu, no mackerel, no salmon, no trout, no prawns, nothing that remotely reflects the raw materials of the region.

For lunch I note there was mince or stewing steak followed by jelly and fruit, ice cream and fruit or apple crumble and custard. A menu reminiscent of school dinners. On deck a couple are eating sandwiches and taking tea from a Thermos. They are from Stornoway and have been visiting relations in Inverness. It's not that they don't like the food in the cafeteria, they say, they think the prices are too high. 'Sixteen pence for a cup of tea,' says the wife, 'terrible isn't it?' I thought the tea was the best thing about my supper. It was hot and not at all bad. The disposable cup wasn't noticeably gracious but it went well with the empty Coke tins and abandoned crisp packets that covered the tables.

In the forward lounge there is a television set on the bulkhead tuned to ITV. The ship is packed with people, every seat is taken. There is some mindless quiz programme which seems to be taking place on a canal longboat in homage to the holiday season. 'What', says the quizmaster, 'was the name of the radio programme on which Cliff Michelmore met Jean Metcalfe? No, I can't help you on this one . . . five more seconds. . . .' Lucky the passengers who have fallen asleep, although come to think of it actually being able to drop off presents a problem – with TV in the forward lounge, taped music in the other one, the only place remotely peaceful is the cafeteria.

I retire there with a green cloth-covered book which back in 1949 became the main topic of conversation in Stornoway for over a year. It was written by the same Alasdair Alpin Macgregor who had before the war captured my imagination with his enraptured view of the Western Isles. But this bilious book, published by Robert Hale in their County Series, revealed Alasdair as not the gentle poet of the islands but their scourge and almost neurotically unbalanced critic. It was as if an innocent wide-eyed lamb had suddenly turned into a mad dog. Every aspect of the islands which he had once keened and mooned over was savaged. It was a sad episode in his life and the story of how it happened is a sad one too.

Alasdair was born in 1899, the son of an eccentric Edinburgh figure, Colonel John Macgregor. 'My mother', said Alasdair on the second occasion I met him, 'was a streetwalker.' A great man for one-liners was Alasdair; at one time he had been President of the League for the Prohibition of Cruel Sports. A vegetarian, teetotaller and uncompromising anti-vivisectionist, he had a profound feeling for the rights of the individual. We were having dinner in his house in Upper Cheyne Row one evening in 1969 when he told me how the week before he had publicly silenced a magistrate in Hampshire. Alasdair, a passionate humanist, had been appearing as a witness in some minor traffic incident and arrived early on the scene to hear a magistrate hectoring a witness who refused to take the oath.

'The man', said Alasdair, 'wished to affirm. "Why do you refuse to take the oath?" said the magistrate. Well I wasn't going to put up with that. I stood up in the court and reminded him that it was the right of every citizen to affirm without being cross-examined as to their motives in so doing. Consternation! But I wasn't having it. "I want a solemn promise from you", I said to the magistrate, "that you will never again hector and bully a witness in this disgraceful fashion." Well of course the wretched man was flustered, there was nothing he could say. But by golly that taught him a lesson!'

Alasdair, then, was made of stern stuff but when it came to his beloved Hebrides he melted at the knees, his heart became as soft as marshmallow and his sentences quivered sensitively like so much jelly. He carved out a small and rewarding niche for himself writing undemandingly sentimental pieces for the *Scotsman, Glasgow Herald, Oban Times, Edinburgh Evening News, Scottish Country Life,* and many another journal about the Hebridean islands. When he began to publish these articles in book form he found it necessary to append a glossary so that the uninitiated might fully understand his drift. His vocabulary was in its way as esoteric as Spenser's in *The Faerie Queene.*

Forby, he wrote when he meant besides, *fornent* when he meant in front of. *Erst* was formerly and *yonter* meant further. In this spurious language further confused with Celtic Revival inversions and fey subjunctives ('Fain would I tell you . . . well repaid would I be') Alasdair spun his tales of yore and enrobed them in the purplest of prose.

At times he unconsciously parodied himself and his picturesque perorations were always worth treasuring. 'Twilight it is,' he wrote at the end of *Over the Sea to Skye or Ramblings in an Elfin Isle,* 'and the day is done. And into the rest-seeking soul steals the peace that is begotten of eventide and a sense of the omnipresence and omnipotence of the Supreme Artist who designed this magic scene and whose wondrous works we can never fathom.'

Alasdair, with his Patience MacStrong platitudes and his effortless weaving of the MacTrite, was ripe for parody and it fell to a fellow author, Compton Mackenzie, to perform the surgery. It was done cruelly and without anaesthetic. By then Alasdair rather regarded himself as the official chronicler of the Hebrides. *Behold the Hebrides, Summer Days Among the*

Western Isles, Searching the Hebrides with a Camera and *The Haunted Isles* had presented a highly glamourised portrait of the natives: simple, lovable, wreathed in myth and legend, eternally engaged in the telling of romantic tales and the singing of songs over the peat-fire flame.

Mackenzie had already had a dig at Alasdair in 1936 when he wrote in John Lorne Campbell's *The Book of Barra* (Routledge, 1936) of 'the ill-told tales of dubious truth and incontestable monotony with which the topographer of today is inclined to hide as with a flour-thickened gravy the stringy fare he offered.' But it was his creation of the fictional character of Hamish Hamilton Mackay which stung Alasdair to the heart. By then he and Compton Mackenzie were established in the public eye as the two most authoritative writers on Hebridean matters. And now Alasdair had been, as it were, professionally assassinated.

By one of those grim ironies which the Great Author permits himself it was Mackenzie's hopeless struggle to meet his literary deadlines that gave Alasdair his chance to strike back and, as he thought, re-establish his supremacy in matters Hebridean. Hale approached Mackenzie to write the volume about the Western Isles in the anodyne County Books series. Mackenzie was too bogged down in novels to do it and it was then that Hale turned to Alasdair. It was like putting a sawn-off shot gun in the hands of a spurned lover. Alasdair fired indiscriminately from the hip and the shot peppered the whole archipelago from the Butt of Lewis to Barra – particularly Barra where Catholic Mackenzie had made his home and whose causes he so vigorously espoused.

In 350 pages of indiscriminate vilification he diminished the people, accused them of depravity, laziness, lack of cleanliness, immorality, fecklessness, greediness and drunkenness. It was a hysterical book and it undoubtedly did a great deal of harm – perhaps even more harm than Alasdair's earlier works which had painted the islands as a haunt of simple-minded but warm-hearted peasants.

The people of Lewis were quick to reply. The Lewis Association, which had been formed in 1943 to promote the development of the island, prepared a 14,000-word rebuttal of *The Western Isles* and the readers of the *Stornoway Gazette* had a grand and self-righteous time. 'Sir,' wrote an indignant reader, 'our Public Enemy No. 1 is not Stalin it is Alasdair Alpin MacGregor!' As the *Gazette* put it: '*The Western Isles* will give pain and offence to thousands of decent, honest, law-abiding Isles folk in all parts of the world and will make it difficult for young men to find work and for young women to gain respect. It will leave a train of slander and suspicion wherever it is read and it will make the work of all genuine reformers and friends of the islands difficult for years to come.'

What particularly angered the *Gazette* was the way in which Alasdair had based much of his criticism on local court cases reported verbatim in the paper. 'How can we discuss our intimate affairs with any freedom', it asked, 'if we are made to feel that Mr MacGregor sits in Chelsea, a literary peeping Tom sniffing out whatever scandal his nose can lead him to secure in the knowledge that a community cannot sue for damages and that smut and slander pay?'

There was humour as well as outrage in the correspondence columns and I have a strong suspicion that Compton Mackenzie himself, or maybe Hamish Hamilton Mackay, may well have written this letter which appeared on 23 December 1949 and was signed 'One of the Peasants':

Sad, sad is the heart of me when I hear that a man and the name that is on him is MacGregor, has been writing about the people in the islands and putting hard words in his book about the customs and doings of the people.

Surely the voice of them that tread lightly on the westering wind will be seeping through Chelsea and into the heart of him and surely the spirits of his ancestors will be putting a dread on him.

Many are the days that have died since Mr. MacGregor last put his foot somewhere 'on the bourne of the terrestrial sunset or the threshold of Tir Nan Og' and will he be no more coming to Lamishadder which is 'the name they put on the place of the stepping stones when in time of summer the warm air is scented with crimson clover and sheaves of meadow sweet'

I am thinking that he will not be coming again and it is the seabirds that will be crying with mournful voices and the waves that will be beating themselves on the primeval rocks in sorrow.

Ah well, it is the shillings of people like us that have been lining the pockets of the great people like Mr. MacGregor since the beginning of time and I am sure that it is thankful we should be that he still allows Macbrayne's steamers to call so that everyone can leave this bad, bad place and go to the great cities to be purified.

The book hurt. Despite official calls for the publishers to withdraw it from circulation it continued in print and I don't think John Lorne Campbell of Canna exaggerated when he said in 1975 (*The Scots Magazine*, September 1975):

The Western Isles represented a savage bite by MacGregor at the hand which had fed him. It was meant to do harm to the Islands, and it did do harm; one can still trace its influence today in the contemptuous attitude towards the Isles that is clearly felt in circles in institutions like the Scottish Office or the Scottish Transport Group.

Alasdair remained unrepentant, but he was careful never to set foot in the Western Isles again. Seventeen years after his great tirade appeared he wrote another book of reminiscences about his earlier wanderings in the west and there was a small hint of an apology. He quoted Cowper's line 'England with all thy faults, I love thee still!' and added: 'That is just how I feel about the Hebrides. We can deplore without necessarily sacrificing affection. We can, in dreams, behold them, memorably and felicitously, and with a secret yearning, maybe with a sob at the heart and a moistening of the eye, as we surrender to the enchantment.' Even at the end soft-centred Hamish Hamilton Mackay lived on.

I must remember his fate. No biting of hands on this trip. Up on deck Lewis looms large and the Eye peninsula, a low hostile looking shore. Ahead are the lights of the Burgh of Stornoway.

It's nearly ten before we tie up. I make straight for Mrs John Macarthur's guesthouse in St James Street, highly commended to me by a Lewis friend in Portree. 'Spotlessly clean,' she said, 'you couldn't do better.'

'Can I get you a pot of tea?' says Mrs Macarthur when I come down after a wash. There are five-star hotels where you wouldn't get a cup of tea at this hour let alone what Mrs Macarthur appears with – a tray full of flowered china, hot sausage rolls, pancakes lathered with crowdie, homemade shortbread. The tea is boiling hot. I have come home.

2

A POPULATION SKILLED IN EPISTEMOLOGY

STORNOWAY TO LEURBOST

There is no Sunday anywhere in the world like the Sunday of Stornoway. Nor indeed is there religious observance elsewhere on such an impressive and enthusiastic scale. Before the day is out three thousand worshippers will have passed into the Free Church in Kenneth Street.

It will not be possible today to play golf or tennis; neither will you be able to swim or dance or enter any shop. At the lower end of the town the children's swings are in chains. And if the prospect of a day of enforced rest makes you restless then neither will it be possible to leave the island. The next plane will not take off until Monday and the *Suilven* will remain tied up until Monday too.

It is a mistaken notion that this Biblically uncompromising attitude to the Sabbath stretches back into the early days of the Free Church. The full rigours of the Stornoway Sunday were not enacted until the 1930s. Until then the steamer left for Kyle and Mallaig on Saturday night. As the result of pressure from the Free Church and the collection of 10,000 signatures, MacBrayne's altered the sailing to 0030 on Monday morning. Later in the 1960s the Church was to have a complete victory on Sunday flying and in the 1970s land at Arnish was only leased by the Stornoway Trust to Fred Olsen Ltd on condition that there was no Sunday working in the fabrication yard.

Lewis has a population skilled in epistemology and the Bible satisfactorily furnishes answers for all occasions. At the time of my visit to Lewis the House of Commons had once again rejected by a large majority the restoration of capital punishment. I was told on several occasions that the official policy of the Free Church was contained in Genesis, chapter nine: 'whoso sheddeth man's blood by man shall his blood be shed.' But closer inquiry revealed that the Church was in a state of disarray on this subject. The view of the uncompromising majority was succinctly put by the MP for the Western Isles, himself a member of the Free Church, Donald Stewart.

He told the *West Highland Free Press* that he was in favour of hanging for all categories of murder: 'I think that is the punishment laid down on religious grounds. I think life is so precious that the taking of it should mean that penalty.' But Mr Stewart was mistaken in believing that his Church had pronounced officially on the matter. The *Monthly Record* of the Free Church, which represents the liberal wing, questioned the mandate given by the Bible:

> It is argued, for example, that the Mosaic law supported capital punishment. Of course it did. But if we apply Moses *simpliciter* we must bring back hanging not only for murder but also for blasphemy, adultery, disobedience to parents, dealing in the occult, breaking the Sabbath and homosexuality. Do we seriously want to reinstate all this?

There is a wild fringe of the Church in Lewis which would indeed welcome the most rigid application of Jehovah's wrath on all offences against the law of Moses, but Professor Donald Macleod, Principal of the Free Church, was troubled by the draconian image which the Church presented to the public. 'During the public debate on hanging,' he wrote, 'we somehow managed to convey to the media the notion that an official and unanimous decision had been taken to ask our people to write to their MPs urging them to support the restoration of the death penalty.' He reckoned that although 60 per cent of Free Church members might welcome its return, 40 per cent were perhaps opposed to hanging.

If there was debate in the Free Church, the Free Presbyterian Church was in no doubt at all. Their religion and morals committee reaffirmed its usual unforgiving attitude to unjust murder: 'the nation incurs guilt when the powers-that-be refuse to exercise their God-given duty of the power of the sword in avenging the evildoer.'

I recall staying with a Free Church couple when a particularly brutal murder was headline news in the papers. A man was helping the police with their enquiries after a series of sexually assaulted corpses had been found and most of the country had already got him in the dock.

'When a person admits to his guilt,' said the husband, 'what's the point? He's no use to man or beast!'

'You don't believe in repentance or redemption?'

'No. Get rid of him.'

'You don't believe. . . .'

'I don't believe in keeping him on the surface of the earth at all. Get him under the ground!'

His wife nods her head supportively and says we live in terrible times. I appeal to her: surely the Bible teaches hope and forgiveness?

'Well,' says her husband looking at me fiercely, 'my Bible teaches me an eye for an eye and a tooth for a tooth.'

'But the New Testament. . . .'

'. . . and the Shorter Catechism teaches thou shalt not kill. It's the sixth commandment. Isn't it the sixth?'

I clutch at rational straws. 'But if the commandment says thou shalt not kill you can't really *hang* a man?'

The old man points at the light bulb in the ceiling and says gnomically: 'It's like this electricity. It goes round in a circle, so where's the end to it? I can't see the point of keeping people alive who admit they have murdered eight or nine people.'

And we leave it there while the kettle boils.

Both the Church of Scotland and the Roman Catholic church came out against hanging, which left the Free Churches publicly identified with the forces of reaction. It is a stance which many would see not as reactionary at all but divinely inspired. Their strenuous political and religious battle to keep the Sabbath holy is part of a larger campaign to defend the Bible and particularly the Old Testament to its very last and literal word.

In Stornoway I became involved in a discussion on this topic with a persuasive lady who was able to cite Biblical authority not only for the death penalty but for Hitler's policy of genocide against the Jews. I have forgotten in the heat of the moment which particular bits of the Old Testament she dredged up to support her views but she left no doubt in my mind that the gas chambers of Belsen were divinely sanctioned. 'They took His life,' she said, 'and it is written, an eye for an eye and a tooth for a tooth. Don't you read your Bible? It's all written there plainly and you would be better off observing the Sabbath yourself as your relatives do!'

Although even in Stornoway the observance of the Lord's Day is not as total as it was, at eight in the morning under a shining sun nobody apart from myself and a tourist walking a dog is abroad. The town clock says it's five past five.

By nine I have seen only three cars; on Sunday Stornoway comes slowly to life. I turn into Cromwell Street. You might expect to find a Cromwell Street in Huntingdon where the Protector was born, but in this Hebridean fishing port which has always valued its freedom and independence it's surely a bit strange?

Long before Sir James Matheson built the incongruously Tudor Lews

Castle in the 1840s there was an earlier stronghold poised on the shore; in 1882 it was finally rubbled and re-emerged in the commercial guise of the Maritime Office of No. 1 Wharf. It was this fortress, originally built in the thirteenth century by the Nicolsons and then seized by the Macleods, which became a symbol of supremacy. It was besieged by the Earl of Huntly in 1506, bombarded by the artillery of the Duke of Argyll in 1554, taken by the Mackenzies of Kintail in 1610 and it subsequently changed hands with the frequency with which uninhabited islands and sporting estates change hands today.

Cromwell, destined to bequeath his name to the main shopping street (how sad to be commemorated only by the Co-op and Woolworth's), sent a small garrison to Lewis in the thick of the Civil War to seize the castle. They battered it down and occupied what was left but got short shrift, being massacred in one bloodstained night by the Macleods – or so the legend goes.

I retail these events only to remind myself that Stornoway, a very stolid-looking town, has had a hectic and squally past. Indeed when Victoria came to the throne it had been a burgh-of-barony for over 250 years and was fairly flourishing. It had a saw mill, a rope works, a mill for carding wool, a corn mill, an extensive distillery, all, as a contemporary report put it 'constructed in a style not much inferior to the best buildings of their class in Scotland'. There were four inns and a score of dram shops – essential in a port which was the hub for 1,500 fishing boats. It was the rich fishings of Lewis that nearly put an end to the natives of the island in the time of James VI who might be said to have invented the slogan 'Scotland for the Lowlanders'.

Always chronically short of money he commissioned his cousin to gather together a bunch of hooligans and chancers known as the Fife Adventurers to liberate Lewis and such other parts of the Hebrides as they might wish using whatever 'slaughter, mutilation, fyre-raising or utheris inconvenieities' they might deem necessary to crush and extirpate the inhabitants. Six hundred colonists landed on the shores of Lewis in November 1598 and began building themselves a town. They found the terrain inhospitable and the natives hostile. Eventually they were thrashed and sent packing by the Macleods. When they tried to re-establish themselves in 1605 and again in 1609 they met the same fate and never came back. The policy of supplanting the locals with Lowlanders and even English settlers was a dismal failure.

A strong smell of fish oil surrounds the piers and a hum of electric motors emanates from Rolf-Olsen (Stornoway) Ltd, latter-day Norse invaders. Herring and Fish Processors it says, Curers, Smokers, Cold Storage, Ice

Suppliers. By 9.30 the town is humming too. I have seen ten people. Two of them are looking at the *Suilven* tied up tidily alongside the dock – that's humming as well.

It's warm in the sun; overhead the gulls dip and cry. One of them alights on the beach on the far side of the road opposite the Tourist Office. I wander over. It is the kind of beach which would get a Highly Commended in any national Dirty Foreshore contest. The gull pecks fitfully at a milk carton and eyes the other flotsam of the fast-food age. There's a polypropylene tray that once held chips or maybe a Bar-B-Q'd chicken wing. I note a carefully screw-topped Schweppes orange drink bottle that is doomed to go on floating back and forth on the tide until someone smashes it. There's a length of rubber cable, an old armchair with the stuffing hanging out, some blue plastic fish boxes, bits of nylon rope and netting, plastic bags, rubber tyres, a segment of a plywood and foam sofa – nothing really that two lads and a van couldn't whisk up to the rubbish dump in half an hour.

The gull flies off disappointed and I turn back to Mary Macarthur's guest house in James Street. Already at the breakfast table are two fellow guests. She is a GP and her husband, a consultant in nephritis, is doing a locum at the hospital. There's grapefruit juice, porridge, homemade oatcakes, sausage, bacon, egg, black pudding and white pudding, fried tomatoes, tea, toast and marmalade – the sort of breakfast that pre-empts the need for lunch.

When they first came, the doctors had arrived, as I had, on a Saturday night and on the Sunday found it difficult to get anything to eat. Now, said Mrs GP, they were into the way of things, eating in other people's houses. 'It's my husband's birthday today and Mrs Macarthur is preparing a dinner for us.'

Getting a drink in the town on a Sunday is not altogether impossible. If you are a bona fide resident in one of the hotels or if you go for a meal you can have an alcoholic drink with it. Young people, I had heard, go out on Sundays to the RAF Club. There are ways and means. 'If you're known,' a Stornowegian on the *Suilven* told me, 'you would have no trouble slipping in somewhere and getting a pint.' Once there had been a pub which charged you 30p to come in through the back door on the Sabbath, then another followed suit, 'but the Church objected and the brewers stepped in and put a stop to it.'

After breakfast I take a turn into the woodlands that surround the castle. It must be the finest park, for all I know the only one, in the Highlands and

Islands and all the more unexpected in Lewis which is almost entirely treeless.

Although the Western Isles is the heartland of the Gaelic language Stornoway itself has always been a very English town. Incomers dominate the scene and Gaelic fights a rearguard action in offices and shops. A further erosion is on the way. £40 million is to be spent on extending the runway at Stornoway airport and erecting a NATO base. Protest is vociferous, particularly from those who have come to the Hebrides to escape from the pressures of life down south. Suddenly, or so they feel, they find themselves in a potential nuclear target zone. The Ministry of Defence revealed its plans for Stornoway in 1979 and within a short space of time 43,000 signatures had been put on a petition to the Secretary of State for Scotland. Keep NATO Out is now as well-organised a campaign as the one mounted in Orkney a few years ago to prevent prospecting for uranium. Never before have the islands flexed their muscles so independently.

The Western Isles had a brush with the nuclear age when the EEC started investigating how its member states could bury their nuclear rubbish. In 1979 the Environmental Secretary revealed that there were six possible sites in the Western Isles. As a result HAND (Hebrides Against Nuclear Dumping) was formed and that battle is running concurrently with the anti-NATO campaign.

The NATO base, if and when it is built, will be used initially by Buccaneer, Phantom and Tornado fighter aircraft and Stornoway will become a major staging post for service personnel and military reinforcements travelling to Europe. It has been worked out that up to 400 RAF men and their families will descend on Lewis. Even more alarmingly, some observers believe that Stornoway is already a fall-back base for nuclear bombers and for the storage of nuclear weapons. The denials are fierce but in the islands they are used to official disclaimers followed by the gradual encroachment of the military.

There is fighting talk. Brian Wilson, the Labour party candidate at the forthcoming General Election, describes the military installations which already litter the western seaboard. There is the American Polaris/Poseidon base at Holy Loch, the British Polaris base at Faslane, the nuclear armament depot at Coulport, the nuclear warhead store at Glen Douglas, the US Navy nuclear weapons store at Macrihanish.

'These instalments', he writes, 'represent an obscene and inconceivably expensive over-reaction to the possibility of nuclear war.' The massive military presence in Stornoway, it's generally agreed, will make life intolerable. No wonder the feeling is growing that Whitehall regards the Western Isles as expendable; an area with such a small population that if it were 'wasted' then statistically it wouldn't really matter. 'It is wholly conceivable', claims my old friend Frank Thompson, who has written more than most about the Hebrides, 'that the intention of the government is, finally, to create conditions which will cause a movement of the existing population of the islands, to leave vast empty spaces to be used as war-game areas for NATO and other forces.'

Perhaps there's not all that much time left for me to find my roots. My first step is to call on Zena Nicoll. She is the first of many cousins I will meet and over tea and biscuits she gives me a long list of descendants and close relatives of my grandmother . . . Mackenzies, MacIvers and Macleods. Zena teaches History at the Nicolson Institute and lives in Jamieson Drive. It's very English, this part of Stornoway. There is a profusion of trees in the gardens, honeysuckle climbs up walls, roses swirl round the bay windows, linen blinds are half pulled down as a tribute to the Sabbath. Neat granite walls, green gates and a general air of house-proudness and modest prosperity is manifested. You could be in the residential area of Stirling, Dunkeld or Inverness.

Zena, or to be more semantically accurate Xina, is short for Alexina which itself is a variation of Alexander. This Gaelic tradition of giving boys' names to girls may seem like a bit of macho chauvinism – relegating a woman to the role of failed man. But this isn't the case. The Angusinas, Dolinas, Alinas, and Wilinas owe their names to the custom of naming a first grandchild after its grandfather; if that first grandchild is a girl then she is still given the grandfather's name but suitably feminised. Now that television has lent glamour to Marilyns, Traceys, Karens and Dawns the 'inas' are a disappearing sorority. My cousin Zena may be the last in a long line; meanwhile she is a fount of knowledge about the family. We start with my mother's aunt.

'You call her Aunt Maggie don't you? Well here she was known as Peggie M'Aonghus, Peggie the daughter of Angus. Aonghus was your grand-mother's father. Your grandmother was Seonaid or Janet.'

'And my wife is a Janet.'

'So that's the name continued. Well they were crofting, fishing people. There was Caitriona who still has two daughters living in Leurbost, Seonag and Seonaid. There was Kate who had Johnnie and Kenneth, they're still living. There was Iain, that's the one son I knew of and his grandchildren are still living in Leurbost. Your grandmother and my grandmother were full cousins. You and my father would be second cousins and so it goes.'

We talk about my great aunt Peggy who came home from Skye at the end of her life. 'I remember her best,' says Zena, 'when she came to live with her sister Mary Ann after she had her leg amputated and she died here. My childhood friend was Mary Ann's daughter; she died when her first child was born. Looking at you I can see the family resemblance.'

Zena tells me about Mary Ann and her gift for making ends meet. 'She was so thrifty she could make clothes out of nothing and food out of nothing. The men, you see, used to go off fishing round Skye; it was the women who worked the croft, the men were away all the time.' But from these crofts there came men of learning. 'My uncle went to university; in that generation quite a number of them went but three of them in our family died of TB. My uncle was the only surviving son and every effort was made to educate him. He became a minister.'

Zena tells me that my closest cousin is not in Leurbost at all but right in the thick of things in Stornoway – he is Norman Mackenzie. That night I have dinner with Norman in the Caberfeidh Hotel where he is treated with courtesy and consideration. But then he ought to be, he owns it. He also owns the seventy-room Seaforth Hotel opposite Mrs Macarthur's guest-house in James Street. He is a man of substance. There are, I gather, other entrepreneurial activities – a quarry, a construction company or maybe two, haulage interests.

We are the same age; he has what I have come to recognise as the pyknic Lewis face and in him I see close resemblances to other members of the family in Skye. Over turkey broth and locally smoked salmon we exchange a lifetime of recollections. Our paths have never crossed before but by two in the morning we are old friends, and our kinship has been charted to the outermost branches of the family tree.

'It's a pity', says Norman, 'my father Murdo isn't here, he knows the whole story of the family. Caitriona, his mother, was the sister of your auntie Peggy and your grandmother Jessie or Seonaid. My father and your mother were first cousins so we are second cousins. Tomorrow you must go to Leurbost. You'll find my father's sisters there – Seonaid Macleod and Seonag Macsween and plenty more cousins I'm sure.'

The road to Leurbost runs over Arnish moor and after the sycamores, horse chestnuts, Monterey cypresses, sugar maples and the great hills of rhododendrons surrounding Lews Castle, this is a cheerless landscape. Where the road turns off to the west coast a garage rises out of the ground with petrol pumps and asbestos roofs. It is a bus depot too, a local centre for the purchase of Datsun cars and no doubt cans of Coca Cola, fan belts, Mars bars and the consumables of the motoring age.

I turn off left for Leurbost. At the entrance to the township are six modern bungalows assembled from kits constructed on the mainland. They are characterless, pebble-dashed and trim. Here a carriage lamp, there a rockery, curtains are ruched, they give promise of tubular chimes in the hall. They are as appropriate in Leurbost as they would be in Lowestoft or Llangollen.

But the house I'm going to is very much part of the scenery; the walls are whitewashed and the roof is corrugated iron painted a bright red. Here lives Seonaid, who looks so much like my mother that it is a physical shock when she opens her arms to greet me. A perfect stranger and yet instantly someone whom I feel I've known all my life. I follow her into the neat small house. Seonaid is in her mid-eighties. 'You'll take a cup of tea,' she says and goes to put the kettle on. Then as it boils she looks at me.

'After all these years, just fancy. Wait till I show you my mother's photo,' and she finds an old faded picture which is almost an identikit of my grandmother's portrait done at the turn of the century. 'I'm called after your mother. Your mother is my auntie. This picture of my mother was done in Argyle Street in Glasgow. I was in service there. You know your grandfather's croft and my grandfather's croft went to some people called Mackinnon. I was a Mackenzie.' Seonaid pours our tea and I ask her what she remembers of her early life.

'Most of the girls, like me, went into service or nursing, the boys went to the shipyards or to sea. In those days we grew corn and potatoes and vegetables. There's not one croft worked now. All you see is, what do you call that stuff, rushes?'

More relatives arrive, more tea is poured. Photographs are produced and kinships are explored. I am sent down the road to see Calum Maclean who lives in a house perched above the loch. Half his life has been spent at sea as a ship's quartermaster. He has the huge fists of a man used to handling wire hawsers. 'I'm a cousin too,' he says, 'your granny was my great aunt, my father and auntie Peggy were first cousins.'

Calum tells me there are sixty crofts in Leurbost, 'but I can't say they're being worked, all of them.' His own garden is full of vegetables and flowers. Calum is retired with ample time on his hands to grow things but there's no point in having a boat: 'The bay used to be full of fish but there's nothing now. We'll take a turn down to the cemetery if you like but you ought to see the old family house, what's left of it, first.'

What's left of 55 Leurbost is no more than a mound of stones. Neighbours come out and claim remote familial ties. We all look at the pile of rubble where my grandmother was born. Could my people have lived in such primitive and deprived conditions? 'Well you're not seeing it at its best,' says Calum, 'it would have been thatched and more trim.' Half the stones have been taken away to build a road; someone is using the remaining end as a store for fleeces. My roots are far from imposing.

'At the back there', says Calum, pointing, 'is part of another old black house, it was one of the Macraes that was there – they were also members of the family.'

'And the house with the tin roof?' I point to another tumble-down dwelling.

'That was where Ma Thompson your auntie lived with her sister Mary Ann. It was thatched too before the iron roof. It was lived in until fifteen years ago.'

I go back and stand inside the derelict tumbled walls of 55 Leurbost. I find it impossible to visualise what kind of life could have gone on inside that small bothy a hundred years ago. A home it must have been, but you could not describe it as a house. That word conjures up solid walls, windows, fireplaces, a staircase, rooms with floors. A dwelling is a better word. Stones piled one on the other to make a reach-me-down shelter. At one end the family, at the other end cattle; in the middle of the earth floor a peat fire and in the thatch above a hole to let the smoke out. There are descriptions enough of such hovels; they left an indelible impression on Victorian travellers.

William Rea, arriving in 1890 to take up a post as a schoolmaster at Garrynamonie in South Uist, recalled the shock which he, a young man from Birmingham, felt when he first stepped ashore: 'After a mile or so searching the road right and left for dwelling houses, and only seeing in the fast failing light what I took to be large isolated heaps of stones or earth, I burst out: "But where are the houses?" Pointing to one of the black-looking heaps I had noticed, my companion replied, "These are the houses!"'

There was no shortage of stones and improvisation secured the rest. Poles raised and lashed across the top of the walls and covered with turves, heather and moss made the roof. The chimney was a herring barrel with the end knocked out. Box beds in the wall, a few stools, and a table knocked together from driftwood.

Perhaps my grandmother's parents had acquired a little money. In that case the floor might have been raised on boards instead of being earth.

There could have been a window made of glass, perhaps furniture brought in from Glasgow, a dresser, a rocking chair, an Ansonia eight-day clock on the wall. I can only surmise about all this. There's no one who really remembers.

Was it like the house Joseph and Elizabeth Pennell described on their depressing journey to the Hebrides in 1888? At Tarbert, they saw a hut 'burrowed out like a rabbit-hole, its thatched roof set upon the grass'. The Pennells had been struck by the marked difference in life style between the estate owners and their tenants:

> Just below in the loch Lady Scott's steam-yacht came and went. Beyond, her deer forest, a range of black mountains, stretched for miles. Within sight and low on the water were the thick woods, in the heart of which stands her shooting-lodge. The contrast gave the last bitter touch to the condition of the people. They starve on tiny crofts, their only homes; their landlord holds broad acres as playground for a few short weeks.

On Harris, on the Sunday they were there, the Pennells passed a cabin with peat smoke seeping through the thatched roof:

> As we drew near we heard the voice of someone reading aloud. Now it was silenced, and a tall old man in his shirt-sleeves came to the door with an open Bible in his hands. Within, on the left was the dwelling-room of the household; on the right, the stable, cattle and the family share the only entrance. Into the room, through a single pane of glass, one ray of daylight fell across the Rembrandt-like shadows. On the mud floor, at the far end, a fire of peat burned with a dull red glow and its thick, choking smoke curled in clouds about the rafters and softened the shadows. We could just make out the figures of two women crouching by the fire, the curtained bed in the corner, the spinning wheel opposite. Until you see it for yourself, you could not believe that in our nineteenth-century men still live like this.

Something like that, I suppose, was the way they lived in Leurbost; a dark, damp and unhealthy life. Without proper sanitation typhoid was endemic and tuberculosis as common as the common cold. Dr John Morrison of Ness tells me that when he went to practice in his native Lewis in the early 1930s practically every home still had a wooden shed beside it 'for the tubercular member of the family'.

Ill-nourished, ill-housed and with little or no expectations, that was the way of things when my grandmother was born in 55 Leurbost. There were 113 families living in the township then, along with an unspecified number of paupers. So overcrowded was that thin strip of land on the shores of Loch Leurbost with families who had been evicted from other parts to extend sheep farms and create deer forests, that it was difficult to scratch a living.

The full extent of the misery and degradation the islands had sunk into was detailed in what is probably the most remarkable report since the Domesday Book. In 1882 Gladstone appointed a Commission to enquire into the conditions of the crofters and landless cottars of the Highlands and Islands. The evidence they collected and published in 1884 so aroused the conscience of the nation that two years later a Crofters Act was passed which went some way to redressing the most pressing of their grievances.

The Commissioners finished taking evidence in Skye on Thursday 24 May 1883 and they arrived in Castlebay in Barra on Saturday. During the next fifteen working days they received evidence and interrogated witnesses in Lochboisdale, Benbecula, North Uist, Harris, St Kilda and Lewis. Over a third of a million words of evidence was heard. Each community with a grievance elected a spokesman to put their case before the committee. Factors appeared too, merchants, fish curers, schoolmasters, doctors, ministers and priests.

The Commissioners were led by Lord Napier and Ettrick, who owned 7,000 acres of the most valuable land in Selkirk, among them the famous Traquair and Thirlestane estates. At his right hand was Sir Kenneth Mackenzie of Ross and Cromarty, proprietor of 400,000 acres. Then there was another kenspeckled member of the landowning oligarchy, Donald Cameron of Lochiel, who possessed 100,000 acres. These three men, according to Alexander Mackenzie author of *The History of Highland Clearances*, 'had a powerful influence in determining that the absolute minimum was granted to the crofters.' Sitting with them was Charles Fraser-Mackintosh, Liberal MP for Inverness and a Gaelic scholar, and Sheriff Alexander Nicolson, another Gaelic scholar and Skyeman who wrote the celebrated quatrain:

> Jerusalem, Athens and Rome,
> I would see them before I die,
> But I'd rather not see any one of the three
> Than be exiled for ever from Skye!

He of all members of the Commission should have had a deep sympathy for those fellow islesmen who had been deported from the Hebrides, never to return. Then there was a respected academic, Professor Mackinnon, who held the Chair of Celtic Studies at Edinburgh University.

Such tales of hardship, indignity and harassment were heard that in their final report even Lord Napier, a man whose sympathies would have lain by inheritance with his fellow lairds, was compelled to write: 'the habitations of the people are of a character that would imply physical and moral degradation in the eyes of those who do not know how much decency, courtesy, virtue and even mental refinement, survive amid the sordid surroundings of a Highland hovel.'

From these hovels the crofters came forth to stand before the Commissioners and recite their miseries. Reading the minutes is like being swept into the pages of a Kafka novel. Here was victimisation and exploitation on an epic scale; it was unhindered by the law, for very often it was the absentee landowners and their all-too-present factors who made the laws and exacted punishment on those who broke them. It was colonialism of the worst kind. There was no appeal. If you didn't like the way things were then there was no need for you to stay.

This repressive regime under which my grandmother and her family lived had come about gradually over the years. At the beginning of the nineteenth century there was a great demand in the islands for seaware – kelp as it was called. It was burnt into an alkaline ash and used in the manufacture of glass and soap. The imported rival to kelp was barilla which came from the Continent. The Seven Years War, the American War of Independence and the Napoleonic wars restricted supplies of barilla from abroad and for something like 70 years Hebridean kelp fetched astonishingly high prices. The emigrations of the eighteenth century were halted; labour to gather the seaweed was more welcome than ever, and as a result the population increased dramatically. In the Hebrides it rose from 40,000 in the 1750s to 90,000 in the 1840s. Then almost overnight the bottom fell out of the kelp market. The Napoleonic wars ended and the duties on the import of barilla disappeared. The Germans discovered huge deposits of sulphate of potash – seaweed was no longer wanted and no longer the hands that cut it.

But at this time the demand for wool and mutton in the industrial south had increased. Sheep came to be seen as the saviour of a calamitous situation. The black cattle were disposed of and sheep farms took their place. Rents went up; the evictions began. Thousands of islanders were assisted to emigrate and those who wouldn't go were banished to the peripheries of the land. They were no longer wanted and scarcely tolerated. New landowners arrived with ruthless measures. In time sheep farms gave place to even more lucrative deer forests and sporting estates and always the indigenous population were hounded and banished to the poorest part of the land where overcrowding stifled all enterprise.

In the 1850s eviction and forced emigration reached its peak; famine and poverty, injustice and a black despair hung over the islands. Revolt was slow in coming. It was certainly sparked off by similar hardships in Ireland. Journalists and liberal reformers came to the Hebrides and were appalled by what they saw. 'Agitators' awakened the islanders to their rights; anger began to swell at long last.

In nearby Skye the crofters refused to pay their rents; police were called in, warships despatched. And it was then that Gladstone appointed his Royal Commission to investigate the causes of such open revolt among people noted for their humility and resignation. That's how Lord Napier and his colleagues came to be in the Outer Isles in May 1883 to probe what they subsequently described as 'a state of misery, of wrong-doing, and of patient long-suffering, without parallel in the history of our country'.

There are some magnificent passages in the minutes of evidence; words that even a hundred years later ring like a poem of defiance. What must be remembered is that the native tongue of almost all the people who gave evidence was Gaelic; those with English spoke it as a second and often inadequate means of expressing their deeply felt grievances.

Donald Martin, a 61-year-old crofter and mason of Tolsta in Lewis, stood before Lord Napier on 5 June. 'I do not', he said quietly, 'intend to say much.' What he said chills the blood to this day:

> I have seen the people reduced to such poverty that they were obliged to feed themselves upon dulse from the shore. I see them now reduced to such a hard condition that I can compare them to nothing but the lepers at the gates of Samaria – death before them and death behind them. I see no prospect of improvement in their condition. If one tack is set free, another tacksman comes into it to confront the people as the Philistines did who came out to battle with the people of Israel. The old people cannot be sent away without the young people. It is only the young people who can go, and it is only they who can support the old people. If the young people go, the old people will die; and it is hard for them to see the sheep and the deer enjoying the price of their fathers' blood. I have not much more to say.

Witnesses described how they had been cleared from land that their ancestors had farmed, how congestion had made it impossible for them to graze their cows or sheep, how even their most simple activities had been proscribed. 'Shootings and fishings', said Angus Campbell, a crofter of North Bragar, 'are let over all our land to a sportsman. A gamekeeper is settled among us with a house and piece of land. We cannot have dogs and a child must not cast a stone into the river. Sixty head of cattle were at one time taken from us and not accounted for.' Campbell claimed the crofters were engaged in an unwinnable confrontation: 'The factor is final judge – no appeal.'

Many witnesses talked of the old days before they were dispossessed of their land and herded together. Malcolm M'Phail of South Shawbost told the commissioners how his 'father and grandfather lived upon milk and butter and flesh and meal whereas I live upon meal, hot water and sugar. My father had a croft of £5 and such was the produce of it that not only did we not buy anything, but we were scarcely able to consume the produce at that time.'

To complain was of no avail. Malcolm M'Lean of Swainbost described how his people had been deprived of their hill pasture which had been given to a sheep farmer. 'The people asked the chamberlain what he was then going to do with them when they had no homes and he pointed to the sea and told them their home was there.'

Other witnesses described how they were perpetually in debt to the fish curers who supplied them with boats and then paid them in kind. They talked of the lack of roads which meant carrying their peats on their backs for miles; of lack of ground to grow vegetables and always of the congestion that followed their eviction from fertile land given over to sheep. 'We poor people', said Alexander Macdonald of Crowlista, 'have been sent to a headland of the sea where it was not worth while to send sheep forty years ago and that was the reason we were sent there. We were crowded all together upon it. There are now so many poor that there are twenty-three crofters in the township who have only one cow each, and not one of them can say it is his own cow after all.'

Frequently there was no grass on which to feed a cow, nowhere to cut peats; even gathering whelks from the shore was subject to a charge. And this was on land to which the people believed they had an historic and inalienable right. They believed passionately, perhaps wrongly, that if the land were given back to them they could all survive.

'Your demand then', asked Lord Napier of Angus Paterson a 58-year-old crofter from Kirvig, 'is that you should obtain more land?'

'That the land', replied Angus, 'should be given to the sons of men which was owned by their fathers, and for which their ancestors shed their blood.'

On Tuesday 12 June 1883 the Commissioners gathered in Keose on the north shore of Loch Erisort and among those who came to give evidence was Kenneth Macdonald, a crofter and merchant from Leurbost. He had been elected by the people of Leurbost, to cite their grievances. The list was long.

'Who made out the paper which you present to us?' asked Lord Napier.

'I have written it myself.'

'Is it on behalf of the township or on behalf of yourself?'

'The one portion of it concerns the affairs of the township and the other concerns a matter of my own in which I was not dealt with in a Christian fashion.'

'Was the part of it that concerns the township read to all the people of the township?'

'I read it to a large number of them. I did not get them all gathered to read it.'

'How many would there be gathered to hear it?'

'It was not read at a meeting but to everyone that met me.'

Almost every witness who came before the Commissioners was cross-examined in this manner. It was the general belief of the land-owning classes that the crofters themselves were quite content with their lot until strangers came into the islands and began to orchestrate their grievances. Prominent among the 'agitators' as they were described was John Murdoch who founded *The Highlander* in 1873. Born in Nairn in 1818, Murdoch had spent some time in Dublin where he involved himself in the Irish struggle for land reform.

He was known in the islands as *Murchadh na Feilidh*, Murdoch of the Kilt, because he saw the wearing of the once proscribed tartan as a symbol of resistance. Murdoch found the people afraid to attend his meetings for fear of reprisal from their landlords but over the years he managed through the paper, and with the help of ardent Celts like Professor John Stuart Blackie, and MPs like Dr Charles Cameron, who was also chairman of the Federation of Celtic Societies, to stir the crofters into action.

Murdoch preached to the crofters the doctrine that 'the land was theirs and that landlordism was a violent encroachment upon the divine rights of the people.' And there was always the Bible to back them up: 'The earth is the Lord's and the fulness thereof. . . . Woe unto them that join house to house, that lay field to field. . . . The earth He hath given to the children of men.' Murdoch's long campaign came to fruition with the formation of a Highland Land Law Reform Association. For a man of property like Lord Napier Murdoch's presence in the islands could only be construed as a threat and a danger to the status quo.

'Were there any outside people at your meetings helping you?' Napier asked Kenneth Macdonald of Leurbost.

'No, not at the meetings that were held in connection with this matter.'

'What other meetings do you refer to?'

'I saw Mr Murdoch one day addressing the people.'

'Did Mr Murdoch's address influence the people much?'

'The minds of the people before the arrival of Mr Murdoch were stirred up in some way but until they heard him they did not even understand their own minds on this question so well as they did afterwards.'

And there Lord Napier wisely left it. 'We will hear the paper,' he said.

Kenneth Macdonald summarised the injustices the township had suffered, the gradually increasing rents, the petty fines, 'such as fining a man for a big lip. For instance, Widow Esa MacIver, No 21 Leurbost, receipts can be produced to prove that she paid double poor rate in 1868. Fined for Cleas-cro plantation fence in 1871; fined for Arnish deer forest fence in 1873. Two girls and three boys from Leurbost have been taken to the fiscal's office under the control of a policeman for taking oysters out of the ebb in 1864; mussels and wilkies were taxed.'

Sheriff Nicolson questioned Macdonald about the overcrowding and the building of illegal dwellings to house cottars and squatters. 'All these houses were built in spite of the regulation?'

'I saw one built in spite of the regulation. This man was called to account for it.'

What was done to him?' asked Nicolson.

'His father-in-law was summoned out of the land. Mr Munro made the peace by compelling him to pay £5, and Mr Munro threw down the house next year and the constable broke the furniture and everything that was there and scattered it.'

Macdonald told the six men behind the table that he thought each of the crofters had a cow, some had three cows, there were others without sheep. He described how they were reduced to cultivating rocky and stony places and bogland. He gave place to Donald Mackenzie a 68-year-old crofter-fisherman from Crossbost, the township two miles down the road. There were fifty-one families living in Crossbost, tenants and cottars, but only the twenty-one tenants paid rent. Most of the people had been driven to the shore here in the 1840s from Lochshell ten miles to the south. Their expulsion had been brutal: 'The fire was drowned on the hearths by the officers of the estate. They were fined £50 sterling for not leaving the villages on the appointed day. The people of the two villages were put to a smaller village than either of the two they were driven from.'

When the people first arrived in Crossbost they had a small village five miles away where they could herd their cattle. Then it was taken from them but nothing was taken from the rent. Then they lost another piece of land, again there was no reduction in the rent. They looked back on Lochshell with envy: 'It was a very good place, we had plenty cattle and sheep there.' Now their old land was being farmed by one man.

'Would you like to get that back?' asked Lord Napier.

'That is what we desire. Here we are shut in like sheep in a fank.'

Finally it was the turn of George Macrae a 49-year-old crofter and fisherman from the small township on the shores of Loch Grimshader a mile or so north of Crossbost. The story was similar to many the commissioners had already heard throughout the length of the Outer Isles. A shortage of land, no pasture to graze cattle or sheep; they too felt themselves penned in like animals.

The gamekeepers and the herd have drowned and destroyed both our cattle and our sheep. In order to find out whether this was gamekeeper law or chamberlain law, I was appointed to meet the gamekeepers here about a month ago. The head gamekeeper upon the whole estate told me he had the full authority to do whatever he pleased in the matter, to which I replied that if he had such authority he might use it ill as he had already done.

Then Macrae told the commissioners that only two weeks previously when all the townships were 'in the very hurry of the spring work', they found that their moor had been set on fire. A constable had gone to Stornoway to find out who had started the fire and Sir James Matheson's head clerk told him that his gamekeepers might burn heather wherever they pleased.

'It is', said Macrae, 'a most oppressive and terrible thing for us, because the very place that was burned was the place that kept alive our cattle during the winter in snow time. The fire came into our peat moss near our crofts and some portion of the township was afraid even of their houses.' Macrae complained too about the deer which roamed freely round the township eating their corn.

'We have to watch by night ever since the corn comes in the ear until it is stacked in our stackyard to prevent the deer from utterly destroying it.'

'How long is it', asked Lord Napier, 'since the deer began to do this?'

'They commenced about five years ago and they are getting worse.'

The commissioners spent one further day taking evidence from twelve more witnesses at Tarbert in Harris and then they left for Shetland. The following year their report was published and in 1886 the Crofters Act gave security of tenure to crofters and the right to claim compensation from their landlord for any improvements made. They were entitled to pass their small patches of land to their descendants and a Crofters Commission was created to fix fair rents and generally administer the Act.

The legislation did not assuage land hunger and a series of clashes with the forces of law and order continued well into the twentieth century. Deer were slaughtered and dykes and fences torn down in an effort to re-occupy land from which their ancestors had been driven. The Crofters Act was little more than the prelude to the redressing of injustice.

I ask Calum Dan how Leurbost is thriving today, after all that agitation and all the hard-won legislation to establish the people's right to their land.

'Well we have 60 crofts here now but I can't say they are being worked, all of them. You'll see as we go down to Crossbost that there's not that much planted these days.' The cemetery is as overgrown as some of the crofts; the grass is waist-high and you have to pick your way carefully to avoid stumbling on old mounds.

The sun, in the sky, burns down and the sea is mirror calm.

'This M. Maclean of HMS *Snipe*,' I ask Calum pointing to a war grave, 'would he have been a relative?'

'Yes, and there's another one here. He was your great uncle's boy, you remember John? Well this was Roderick his son.' Calum reads the inscription. 'In loving memory of our dear son Lance Corporal R. Maclean, 2nd Gordon Highlanders, who died at Dewsbury War Hospital on Sunday 8th June 1919 aged 25 years. And then in Gaelic it says "until daybreak and shadows flee away".'

As we walk through the cemetery, again and again my eye falls on granite stones with the date 1 January 1919. They are all, without exception, naval ratings and a crossed anchor stands above the name and number of each one who perished. Eight hundred died in the Great War which had ended on 11 November 1918. But then early on the morning of 1 January over 200 more were drowned within sight of the shore close to Stornoway harbour. Eleven of them came from Leurbost.

It was without doubt the most tragic disaster that had ever overwhelmed the Outer Isles. Towards the end of December hundreds of men still in the services were given special leave to spend Hogmanay with their families. On the last day of the year about 500 soldiers, sailors and civilians were waiting at Kyle of Lochalsh to cross the Minch. At that time the steamer being used on the run between Kyle and Stornoway was the 280 ton *Sheila* which had been doing the trip for fifteen years.

The *Sheila* could not take all the passengers and HM Yacht *Iolaire* with a crew of 23 was sent from Stornoway to pick up the 260 naval ratings who would otherwise be left behind. Some of them were boys in their teens returning to Lewis for their first leave after enlistment; but the majority had served for most of the war. Some were veterans who were coming home for the first time since they were called up in August 1914.

Two hours away from Stornoway midnight struck and there was great excitement and singing to welcome the New Year. As they neared the light on Arnish point and the entrance to the harbour of Stornoway everyone began collecting their kit and getting ready to disembark. At five minutes to two there was a sudden crash and the ship ran aground. The land was only a few yards away and the stern of the *Iolaire* was only half a dozen yards from a ledge of rock which ran to dry land. Scores of those who leapt overboard in an effort to reach the shore were drowned in the heavy seas. When the alarm was at last raised the *Iolaire* was found lying between the Beasts of Holm and the shore; all but her masts had disappeared.

In the next few days the area round the wreck was dragged with grappling irons and more bodies were brought ashore and laid out on the grass overlooking the shore. All the officers of the *Iolaire* and all but five of the crew perished.

At the public inquiry in Stornoway in February, despite rumours to the contrary which had been rife in the island, the evidence indicated no insobriety on the part of the ship's officers or crew and none of the survivors was able to advance any reason why the ship should have been so disastrously off course. Of the 284 on board the *Iolaire*, 205 perished.

The great blessing of the inquiry was that finally all the gossip and suspicion which had been circulating suggesting that the tragedy had in some way been caused by drink was officially laid to rest. But as Neil Munro wrote in a poem for the Glasgow gathering held in April to raise money for the dependents of those who were lost:

Today in Lewis the lark sings unheeded,
The sparkle of waves in the sea-creeks gladdens no eye,
No dance to the pipe in the croft and no mirth in the sheiling,
Cheerless and leaden the hours of the Spring go by.

Even on a day of blue skies like this one Crossbost and Leurbost could by no stretch of the imagination be described as picturesque. For anyone used to the manicured prettiness of the Lake District or the thatched hollyhock charm of a Devon village, the townships of the Western Isles must seem dour and gaunt. In my grandmother's day the black houses, as they were called, cobbled together from heather, peat turves and stones, would have at least harmonised with a landscape of heather and peat and stone.

The black houses now are roofless, many of them lying beside more modern 'white' houses and even more modern bungalows. None of the townships has, in the English tradition, a village green or a focal point. Where in Sussex or Kent the village clusters protectively round its pond, church and pub, Hebridean townships are strung starkly along the road and behind each house is a long thin strip of land – the croft.

In England the traditional social order is immediately visible to the eye. There is the Georgian rectory or vicarage in its large grounds, here behind a wall is the imposing Queen Anne residence built for the squire, at a respectful distance are the simple cottages of the labouring classes. The Hebridean township represents the visible manifestation of the classless society. All the houses are of the same design and pretension, away on the horizon there may be a shooting lodge but its occupants are not part of the community. If a minister lives close by he too will come from the same background and be Gaelic-speaking. Everyone in the township will have been to the same school and speak in the same classless accents. Although a township may extend for a mile or so along the road there is an intensity of life which may not exist at all in a class-structured English village. There may not be a hall in which people can meet but the old traditions of co-operative help and communal activities are still strong.

The ties of kinship and family are strong as well. The incomer does well to watch his tongue; virtually everyone is related to everyone else by some form of blood or marriage tie. You get the feeling that the extended family was invented in Lewis. Perhaps that's why anthropologists and sociologists have been prowling about the Outer Hebrides in recent years. Before I went to Leurbost I picked up a couple of academic works in a Stornoway book shop; the first was written by Dr Judith Ennew (*The Western Isles Today*, Cambridge

University Press, 1980) and for all I know the clachan or village that she describes may well have been Leurbost. Dr Ennew brought to bear on the natives of the Hebrides the same stern and clinical eye that her Cambridge colleagues had already cast on the Skolt Lapps, the Yoruba and the Nayars. Her reception was at times as frosty as it might have been in Papua or among the Kelabits of Borneo. When she started her fieldwork it was in an area which she could only describe as ambivalent in its attitudes to visiting social anthropologists. 'In the first village the children of those families where I appeared to be a most welcome visitor would mock and spit at me in the street. In the second I was, like most strangers, subjected to persistent vandalism of my property.'

I mentioned this alarming occurrence to an academic from Lewis. 'Ah well, you see, the people are very hidebound in the rural parts, they tend to regard academics as a pain in the arse. In the old Viking days they used to put social anthropologists to the sword so you could say things are improving.'

The other essay I leafed through was by Dr Peter Mewett, a piece rich in sociological jargon entitled 'Associational categories and the social location of relationship in a Lewis crofting community' (*Belonging*, ed. Anthony P. Cohen, Manchester University Press, 1982). He somewhat uncharitably dismisses Dr Judith's efforts as 'a spurious theoretical perspective' which relegated to journalism 'what could have been an interesting ethnography'. 'Idiosyncratic and inadequate' is his final verdict on her efforts. Better perhaps to be spat on quietly by children than put down so publicly by a colleague.

Incidentally those who relish anthro-speak might well dip into Dr Mewett's costive pages. On the whole I think I prefer dear old Alasdair Alpin Macgregor. Here is Dr Mewett struggling to put down on paper what he sees as the future of the small Lewis township:

> Incipient class differences have not yet been translated into inter-personalised differentiations between neighbours and co-villagers. . . .
> the combination of an increase in economic differentiation and in the projection of prestige markers, together with a decrease in the multiplexity of social relations will culminate in the emergence of class as a means of classifying impersonal relations.

I was fortunate in not reading all Dr Mewett's comments on kinship before making my pilgrimage to Leurbost: otherwise I think I would have been at a loss even to say hello. According to Mewett, when Lewis folk refer to their 'relatives' they are actually using the word to 'denote an ego-centred bilateral set of consanguineal kin'.

But then down in Leurbost they have always had difficulty in conceptualising their more distant consanguines and mobilising their agnatic emphasis in the ascription of apical stereotypes. I think it's got something to do with the wind. There's a lot of it about.

3

EIGHTY-FIVE MILLION TONS OF PEAT

NESS TO BREASCLETE

A quarter of the 20,000 people of Lewis live in Stornoway, which over a hundred years ago was described by a visiting sportsman as the London of the Hebrides – 'the city of merchants, the grand emporium in those northern climes of cod and ling, herrings and haddock. How cheery and pleasant it looks of a bright morning with its white houses in a sort of amphitheatre round the bay.' Stornoway is still a town of merchants. The merchant princes, as they are known, live in Matheson Road. 'If you've owned a shop for three generations,' I'm told, 'you're the aristocracy.'

Edward Young and his wife Sheila live in the cantonment of the merchants; wide streets, lawns and solid stone villas. Eddie is Rector of the Nicolson Institute to which senior pupils come from all over the Western Isles; the school has a formidable reputation for turning out fine brains so Eddie and his colleagues have an unparalleled influence on the future of the Western Isles. They are creating tomorrow's islanders.

At his suggestion I'm going to start my journey in earnest at the most northern township of all, Eoropie. We decide to make a picnic of it; Sheila packs a basket of food, I bring a bottle of white wine from the Co-op, and we set off out of town and up the road to Barvas.

With the best will in the world it would not be accurate to describe the landscape of Lewis as a bonny one; it is severe, sterile even, Wuthering Heights more than Arcadia. The island is blanketed with peat moors and what is not peat is water. Only one acre in 50 is capable of yielding crops. In fairness, Lewismen with long memories will tell you that it was Magnus Bare-leg, an ill-disposed Norseman, who burnt everything that grew in 1098.

Even if the Norse hadn't fired the existing woodland it would never have amounted to much. Fierce winds hose the island with sea spray for a large part of the year and saltburn shrivels leaves. When Lady Matheson planted her woodlands round Lews Castle she had to import soil from the mainland to establish the trees and they were a long time growing on that windy promontory.

It's been worked out that there must be 85 million tons of peat lying on Lewis. Over the years scores of thousands of tons have been cut and burnt as fuel; beside each house you'll see the peat stack and throughout the islands the pungent smell of peat smoke wafts towards you on the wind long before you see a house. The land has been scored by generations of peat cutting. Water collects in the impermeable bottoms of these banks and in the winter when the wind bends the grass flat and black clouds race over the moors the prospects are bleak.

Today, though, as we drive up to Eoropie at the Butt of Lewis the skies are blue. I ask a local how it's pronounced; 'Yorr*erpee,*' he says. Here is the second most historic ecclesiastical building in the Long Island – the church of St Molua which educated guesses suggest was built in the twelfth century. It stands in a field and is looked after by the Episcopal Church of Scotland. The church has been re-roofed and equipped with an incongruous modern altar and a pulpit like a pillbox.

I'm more impressed with the architecture of Port of Ness which has a massive stone harbour. I examine the natives to see if any of them have matted hair but there are no vestigial signs of the phenomenon which Macculloch noted in the early part of the nineteenth century when he was exploring the islands. He claimed the men of Ness were a race apart, 'being of pure Danish origin although speaking unmixed Gaelic. Fat and fair with the ruddy complexions and the blue eyes of their race their manners appeared peculiarly mild and pleasing, although their aspect seemed at first sight, rude enough; their hair being matted, as if from birth it had never been profaned by comb or scissors.' Macculloch was quite taken by this matted hair. 'It must have descended with them', he observed, 'from the most ancient times.'

What the men of Ness still have which distinguishes them from people in other parts is a carefully preserved taste for the meat of the gannet or *guga*. This summer their annual cull of the birds on Sgula Sgeir had come in for criticism from the RSPB which had already successfully reduced the slaughter from the customary 3000 birds to 2000. The men of Ness have politely pointed out that during the five summers of wartime when no birds were taken at all the numbers of breeding pairs dropped to 200. Culling, they claim, keeps the numbers up. But the RSPB now wants the annual August hunt stopped altogether. It's part of their global strategy to prevent songbirds from being shot at by the French and Italians. They don't want a lot of wretched foreigners telling them that eating sparrows and thrushes is no more offensive than eating gannets.

But for the men of Port of Ness the annual expedition to Sgula Sgeir is as important as running the bulls in Pamplona or headhunting in Borneo. It calls for skill and physical strength and it must be seen to be done. A spokesman for the community has told the RSPB to mind its own business. When the English stop killing five million turkeys for Christmas, says William Macleod, they'll stop catching guga.

The hunters pursue the guga around the dizzy cliffs with nooses on the end of long poles. The August jaunt to the gannet island forty miles to the north has been going on for centuries. Dean Monro writing in the sixteenth century described the island 'full of Wylde foulis, and men out of the parochin of Nesse in Lewis use to sail ther, and to stay ther sevin or aught dayes and to fetch hame with thame their boitt full of dray wilde foulis with wyld foulis fedders.'

There is always an over-subscribed waiting list for guga and it is despatched by post to Lewismen in distant parts. The guga were traditionally salted and put away for the winter; a friend of mine who has eaten guga testifies to its tensile strength and toughness; 'more a tribute to tradition', he says, 'than a gourmet feast. It tastes a bit like sea saturated duck. Indeed in Barra they used to call gannet Mingulay duck.'

There is another singularity about the people of Ness; they are the only community in Britain to have compiled their own telephone directory. In the gaeltacht there are so few given names and surnames that without the bestowal of patronymics and nicknames confusion would reign. At the simplest level when there are three or four men called Donald Macleod living in a township one may be known as Donald John (Donald son of John), another as Donald Alex and the third Donald Angus. Often a job designation – Donald the post, Donald the ferry – does the trick or a physical description – a red-haired Donald will be *Domhnall Ruadh*, Donald Red. One man in Ness with very black hair and a dark skin is known as 'Zebo' after a proprietary grate cleaner.

Usually the patronymics and nicknames are Gaelic in origin – *Seonag a' Phigean, Aonghas Tola, Domhnall an Torrachan, Shifildh, Am Blondaidh* – but now and again the English is left untranslated. R. Morrison of Lower Shader is known as Ruaridh Sir, W. Morrison of Borve is Uilleam Malt, Mary Macdonald is Mairi Mhurchaidh Scap, Murdo Morrison is Freckles, Norman Macleod is Split.

There is wit in these nicknames, sometimes a little gentle mockery. In Skye a few years ago a young man decided to go round the world. The preparations were a subject of public discussion for months; the plans constantly changed. Visas were acquired and after a flurry of emotional farewells the lad set off on his global tour. He got as far as Inverness and decided to come home. Thereafter he was known as 'Gulliver'.

For the non-Gaelic speaking outsider names present a further difficulty; many bear no verbal relationship to their English equivalent – Hector is *Eachainn*, James is *Seumas*, Flora is *Fionnghal*, Julia is *Sile*, Rachel is *Raonaild*. Thus when Scotland's leading Gaelic poet was lecturing at Edinburgh University his English-speaking students knew him as Sam Maclean; in Gaelic the name on the dustjacket of his books is *Somhairle MacGhill-Eain*. Similarly the Finlay Macleod of Shawbost who writes in the *Times Educational Supplement* in English is the same man as the Gaelic columnist of the *West Highland Free Press, Fionnlagh Macleoid*.

Some years ago I went to a semi-detached house in Surbiton to interview, on behalf of the BBC, a Gaelic activist who was most insistent that I should be aware of my identity in Gaelic. My first name is a corruption of Roderick, *Ruaraidh*, and I had been given my mother's maiden name, Macdonald, as a middle name. I emerged from the house as *Ruaraidh Dohmnallach Mac a' Chubair*, a mouthful which I have kept quiet about ever since. Being one person in these hard times is difficult enough, opting for voluntary schizophrenia seems the height of folly. But most Hebrideans have no option at all, a dual identity is thrust upon them at birth. The best description of the confusion that results has been given by Martin Macdonald who runs Radio Highland (*Jock Tamson's Bairns*, edited by Trevor Royle, Hamish Hamilton, 1977). He is known in Gaelic circles as *Martainn Iain Domhnallach* but his birth certificate identifies him as Martin John Macdonald. It didn't really matter too much until he was called up for National Service when he found that one of his selves had been exempted to continue his university studies and the other was scheduled for instant despatch to an army training depot. It was more than the civil servant who dealt with his case in Edinburgh could comprehend:

Iain, I explained, was a Gaelic name. He nodded. John had been its accepted English translation or equivalent for centuries. Again the nod. But, down the years Ian, an anglicised form of Iain, had emerged as an English name in its own right. No nod this time, merely a wary indication of the head. I quickly abandoned a foray down an even more convoluted byway which might or might not explain how every John in the Bible surfaced in Gaelic as Eoin and went for the clincher. Ergo, Iain = John Q.E.D.

Wisely he didn't bring up the spelling of his first name, a move which would only have added to the ambiguity. Many of his childhood friends were Martainns in their own community and Martin at school 'and always the Martainns had to make the essential compromise to bridge the two. Through long conditioning and acceptance the community was no longer conscious of a clash nor, during our schooldays, were we. But looking back I can see that tensions existed between our dual worlds. And since those tensions concerned identity, and identity is crucial, they must have left a mark.' No one who seeks to understand the Gaelic ethos should neglect the profoundly unsettling shadow that the domination of English has cast over these islands.

But on this hot day in Ness it's flies that are on my mind not the Anglo-Saxon legacy. We eat our lunch on the dunes of Eoropie standing up. There is a terrible plague of bluebottles hatched out perhaps by the unusual heat of the sun. We try sitting on the rocks but the flies circle and descend in angry squadrons. Standing you can at least dodge and weave about.

Eddie comes from Northumbria which like Lewis has roots going back into Viking times, and he tells me that when he arrived at the Nicolson he went out of his way to tread carefully. Was Stornoway something of a culture shock? 'No, but you have to recognise the fact that you are coming into an integral community with its own traditions and its own beliefs to which it generally seems to adhere and you should be aware of this before you start making changes or suggesting any alterations. That's only common sense, it would be the rule if you moved into any small community, not only Lewis.'

'People use the word reactionary when they talk about Lewis attitudes. Would you use that word?'

'Of the community?'

'Yes.'

Eddie thinks for some moments.

'No, I don't think I would. What I would say is that there are people who firmly believe that what they might call the old ways are right and that is entirely their right to believe what they think. And if somebody from outside says they're reactionary then that's entirely the judgment of someone from the outside.'

There is a touch of the diplomat and the Delphic about Eddie's careful replies to my questions.

1 Car ferry MV *Suilven* approaching Ullapool pier

2 Lews Castle Technical College, Stornoway. Piping instruction

3 Relatives, Leurbost, Lewis: Joan (Seonag Nicsuain), Murdo (Murchadh MacChoinnich) and Jessie (Seonaid Nicleoid)

4 Graves of *Iolaire* victims, Crossbost, Lewis

5 Peats drying, near Balallan, Lewis
6 Man walking, Balallan, Lewis

7 Frau Beatrice Schulz's tea-room, Callanish, Lewis

8 Ness Bay, Lewis

9 Clach an Truiseil, Balantrushal, Lewis
10 Clach Micleoid, Macleod's Stone, Nisabost, Harris

11 View from the car, Valtos Bay, Lewis
12 Sheep shearing, Valtos Bay, Lewis

13 Amhuinnsuidhe Castle, Harris, looking to Taransay

14 Jetty, Harris, looking to Scarp

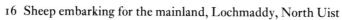

15 Marion Campbell BEM, of Plocrapool, Harris, treading wool

16 Sheep embarking for the mainland, Lochmaddy, North Uist

'Do you think it's right then', I probe, 'for a small religious minority to impose their views on the whole community?'

'What you call the small minority would say that they represent the large majority and that if you were to stop observing the Sabbath, say, then that would threaten the whole *mores* of the community and it would precipitate attacks from all sorts of other modern forces.'

'Do you think that tourism if it got the same kind of hold it has in Skye might destroy Lewis culture?'

'No, tourism properly handled would not. In fact the kind of visitor we normally attract is the more responsible sort of person who is looking for the peace and tranquillity which sometimes occurs in the Western Isles and not necessarily looking for an all-night disco.'

I ask Eddie, who is a cultivated man, what are the bonuses of living in a community with no cinema, no theatre, no art galleries and museums, none of the cultural amenities of Edinburgh or Glasgow.

'It's difficult to mention them all but perhaps the greatest pleasure is belonging to an actual living community which although it's changing and developing in both good and bad ways still gives you the sense of being an individual – that's a source of strength. Secondly you work just as hard here as anywhere else but you recover more quickly because of the environment. And there's another thing – people judge you not for what position you hold but as an individual.'

'And the pace of life?'

'I don't think it's slow – I think life is more *intelligently* paced. The crofter can work desperately hard but he's always got time to turn round and talk to you and give you your true worth as an individual – maybe that's what gives visitors the illusion that life is easy paced here. It's simply that people are courteous to one another.'

I am to find this courtesy all over the islands – the courtesy of not rushing you, of listening not with deference but with the interest of equality. I also find an understandable contempt for newsmen who misrepresent their way of life. On the way back to Stornoway we stop at the Cross Inn for a cup of tea. It's run by a mainland Scot called Tom Paterson. When he finds out that I'm a journalist he clams up. 'You'll never get any truth from a journalist,' he says and retreats into the kitchen. Eddie tells me that some years previously Tom had been interviewed by a visiting television team from London. 'It's a sad fact that all too often TV people only come here when there's some conflict in the community and they tend to magnify the problems.'

When Tom comes back he tells me a long story about the way in which his views were misrepresented. When the filmed report was shown he seemed to be saying that there was too much drinking going on and that didn't do him any good locally. 'I'll tell you one thing', he says angrily, 'they were making out that all we did here was drink all day but I've never seen such a bunch of alcoholics as themselves, they got through *bottles* of brandy!'

The national reputation of the islands and Lewis in particular as one of the hardest-drinking parts of Britain may partly stem from the controversy which always surrounds the granting of new licences. The churches on principle oppose any extension of licensed premises, veto polls are organised, and the fierce arguments against the opening of a hotel bar naturally lead the rest of the country to believe that intemperance is a grave problem.

In the 1970s press and television highlighted the more farcical side of the repressive attitude of the Free churches to overt drinking and they made great play with the absurdities that attended drinking in Lewis. The men of a remote township who wished to indulge in the kind of social drinking that occurs nightly in an English village pub were forced into clandestine and illegal practices which excited ridicule when shown on television. The men would club together, send an emissary into Stornoway to buy beer and whisky, and then sneak off to some shack out of sight of the police to drink it. These tumbledown 'bothans' where the drinking took place were uncomfortable and the whole operation was socially and morally degrading. The notion that grown men should have to conceal their drinking could only be tolerated in a society which is deeply riven about its attitude to alcohol. And Lewis came badly out of the publicity that attended the churches' attempts to curb intemperance.

The struggle between mild social drinking and the wild excesses which the culture of the islands seems to stimulate is a divisive one. In a chain of islands where there are no cinemas, theatres, concert halls or any of the social amenities found in other parts of the country drinking may well be the only diversion available. The pattern of life where people go late to bed tends to encourage ceilidhs and conviviality and it is the accepted norm that a visitor should not turn up empty-handed. There is a far greater tendency to carry on drinking after hours than in urban communities where there are trains and buses to be caught in the morning, cards to be punched at factory gates. The stamina for staying up is notable but when the Hebridean dawn may bring bucketing rain and gale force winds late-to-bed and late-to-rise is far from inconvenient.

Friday-night dances often astonish visitors. They never begin until the bars close. The custom is to take a supply of drink, known as a 'carry-out', with you. A stream of customers leaving the local hotel bar on a Friday dance night is not unlike a horde of passengers disembarking from a cross-channel steamer laden with plastic bags of duty-free drinks. On nights when there is no dance a carry-out in the shape of a few cans of beer and a half bottle of whisky will be taken to a neighbour's house and the 'crack' that ensues may last into the small hours.

Not everyone drinks; not everyone ceilidhs until dawn; but in a small community those who are heavy drinkers or have a drink problem tend to stand out. A drunken man in Oxford Street is lost in the dense throng; a drunk weaving down a street in Stornoway in mid-afternoon is all too obviously visible. Ironically on one of my forays to the Western Isles I caught the night sleeper from Euston and saw more victims of drink between platforms one and thirteen in two minutes than I saw between Stornoway and Rodel in two weeks.

Statistically, it is said, there is more intemperance in the Western Isles than in comparable communities on the mainland. Statistically too the Western Isles is held to have more than the national average of depressive illness, but it would be misleading to weave fantasies from such information. The accepted myth of the gloomy Celt burdened with guilt and rendered inert by apathy is not borne out in reality.

The brightness and the achievements of Eddie's pupils at the Nicolson do not suggest a legacy of mental or intellectual deprivation. 'Quite the contrary,' he says. But how strongly are their attitudes influenced by their environment? I had a long talk with the Youngs about the way in which young people in the islands see themselves in relation to the rest of the world and some months later Eddie sent me the results of a survey which the English department had carried out among 330 pupils in classes five and six. I had particularly asked for questions which would indicate what the movement of the youngsters would be when they left school. Would they stay in the islands or be lost altogether as so many bright people before them?

It was a fascinating survey and it provided some unexpected answers. Sixty-six per cent of pupils approved of capital punishment for murder and the same percentage admitted they were either indifferent to or intolerant of the various peace movements active in Stornoway and the rest of Britain; 40 per cent felt a nuclear war during their lifetime was possible. A significantly high proportion of students thought that abortion and divorce were too readily available, that everyone should work for a living and have a duty towards the unemployed, the sick, the elderly and single-parent families;

that corporal punishment should be retained in school.

Predictably the questions on religion revealed a high degree of conformity. Ninety per cent believed in God and 56 per cent claimed regular church attendance. When offered a political scale moving from Fascist through Conservative to Moderate, Socialist and Communist the majority pronounced themselves to be of Moderate opinion veering to Socialism.

Fifty-six per cent of the Nicolson students expected to take up professional work after leaving school; 25 per cent thought they would go into business or office work; 13 per cent said they expect to take up a skilled trade.

Only 57 per cent claimed to speak Gaelic. Four out of ten had no Gaelic at all. More girls (67 per cent) than boys (42 per cent) spoke Gaelic, which might bode well for the next generation of pre-school children. Depressingly, a majority (70 per cent) saw themselves living permanently either on the Scottish mainland (53 per cent), in England (4 per cent) or abroad (12.5 per cent).

Although the attitudes were more conventional than those you would expect in a comparable comprehensive on the Scottish mainland or in England there was a spark of rebellion in answer to the question 'Is violence ever justified in seeking political change?' Thirty-three per cent thought it was. Surprisingly too when asked which was the strongest influence on their lives (parents, school, church or state) only 6 per cent named organised religion; 73 per cent thought it was their parents who were the most effective in controlling their actions and reactions.

The following day I drive west to Shawbost to call on Finlay Macleod, a former Deputy Director of Education in Lewis who left his job to concentrate on writing. Finlay is a Gaelic activist; his wife Norma is Director of Social Work and a noted Gaelic singer. The Macleod's house is close to the tweed mill, one of the three big mills in Lewis which are the base of the Harris tweed industry. These mills employ about 450 people processing mainland wool from Cheviot, Cross Bred and Blackfaced sheep. It is scoured, dyed and dried and then converted into yarn for weaving. It is this yarn which is sent out along with the weft to the 650 weavers who, pedalling away on their Hattersley looms, actually weave the tweed.

There is only one weaver left who makes tweed in the old way and that's the remarkable Marion Campbell of Plocrapool who uses an old wooden loom with a hand-operated shuttle. She is also the last woman in the islands to spin her own wool, design her own patterns and dye her sheep fleeces using flowers, mosses, lichen and peat. She hand-washes it and then shrinks the tweed in her hands in the traditional way. She began weaving when she left school at 14 and over 60 years later she still cannot make enough tweed to meet international demand.

Contrary to popular belief the tweed industry is still little more than a century old. Two Hebridean landowners Lady Dunmore and Lady Gordon Cathcart were instrumental in bringing island tweed to the fashion houses of London and it was the Dunmore family arms, an orb surmounted by a Maltese cross, which was chosen as the symbol of genuine island tweed when the Harris Tweed Association was founded in 1909. The most significant step forward came in 1934 when the weavers agreed that the time-consuming process of spinning and dyeing should be done in factories. Production jumped from 95,000 yards in 1934 to just under 1½ million yards in 1935. The output these days is about 4.5 million yards.

Finlay, though, has been instrumental in starting another industry in Shawbost; one that is non-productive in terms of material gain but essential, he believes, if the identity and heritage of Lewis is to be preserved. He has set up a centre for the collection of relics, photographs and written material from the past; the kind of things which are all too often thrown out and forgotten about. It is at once an exhibition, an archive and a focus for the entire neighbourhood.

'The kind of things we're doing', says Finlay unlocking the door of the building which contains all this material, 'is to record the names of the owners of crofts, people who moved here who had been cleared from Uig for instance. These kind of things.'

The project is now in its second year and at the moment three people are working full-time. 'I've got a geology graduate who is well-versed in ornithology and who knows the islands well and two local girls on the clerical side. On the historical side there were four people, but that's in abeyance at the moment. We're hoping to re-start it with five people.'

Finlay leafs through files and documents. 'These are transcriptions of interviews with local people – their own lifetime of experience. Some of it is in Gaelic, some in English. This one is on fishing; here are stories of fishing girls, their experiences when they went to the mainland curing herring. We're building up a composite account of the past – extracts from papers, the school register; a wealth of information.'

Finlay shows me some more work in progress charting where the Shawbost sheilings used to be, the inland grazing moors where the women took the cattle in the summer. 'Here are the raiders of Dalbeg. We're concentrating on quite a small area – Shawbost, Bragar, Arnol, Dalbeg, but

45

for ornithology we cover the whole of the Western Isles.'

'And who is it intended for?'

'For anyone and everyone, local people, students. There are other groups working like this in Harris, South Uist, up in Ness where you were yesterday. In Tong someone is writing the history of Tong school. There's a lot of interest in Uig.'

Finlay writes a column in the *West Highland Free Press*, he writes for the *Times Educational Supplement*, and he is also chairman of Acair, the first-ever bilingual educational publishing house. It was set up in Stornoway in 1977 to provide books for Gaelic-speaking schoolchildren and is financed jointly by the Highlands and Islands Development board, An Comunn Gaidhealach and Comhairle nan Eilean.

I shall hear a lot on this journey about the new spirit breathed into the islands by the formation in 1975 of the multi-purpose, one-tiered, non-political, Western Isles Islands Council which gave itself the Gaelic name of Comhairle nan Eilean. Before then the four parishes of Lewis were run by the Ross and Cromarty County Council from Dingwall and Harris and the Southern Isles were administered by Inverness County Council from Inverness. It was a divisive arrangement and one which left the Outer Hebrides feeling at times that economically and politically they had been cast into outer darkness.

Although the formation of Comhairle gave the islands the feeling that they had at last achieved a new geographical entity, did that necessarily give the people a greater say in their destiny? Has devolution meant more power for the people or have they just exchanged two sets of officials in Dingwall and Inverness for one set in Stornoway?

According to a relative of mine, Kenneth MacIver, who has made a recent study of these matters, the reorganisation precipitated a shift of power from the hands of the Councillors towards the top officials of Comhairle. 'In general,' he claims, 'reorganisation brought local government closer to the people but it also brought an increased bureaucratic and de-personalised nature to the relations between the public, Councillors and Officials . . . along with a massive increase in the size of the structure this resulted in local government becoming more remote and detached.'

It appeared to him after fairly intensive research that the real power lay not with the democratically elected councillors but with the career officials. The majority of councillors are middle-aged or elderly; the majority of the officials are young. The power of the officials was further increased by their almost complete control of the political agenda. They control the information reaching councillors, they define and present the issues, they recommend the course of action to be taken. The Chief Executive told MacIver: 'In June I presented the capital expenditure for the past year and the future predictions for the coming financial year. This allocation of resources involved a good deal of decision, or at least recommendation for approval, on my part and on the part of the Director of Finance. However there was no debate or discussion at all and our recommendations were unanimously approved. Now, was this approval or had the councillors any idea of what was going on?'

The professionalism of the bureaucrats and the amateur status of the councillors very often leads the elected representatives of the people to seize desperately at some trivial issue they can comprehend while the really vital decisions go through unchallenged. 'I can go along to a committee meeting', the Chief Executive told MacIver, 'with two issues – one involving £50 for traffic wardens' caps and the other involving £10,000 of complicated loan and banking charges. They will debate the first issue for an hour and pass the second on a nod.'

The Director of Housing also commented on the inability of most councillors to understand the facts and figures being presented to them by the paid officials. 'You can notice the involvement of councillors at the meetings', said the Director of Housing, 'where a major policy document of 12 pages would rarely be discussed at any length while you put up a one-line report on a small local matter and it may be discussed for an hour.'

It would be tempting to argue that the actual running of the Western Isles lies effectively with professional civil servants not with the people. It was a point I put to a close but detached observer of the scene. 'It's far more complex than that; you cannot be simplistic. First of all there are no party politics in the Council, no class axes to grind. Secondly whereas in a comparable area in England you would have among your Councillors all sorts of professional expertise – lawyers, accountants, engineers, academics, journalists, potential MPs sharpening their wits in debate, here you've got a predominance of people whose expertise is confined to running a croft or driving a van. I'm not being elitist but in the islands we just don't have an indigenous questioning, educated middle class who will go through every fact and figure with a toothcomb and keep the officials on their toes. Unfortunately, the Lewis high-flyers have flown off to the mainland.'

Certainly in its short life Comhairle has spent huge sums of money, nodded through by delighted councillors on all manner of improving projects. So carried away were they with the need to invest in the islands that

I'm told a quarter of their income is now going to meet crippling loan charges.

But have they tackled the really big issues? It is likely that bureaucrats would shy away from any proposals to upset the traditional status quo. A discussion of the size of traffic wardens' caps no doubt has its part to play in the democratic process but many people believe that for the Western Isles to plan its future to the best advantage the ownership of land should, at the very least, be subject to scrutiny.

A big opportunity was lost when Lord Leverhulme sold Lewis in 1923. He had bought the island in 1918 and founded the Lewis & Harris Welfare & Development Company. His great vision was to promote Stornoway to be the leading fishing and fish-processing centre of Britain. To this end he set up a chain of 400 retail fish shops on the mainland – MacFisheries Ltd, the biggest fishmongery Britain had ever seen. When Leverhulme pulled out of Lewis he gave Lews Castle and all his property in Stornoway to the townsfolk; he offered all the crofting land as a gift to the people and the rest of the island to the Lewis District Committee.

Only 41 crofters accepted his gift, and although a Stornoway Trust was created to administer Leverhulme's land in the Burgh the rest of Lewis was sold to speculators and syndicates and it has been changing hands ever more lucratively ever since. Every now and again the Western Isles hits the headlines particularly when an estate or an island is sold to some unusual foreigner – an Egyptian property developer for instance, or a Hong Kong-based syndicate of asset strippers. Indeed the most striking fact about the Western Isles today is the way in which large bits of it are constantly changing hands, sometimes in a very private and unrecorded manner.

The unenviable legacy left by the growth first of sheep farms then of deer forests has dogged the history of the islands for over a century and a half. The fact that large tracts of land were reserved for peripatetic sporting tenants created a conflict of interest which survives to this day. When a Victorian gentleman paid good money to come and shoot and fish he expected to have an unfettered run of the land he had rented. He was in no mood to let a few ignorant peasants stand in his way, especially when most of the time he couldn't get a sensible or civilised word out of them.

Many of the tenants were military men used to being obeyed. As in India, they treated the natives with amused condescension mingled with exasperation which sometimes flared into contempt. 'Taking them as a whole', wrote the huntin' and shootin' authority C. V. A. Peel in 1901, 'the crofters are an ignorant lot of creatures and the less said about them the better.'

Much of the pleasure of shooting in the Outer Hebrides, he said, had been spoilt by their antics: 'it is not conductive to sport to be followed by a gang of men and ordered out of the country, nor is it pleasant to be cursed in Gaelic by a crowd of irate old women, even if you do not understand every word they say. They were especially insolent and troublesome in Benbecula and Barra.'

Although men like Peel must have walked about with their eyes more than usually open, if only looking for something to slaughter, they seldom made the connection between the appropriation of the land for private pleasure and the mounting discontent of the people. There was evidence in plenty. Peel himself started out one morning with his stalker to look for deer along the precipices. They met nobody but a shepherd returning from the sheep market.

'Weel, Sandy, and how goes it in the town today?' asks the stalker; but the shepherd has evidently sold his sheep badly and he answers: 'Bard, very bard; nothing in the town but famine and English – famine and English!'

Much of the evidence heard by the members of the Napier Commission focussed on what the islanders saw as the appropriation of land traditionally theirs for the exclusive use of wealthy outsiders. The demands of the sportsmen and the crofter were irreconcilable and they remain largely so to this day. The sportsmen wanted and still want a wilderness inhabited only by wildlife; people other than those directly employed in the conservation of game are, as Peel so bluntly stated, a nuisance.

Giving evidence to the Commission Roderick Mackenzie, a 75-year-old crofter of Nether Coll, claimed that he and his neighbours were 'so pressed by sportsmen and their gamekeepers, that we are not allowed to walk without the fear of being taken up as trespassers, even upon the hill pasture for which we pay rent.'

Sheriff Nicolson asked him what he meant by fear of trespassing? 'They keep', said Mackenzie, 'a man out upon the moorland pasture to take up any man or child whom they may find straying there, in case he may be there robbing the nests of the birds.'

Nicolson asked him for the name of the shooting tenant.

'I don't know. He is an English gentleman living in London.'

Why, persisted Nicolson did they take any notice of the gamekeeper?

'Bless you! have I not seen two lads sent for nine weeks to the prison there for robbing a grouse nest, and one of them barely came out alive? Our great complaint is that we are prevented from sending a boy or anybody else out to attend to the cattle.' Mackenzie, when asked if the crofters were afraid of being evicted if they stood up to the gamekeeper, said they were.

'It is lying waste', claimed John MacIver, a 56-year-old crofter from Breasclete, 'the best part of the land throughout the island and the poor people kept in the worst parts of it, when they cannot make a livelihood out of it and the best parts taken from them at every corner.'

Murdo Macdonald, a spokesman for the crofters of Berneray, described how they had been threatened by sportsmen that even if they were walking on their own pastures 'they would put lead into our bodies'. He told Lord Napier: 'I could not think of going to get heather to make ropes for thatching our houses, except during the week we are permitted to do so by the factor.'

All over the islands the Commission heard evidence about the way in which sporting land had been increased at the expense of grazing and farming. As one crofter put it, it was 'the smallness of the land, the dearness of the land, the poor quality of the land' which made life increasingly difficult. As if to rub in the injustice, all the able-bodied men and boys in a township were often compelled to build dykes to keep their stock from straying onto land from which they had been expelled.

These gloomy memories of man's intolerance to man are a part of history. But it is living history. Some justice was done in the 1880s but land hunger continued well into this century. Later in my journey I will meet a man who remembers vividly going on a land raid to a sporting estate after the Great War. They had been promised a land fit for heroes but in the Hebrides as in Flanders they had to fight for every foot of it.

Nobody is forced to steal land in the 1980s but the power of the sporting estates remains, an irritant at the very least and in its most flagrant forms a continuing outrage against the community. In his painstakingly researched book *Who Owns Scotland?*, John MacEwen of Blairgowrie, who spent his life as a forester and has maintained into his nineties a growing concern for the way in which the countryside has been mismanaged, talked about a 'sadistic obsession with game resulting in the almost complete degradation of millions of acres of our land'.

The contemporary apologia of many estate owners is that their property is merely rocks and lochs, completely unsuitable either for habitation or development. One Hebridean landowner put it this way: 'If it weren't for the people who came here in the summer looking for a few trout and a chance to unwind you wouldn't see a soul.' It is not a convincing argument. As John McGrath wrote in his foreword to *Who Owns Scotland?*, much of the land still remains 'archaically run, unprofitable, under-capitalised and socially disastrous.'

I remember back in the 1970s writing a film for BBC Scotland about the use and misuse of the countryside. The programme asked some simple questions. Was it right that vast acreages of land should remain in private hands, sold and resold by speculators with no concern other than profit? We talked to economists, naturalists, farmers and organisations concerned with the future of Scotland. It was felt that our filmed report might lead to the conclusion that the private ownership of land was against the public interest. So, in the BBC's traditional quest for balance, on the day the film was shown it was followed by a studio discussion in which the landowners and those with a stake in preserving the countryside as a sporting sanctuary were invited to put their case for private ownership.

Sitting as it were wearing two hats, one slightly tweedy with fishing flies in it, the other formal and concerned with Scotland's heritage, was Jean Balfour, Chairman of the Scottish Countryside Commission. She and her husband owned the 16,200-acre Scourie estate in Sutherland. It made them small fry alongside the Countess of Sutherland (123,500 acres), the Duke of Westminster (112,700 acres), E. H. Vestey (81,400 acres) and Michael Berry with 62,300 acres, but the Balfours also owned the Balbirnie estates: 6,900 acres of the most valuable land in Fife. Was it possible for someone who owned such a big chunk of Scotland to chair objectively a body whose remit was to develop, improve and enhance the amenities of such land for the good of the community as a whole?

Part of the answer was perhaps given to this rhetorical question in *Hansard* of 3 July 1973 when the Labour MP for Caithness and Sutherland, Robert Maclennan, reminded the House that 'Mrs Balfour, who is a constituent of mine, has spoken of a large area of Sutherland which she owns – the estate of Scourie – as being nothing but rock and water, and therefore, incapable either of being developed or of providing any sort of employment. On the face of it, that is an extraordinarily insensitive description of one of the most interesting ecological areas in the country and a neglect of the possible interests of the community in the nature conservation of that area.'

Mr Maclennan claimed he was quoting her statement because it reflected an attitude of mind 'which one would not expect to see in a person fulfilling such an important public office in Scotland – a "keep out" attitude, because the area is of relatively little interest. Perhaps it is because she has a personal interest in the area that she does not appreciate the public interest in it.'

Like Mr Maclennan I continue to be amazed that those who have inherited a vested interest in the private ownership of the countryside should turn up time and time again on committees set up to examine the use and abuse of the countryside. And I'm amazed too that private individuals by flashing a cheque book should be able to inhibit all social and economic advancement in huge regions of Scotland. The landowning lobby has regrettably in recent years won over liberal-minded support by presenting themselves as conservationists dedicated to the preservation of moors, meadow, mudflats and marshlands. It is an attractive argument bought without reservation by the *Observer Magazine* in December 1984 when they recorded the enterprise of various wealthy folk in snapping up pieces of Britain for their own purposes.

A special accolade was bestowed on the Tory MP and junior government minister Alan Clark for the quick-witted way in which in 1984 he pre-empted 18,000 acres of Sutherland. Mind you it was in the blood. Clark is the son of millionaire art historian Lord Clark and his grandfather, a Glasgow cotton magnate, had bought himself on a whim the whole of the Ardnamurchan peninsula as a holiday home. 'We got the Eriboll estate', Clark told the *Observer* with relish, 'for the price of a couple of dingy semis in the Boltons. There was a proposal to put chalets on some of the western part of the land and to afforest some of the eastern parts; we bought it to keep it as wilderness. It is of course a terrible investment from a financial point of view.'

Neither Mr Clark nor the *Observer Magazine* appeared to be the slightest bit interested in what sort of terrible investment this bit of buccaneering land-grabbing might be for those who wished to live and work in those 18,000 acres. 'Where an individual has the resources', proclaimed Mr Clark, 'he is, I think, serving the long-term interests by keeping a place wild.'

Not everyone fortunately accepts the present system whereby a hundred Clarks with surplus cash and a thirst for acres could effectively freeze all initiative in vast tracts of the Highlands and Islands. The Labour party has advanced some dotty schemes in its time but its Scottish Council must be given full marks for trying to alter the status quo in 1972 when their Executive Committee Working Party produced a blueprint for the national-isation of all land in Scotland. 'Private ownership of land', it said, 'is a medieval concept, designed to ensure the dominance of a self-perpetuating oligarchy. It is an affront to reason for a private individual to claim ownership of mountains, lochs and rivers' – a statement few, except the owners of mountains, lochs and rivers, would logically disagree with.

Twenty miles south of Stornoway as the crow flies is the peninsula of Pairc or Park which was turned into a deer forest in Victorian times. After over a hundred years it still remains in private and alien hands. North

Eishken is owned by a wealthy Pakistani, South Eishken belongs to a Swiss. The road to South Eishken runs over the moors and when it enters the estate there is a hostile display of notices calculated to deter the curious. PRIVATE NO WALKING says one, PRIVATE NO HILL WALKING says another, and the third reads PRIVATE NO FISHING. On the road down to the lodge you pass ruined and unroofed croft houses and untilled ground. The estate covers 57,000 acres and 1,400 red deer roam the moors undisturbed. At the end of the five-mile private road down by the shore lies Eishken lodge and its attendant cottages and steadings.

Surrounding the house is a flourishing vegetable garden and in the kitchen tea is on the go. The guests, mainly Swiss, Austrians and Germans, are out on the hill or fishing the lochs. At various times of the year Eishken offers stalking, grouse, woodcock and snipe, salmon and sea trout and also deep-sea fishing. Stalkers and ponymen are in attendance and the food after a hard day's slaughtering is tempting. On the kitchen table is a big plate of smoked salmon and a basket of lobsters, crabs and langoustines.

The hill lochs are stocked with brown and rainbow trout. In 1983 £750 would entitle you to a week's full board, as much fishing as you like, and the opportunity to go out with the head stalker Tommy Macrae and shoot four stags. 'Tommy', says the brochure, 'like his father and grandfather before him knows the ground intimately and will entertain you with fascinating and amusing tales of the area's history and tradition.'

There is no attempt to disguise the provenance of the operation. When you book you are invited to pay your money into a numbered account in a Zürich bank. The estate gives employment to staff and servants but its long-term profits are salted away elsewhere.

More and more people are beginning to question the advisability of allowing so much land in the Highlands and Islands to be abused for private gain. In the evidence which the Federation of Crofters Unions presented to the House of Commons Committee on Scottish Affairs when it was looking into the workings of the Highlands and Islands Development Board, they gave a striking example of the way in which private ownership can paralyse the development of a community. They concentrated on one area – Park in Lewis. Its history, said the submission, 'provides a good example of the disastrous results of the land use policy pursued by private landowners.'

Eishken Estate and its deer forest forms a large part of the Park area. When it was formed in Victorian times thirty communities were destroyed. Congestion and overcrowding led to depopulation. Angus Macleod, secretary of the Federation, whose home village is Calbost, described how the population has declined due to lack of any further prospects. It peaked at 200 in 1901; by 1941 it had sunk to 149. The real decline came after the Second World War. By 1951 there were only 64 people living in Calbost. There were only 16 in 1961 and in 1984 Calbost had shrunk to one household of two people. In 1887 the people of the Park peninsula had raided the deer forest of Eishken. A gunboat was despatched and the raiders withdrew. As Angus Macleod notes: 'Two-thirds of the peninsula is still a deer forest while most of the people have left.'

In 1983 the papers are full of stories about the feuding and fighting among estate owners and local poachers. Two estates in conflict are Grimersta, which owns the best salmon river in the west, and Garynahine. There is a hilarious court case in the Stornoway Sheriff Court in which three members of the Garynahine Estate are fined on charges of illegal fishing. Into the witness box come peers of the realm, water bailiffs, crofters and company directors. Like a latter-day Gilbert and Sullivan farce the trial grinds on. It is what Brian Wilson describes in the *Free Press* as 'the annual poaching pantomime with a rich range of character-actors flitting across the stage'.

But Wilson uses the occasion for his statutory polemic against private landowners.

> What possible public interest is served? The answer is none. The fact that so much legal drama should attach to the catching of a few fish which lie there surrounded by solemnity defrosting in the courtroom heat owes nothing to justice or common sense and everything to the existence of archaic laws written by the landlords for the landlords.

Wilson wants community ownership and management, a move which would prevent the coming and going of anonymous owners from overseas and perhaps put an end to the small private armies employed by the estates to protect their salmon from poachers.

Garynahine is less than a quarter the size of Eishken. It has only 12,500 acres but through them runs the famous Blackwater river. It advertises salmon and sea trout, rainbow and brown trout, grouse, snipe, woodcock, pheasant and duck shooting. It leapt into even more prominence in 1983 when it advertised the most expensive timeshare in the world. The owners, an associate company of Taddale Investments who claim their net tangible assets are in excess of £10 million were hoping to sell each of the 52 weeks in the year to potential timesharers at prices ranging from £5,350 to £53,000 a week. In addition each year you would be expected to pay a maintenance fee ranging from £1,136 to £8,246 for your week.

Imagine [runs the prospectus] being the owner of an estate in Scotland where shooting, fishing and all the rural sports are at hand. Imagine taking out your gun and hunting deer, your rod and fishing for salmon or walking up grouse, shooting pheasants for dinner. Imagine sea fishing, trout fishing and at the end of the day coming home to the comfort of your own estate lodge with faithful servants waiting to serve you that drink, a meal and look after your creature comforts.

The brochure recommends the estate to companies 'who could use the property for entertaining their clients and subject to revenue approval the costs may be tax deductible'. Guns can expect up to 200 pheasants a day, salmon up to 18lb in weight have been taken on the river.

I drive down to Garynahine to see this tax avoidance bargain. On the way I give a lift to a local whose car has broken down. 'Pheasants,' he says, 'they can't keep them on the estate, they're wandering all over the road or flying off to the woods in Stornoway. There's no deer, so what would you get for all that money?'

Garynahine lies at the head of Loch Roag, thirteen miles west of Stornoway. The lodge was built in 1720 as an inn and it lies on the main road. It sleeps a maximum of seventeen and has six bathrooms.

'You'll be lucky to get two fish a week,' says the chap I've given a lift to.

'Do the locals poach them all then?'

'I'm not saying who takes them, maybe they've just stopped coming.'

Outside on the lawn four hooded kestrels are chained to stakes, the property of a visiting sportsman. Inside the manager, Andrew Miller Mundy, a tall well-built man, is sitting in his office at the phone. I introduce myself; not as a potential purchaser of a tax deductible bit of timeshare but a passing traveller anxious to find out how the sale is going. He tells me that timeshare is very much in the air and, yes it has been advertised as the most expensive timeshare in the world, but he considers that £53,000 for the best fishing week of the year in perpetuity is quite a reasonable price.

'If you break it down to a syndicate of say ten fishermen all fishing they would only be paying £5,300 each which isn't expensive. And if you divide the maintenance fee by ten then that's only £250 a week, which works out very cheap. And on top of that they've got another five beds in the lodge.'

He tells me that although the estate reckons to get 200 salmon in a good year, at the moment they will be lucky to get a hundred.

'It's one of the quirks of fishing. We had a guy who came from Rhodesia and caught one trout; he went away happy.'

'How many salmon have been caught so far this year?' I ask; the date is
11 August.

'About five,' says Miller Mundy laconically.

'And brown trout?'

'God knows. About twenty.'

'If you admitted that in a prospectus nobody would buy even five minutes?'

'Yes, but you're being a bit unfair. You know the weather up here; the last
two summers have been exceptionally bad for fishing.'

The estate is employing seven men outside, eight in the lodge and another
two part-time employees. 'At the moment we've got eight days' shooting let;
that employs up to 25 beaters at £8 a day.'

It all seems like a gamble but if the syndicate who own Garynahine can
pull it off and sell every week on a timeshare basis they stand to gain £1.5
million – not a bad profit on the £180,000 they paid for the estate.

Indeed, speculation is the motive behind virtually all the land sales in the
Western Isles. In July 1983 the London property firm Portlandfield bought
the 2,000-acre Valtos estate. In October they recouped almost their entire
investment by selling three small offshore islands. The smallest, the 14-acre
island of Shiaram Mor off Uig, went to a Mr Sati Gulhati, the owner of a
chain of London hotels, for £11,000. The 250-acre Rabaidh Mor fetched
£19,000 from an unnamed ornithologist, and the 103-acre Vacsay island was
sold for £9,500.

Some investments make money; some lose. The biggest loss of recent
years in the Western Isles has been the £4 million which the Highlands and
Islands Development Board invested in a fish-processing plant just down the
road from Garynahine at Breasclete. It is a long and sorry story of false
hopes, mismanagement and final collapse. In 1977 the Board joined forces
with a Norwegian entrepreneur and formed a company called Lewis
Stokfisk. It was hoped, by providing a processing plant at Breasclete, to
develop the fishery resources west of Lewis. The factory was expected to
provide 34 full-time jobs and 15 part-time jobs and Breasclete was regarded
as an important part of the Board's overall strategy for fish development.

Today the functional, elegant-looking building lies empty and un-
attended. On the pier a rusty lorry stands with flat tyres. An equally rusty
fishing boat is tied up at the pier. The project has been abandoned.

In a house nearby I talk to Dr Alastair Fraser who gave up his job as
Deputy Rector of the Nicolson Institute to manage the project. He is
scathing about the whole concept. 'It was a sorry, crazy business,' he says
and tells me his side of the story. At the end of 1983 the Receiver sold the

fish-processing equipment at a knockdown price to the Norwegian businessman who had originally persuaded the Board to back him. It was an unprofitable ending to the most disastrous single episode in the Board's history.

I wonder how long the brown futuristic factory will lie on the shores of Loch Roag. It faces another puzzling construction which nobody quite knows the purpose of – the Standing Stones of Callanish, second only to Stonehenge in archaeological importance. They have been there perhaps for 4,000 years. Was it the site of a temple, an astronomical laboratory, a graveyard, a monument to some long-dead king?

Close by the stones, which look like teeth on the skyline, is an old black house which has been converted into a tea room. Perhaps they'll be able to tell me more. They don't really want to tell me anything. The lady in charge, wearing a tartan skirt, turns out to be Frau Beatrice Schulz from Düsseldorf; assisting her with the tea and cakes is her taciturn daughter Dagmar. The house, she says, is 150 years old and was lived in until 1976.

'When we saw this house an old couple still lived in it; that was in 1974. We fell in love with the place.'

Frau Schulz's husband has a photographic business in the Rhineland where they settled after they fled from East Prussia.

'We got to know the lady who owned this place. The roof was all collapsed. She sold it to us and then we started some rather hard business to get planning permission but we didn't give up and after some time we got it. It was really the stories of Callanish and the stones that brought us here.'

The ever-helpful Board gave Frau Schulz a grant to convert the old black house into a tea room. I'm beginning to wonder whether everything of note in this island isn't owned by enterprising aliens – Swiss at Eishken, absconded Norwegians at Breasclete, Germans at Callanish. I ask Frau Schulz what kind of grant she got from the Board and she tells me it's none of my business, and I suppose she's right.

That night I sink back into Lewis hospitality and go and stay with Annie and Kenny MacInnes at Linshader right on the shore of Loch Ceann Hulavig and less than a mile from the stones of Callanish. Their house was built in 1928, four years after Leverhulme's farm was broken into crofts. Kenny has two crofts of 4½ acres each and well over 2,000 sheep. Honeysuckle and roses are growing profusely. There's an apple tree in the garden, a patch of mint, rows of potatoes and at the end of the house, in the byre they built in 1937, there's a cow. When I sit down for my tea fresh milk and homemade butter are brought to the table.

This corner of Lewis is well-farmed and everywhere people are renewing their fences and fanks. The EEC has given £250,000 to build a new road bridge and notices announcing this event have been erected: 'Each one cost £150,' an old man tells me. The Integrated Development Programme in the Western Isles which makes money available for a variety of projects has manifested itself in the biggest fence-building epidemic for years. When a crofter builds a fence using his own labour he gets back 110 per cent of the cost of materials.

'If you've nothing better to do,' a crofter says, tightening a wire, 'then it makes sense to avail yourself of the money – and fences are always useful.'

After supper I sit chatting with Kenny, a man in his mid-60s. He has very vivid memories of his childhood and in a way he seems to regret the passing of the old days, and even more the old ways.

'When I was very, very young I can remember the old black house and the fire in the middle of the floor. And this was a spess-ee-ull place', he gives the word its three full syllables, 'that was looked upon as a place of gathering. Maybe an old bachelor lived there and everyone from the village would come in and they would sit round and if there was no chair you got some peats and piled them one, two, three, four', Kenny builds a peat bench in the air with his hands, 'and you could sit there and they would be discussing what was going on. And maybe there was somebody there who was flush enough to have tobacco and he'd fill his pipe and pass it round.'

'Did that transmit TB do you think?'

'Well you never know; you never know. But once the TB set in, that was it. I lost a brother in 1924 and he was only 11 years old. He got a new pair of boots and somehow the boots cut his heel and it developed into blood poisoning. He was taken to the hospital but there was no penicillin in those days and once you got the poisoning that was it.'

And what were the topics of conversation at these impromptu ceilidhs? Tales of the past, legends, myth, great sagas?

'No, no! It was what were you doing today and if you weren't here last night what were you doing then? How many sheep did you see and all the rest of it. It was the daily paper.'

'And what has replaced that?'

Kenny gives a snort of dismissal. 'Nothing. It's died. It's dead. Gone.'

'Altogether?'

'Yes, completely. In those days there were no dances, there was no bar, that's all they had. Now they're all watching the box; they've all got cars they can nip across to Stornoway and get in the boozers. That's the other downfall; people getting into the pubs and getting drunk.'

'You mean forty years ago there was no drink?'

'You couldn't afford it, and you couldn't get it. I can remember in the parish of Uig when there was four public service vehicles and only three private cars.'

Kenny recalls it as being a much more friendly place in the old days. 'When everyone gathered round the peat fire cracking jokes it was friendly, yes. Before the war, once it was getting dark and we were finished for the day you could go out for a ceilidh and go down the village. Since the war it's a mad rush to beat the clock which you can never do. Work now never seems to end. What's the cause of this I don't know but before the war people were happy. They were finished work when it was twilight and they had the rest of the evening for themselves. Now suppose the chimney was on fire, suppose the house was on fire they'd sit watching that bloody *Crossroads*!'

Like many other persons in the Hebrides, Kenny has travelled all over the world but there were plenty of islands close by he'd never set foot on.

'I'd been as far as Singapore but never been in Skye. So they said how about having two or three days off? Well, what would I want with two or three days off? Anyway I said, "Well I tell you what, there's one place I've never been to and that's Skye." So I took the ferry at Tarbert and my youngest son's wife's uncle lives in Kyleakin and I went straight for Kyleakin – got a bed and breakfast job there. We toured Skye for two days and honest to God we didn't see anyone working on a croft. There was no crops, no potatoes, there was nothing! So we came to the conclusion they must be living on tourists.' Kenny looks at me with wonder but then he says that maybe they have more sense in Skye than in Lewis.

'A week last Monday sheep were fetching 50 pence a pound. You go to the auction in Stornoway and they say "we're not buying today". You take your cattle home and you go back in three or four weeks and it's the same old faces and they know you've been there before. You can't win; so why not park a caravan on your croft? You can let it for £60 a week, no bother!'

We talk about the salmon poaching and Kenny tells me that his grandfather was one of the first ghillies hired at Grimersta in 1886. 'My father took over in 1907. I started in 1946 and I got a pound a day. During the winter my father was weaving on the old handloom. But if you were going to be ghillying you weren't going to be weaving and if you were weaving you weren't going to be ghillying so I packed it up for a pound a day. I sold the loom for £25; now a new loom would cost you well over £2,000. When I stopped weaving in 1964 I was getting £5.80 for a length of tweed, the same length these days is £50. When I was young I used to buy half a bottle of whisky for 6s 6d. That was a day and a half's work because I was getting four shillings a day. Now it only takes about 2½ hours to earn enough money for half a bottle.'

'So we're better off?'

'We're better off yes. But we're not so happy as we were.' Kenny points a scornful finger at the 21-inch screen in the corner of the room. 'Now that's what you're looking at. We don't bother to go out of our houses and that's the downfall of the community here!'

I go up to my bedroom in the attic and swing the Velux window open. The waters on the loch are still and there is just the occasional complaint of a sheep. Have we really lost something, somewhere between the time they stood the stones eight and twelve feet high at Callanish and the building of the great futile brown box beside the sea at Breasclete? And if so, then what?

4

A HARVEST NO MAN SHOULD DESPISE

LINSHADER TO RODEL

After a big breakfast of porridge and bacon and egg I leave lovely Linshader and drive past the Grimersta estate and its river, which is considered by salmon fishermen to offer the finest sport in Europe; local lads regard it as fair game too. Last night was an ideal one for poaching, no moon, and I wonder how many fish were lifted illegally from the river.

The road runs round the steep fjord-like head of Little Loch Roag and past the island's first hydro-electric plant at Gisla, the only man-made intrusion on the empty rolling moors. At Carishader, a stretch of road lined with crofts, the vista of Loch Roag opens up, peppered with islands.

One of them is little more than a 14-acre rock. This is the island which was sold to the Indian-born hotelier for £11,000. When I rang Mr Gulhati after the sale he had only the vaguest idea of where his little bit of the Hebrides was. He told me that he thought he might put a house on it; take his children there for holidays.

'There's nothing there,' I told him, 'no water, no electricity, not a twig!'

'Have you seen this island?' he asked.

'Yes,' I said, 'you might put a few sheep on it.'

'What's the weather like?' he wanted to know.

'Terrible', I said, 'for most of the year; you wouldn't be able to stand upright for the wind!' I don't think it put him off at all.

The selling of these little Hebridean islets is harmless enough, you might say. 'It's only a game,' said a London estate agent who specialises in such auctions; 'people very often buy on impulse. They think it would be a sort of fun thing to own an island specially in the Hebrides – you know it's very romantic and *unusual*.'

Even more unusual is Glen Valtos. There's nothing quite like it anywhere in the Hebrides. It reminds me of one of those canyons in a wild west film in which the Wells Fargo stagecoach is ambushed by Comanches. A bit sinister too, even though there is a small oasis of trees, one of only about five plantations in the whole of Lewis.

Alastair Fraser of Callanish had told me a nice story about this Glen. There was a murder there and it turned out that the blacksmith had done it. He was duly sentenced to be hanged. Asked if he had any statement to make in mitigation he said that as he was the only blacksmith for forty miles and there were three joiners in Valtos it would be a bit shortsighted to hang him. After a bit of thought they hanged one of the joiners.

The glen opens into Uig Bay and one of the most beautiful beaches in the west, overlooked by the townships of Crowlista, Timsgarry and Carnish. Commanding extensive views over two miles of sand is a tall rectangular building with an Italianate tower. This fishing lodge was built for Sir James Matheson and when I was last here in 1980 it was being run as a hotel. I stayed the night and sent a report to the *Good Hotel Guide*. 'There are eleven bedrooms, four with private bathrooms,' my report ran. 'Unfortunately you may arrive to find everyone has had a bath and only lukewarm water is left. You may also arrive on a chill May evening to find that, although the small electric fire in your room has been switched hospitably on it points parsimoniously to "1" when a maximum "9" is called for.' I also recorded two hot water bottles in my bed, fresh vegetables and excellent roast mutton.

Unforgivably, as I found out later, I upset the Davis family who were running it by suggesting that although the beach was breathtaking the house itself was ugly and I noted that there was not a tree or a bit of shrubbery in sight. I also complained about the wretched processed white bread.

In the 1982 *Guide* the editor noted that the resident manager, Richard Davis, had taken umbrage at my words. Nobody else had said the house was ugly. Austere, yes. He also pointed out that 'there are several trees in full view of our front door'. However there had been one bonus from my visit. 'We are glad to learn', wrote *Guide* editor Hilary Rubinstein, 'that the hotel has been making its own home-made bread since the start of the 1981 season.' Something achieved at least.

I thought it might be a nice gesture to go and apologise to Richard Davis for not noticing his several trees and confusing the austere with the ugly. I drove down to the gaunt lodge – I think gaunt is permissible – and rapped on the open door. While I waited I had another look at the house. Come to think of it, it looked exactly like a station hotel with its big windows painted incongruously a royal blue. A well-dressed woman appeared in the entrance hall.

'I was wondering if I could have a room for the night?'

'Well,' said the woman in *Country Life* tones, 'I'm afraid this is a private house.'

I explained that the last time I'd clapped eyes on it it was functioning as a hotel.

'We let it as a whole lodge occasionally but I'm afraid you can't just drop in for the night.'

I asked how much it would be if I took it all, though as she would gather, I wasn't quite ready to take it there and then. 'Well it's £800 for six rods. Actually the fishing has been rather good in the last ten days – now we're just waiting for the rain like the rest of Scotland.'

By this time I'd been invited in. I asked her what had happened to the Davis family and how she came to be there?

'Well they rather gave up after a bit. As for us, well my son was *frightfully* keen to get something and he finally dropped on *this*. Actually we're the grandparents. We've got two sons, they sort of own it between them. They come for about three weeks themselves on and off.' She pronounced the word 'orf' as a shooting hostess might have in palmier Edwardian times.

I left hoping that my entry in the *Good Hotel Guide* hadn't led to the demise of the Davises. I looked back as I shut the cattle gate behind me. It was still an ugly house. I decided to try the old manse at Timsgarry which was being run as a guesthouse by Richard and Joanna Gollin. Richard told me he taught a business course at Lews College during the day and lent a hand waiting at table at night. He also told me a very sad story about the minister who used to live there.

I talked earlier about the Free Church without explaining how it got its title. It came about in 1843 when 480 ministers of the Church of Scotland renounced the Establishment and set up the Free Church. This Disruption, as it was known, was motivated by a desire not to have ministers forced on congregations against their will. The new congregations took to the hillsides to worship until such time as they might collect enough money to build a permanent house of God. Many landowners resolutely refused to provide land, hoping that the people would be discouraged and return to the Established Church.

Richard Gollin tells me that the minister at that time came to rather a sticky end. 'I understand, and I would stress that this is a foreigner from Watford talking, that his congregation departed leaving only his deaf old servant who used to attend church with her cow. Because income was tied strictly to productivity he would have got paid nothing with no parishioners so he gradually started building up an imaginary congregation. It grew so large that Edinburgh were impressed enough to write and say that they were sending someone to have a look at all these faithful adherents to the Church – at which he hanged himself in the stable. Actually I'm a bit suspicious about this because that particular minister is supposed to be buried in the cemetery just beyond the wall there. I checked with the Church of Scotland and it's only in the last twenty years that they've allowed suicides to be buried in a graveyard.'

I climb over the gate into the small graveyard which is knee-high with nettles, hoping to find the poor forsaken minister's memorial. The place is full of stones, most of them rendered illegible by the winter gales, but no reference to a suicide.

There is an American girl and her boyfriend and a couple from Yorkshire staying the night. The house dates from 1783 and the Gollins bought it very cheaply. It shows signs of extensive improvement – 'We got a local authority grant to do it up – this new roof cost £18,000 alone.'

Once again it's thrusting incomers that seem to be making the going. Why, I wonder, does it take someone from Kent or Watford to do all these interesting things? Why not a local? Perhaps you need to be a stranger to have the persistence to get the grants and beaver away successfully. Of course, once you've got the Hebridean bug – as the Gollins patently have – you don't rest until you've found a niche for yourself. It's a bug which bites the most unlikely people.

Later in the day I bump into a couple from Zürich. At first I take him for a Swiss but he tells me that his mother came from Mallaig, his father from Chard in Somerset. Twenty-two years ago he went to live in Switzerland where he met his wife, Hildegard. They have built themselves a bungalow at Ardroil and ask me in for a bite. The bite turns out to be smoked salmon and a superb bottle of riesling. The place is lavishly equipped like an Ideal Home show house. There's a four-poster bed and the very latest kitchen technology.

He was born William Rowe but now as a Bernina executive his name is Rowe-Klaus. What on earth brought him to a tiny township like Ardroil?

'We first came to the Hebrides when the seaman's strike was on. We waited for days in Uig in Skye to get across and when we finally came here we thought it was wonderful. Full of nice people and no stress, that's what we want.'

Hildegard agrees. 'If I were a normal Swiss woman I wouldn't be here but then I'm not, so I like it too.' They both come in the spring to cut peat alongside their neighbours and their sense of belonging is palpable and obviously gives them a deep sense of satisfaction.

'This March', says Willie, 'my neighbour died, in the house over there. They telephoned to tell me. I dropped everything and flew from Zürich for the funeral. Why not? What's 3,000 kilometres when it's your neighbour who's died? We live in an over-organised world. This isn't organised at all and that suits us.'

Willie pours me another glass of riesling and beams at his good fortune to be here in this elaborately organised bungalow in the heart of a disorganised rural community which has welcomed him with open arms. All the wifies now have Bernina sewing machines and Willie and Hildegard have found a friendship here that may well be lacking in Zürich. 'Wonderful people,' says Willie, 'you wouldn't find people like this anywhere in the world.'

I drive back down the road and a few miles further on find a locked gate. Locked gates have a fascination for me, especially ones that say PRIVATE NO ADMITTANCE on them; it is an irresistible invitation to the curious. I get out the Ordnance Survey map and find that the gate bars the road to Morsgail Lodge and Morsgail forest, a vast hinterland of 13,000 acres. Sir James Matheson created it by depriving crofters of their grazing rights in 1850 and despite the recommendations of the Deer Forest Commission it has never been returned to crofting use.

I climb over the gate and start walking up the estate road which runs beside a fast-flowing burn dammed at several stages to create enticing salmon pools. It's about a mile and a half to the lodge which is situated on a knoll above Loch Morsgail. There are scores more lochs on the estate and a network of rivers and burns. Beside the lodge built by Matheson is an eight-wheeled Crayford Argocat in which, if it worked, you could take off into the interior with your rods and guns and not be seen for days.

I'm in luck; a middle-aged man in the crofter's uniform, blue dungarees, is just locking up the back door. Courteously he says I'm welcome to look round the house. 'Not that there's much to see, the roof's done, full of dry rot. The house has been empty for the last eight years – I'd say it was unsaleable.'

Over the years I've been in many a crumbling shooting lodge but this one really has got a doomed air about it. Tin baths and basins have been placed rather hopelessly about to catch water coming from holes in the ceiling. In the kitchen there is the usual collection of jam jars, old kettles, rusty colanders, cane chairs, chipped enamel pie dishes and cracked cups. There are iron bedsteads upstairs, damp flock mattresses, faded curtains hanging at the windows.

The caretaker tells me that the place has been disastrously neglected. 'These days you'd be lucky to get two salmon a week out of the river. It's all nettled out there at the mouth of the loch.'

'You'd need a lot of staff to keep a place like this up.'

'In the old days they had them, as many as they wanted; they used to live in bothies. Then after the war they started coming to work in saloon cars and were wanting to finish at five and be paid overtime and that was the end of it. It was a different life for the rich in the old days.'

He shows me out and I walk back down the road to the padlocked gate. For the first time in my journey the full meaning of speculative landlordism sinks in. Nothing has happened on these thousands of acres for three years. Tenants have come and gone, ghillies have been given small sums of money to perform subservient chores, and no doubt a few local women have been employed in the house over the years – cooking and cleaning and carrying coals and hot water.

But in terms of lasting benefit to the community – nothing. I am reminded of the words of the late Sir Frank Fraser Darling who set up what came to be known as the West Highland Survey at Strontian in Ardnamurchan in 1944. He subtitled his work 'an essay in human ecology' and his conclusion was that 'the Highlands and Islands are largely a devastated terrain . . . any policy which ignores this fact cannot hope to achieve rehabilitation' (*West Highland Survey*, edited by F. Fraser Darling, Oxford University Press, 1955).

Fraser Darling's analysis of the plight of the West Highlands did not make acceptable reading: those in power ignored the findings. He pointed out a path that has never been followed. 'There are three bodies of Scotland', he wrote, 'that should be able to work in close co-operation and to rid their minds of narrowly pragmatic notions. The Department of Agriculture has great power, plantations and land; the Forestry Commission also has power, plantations and land; the Nature Conservancy has little land as yet but may be expected to develop ideas and techniques in conservation and the ecology of land use. We wait for the lead to be given.'

The lead was never given. Not even when the Highlands and Islands Development Board was set up in 1965 did anyone sit down and re-read *West Highland Survey*. Had they done so much more might have been accomplished in the last twenty years. As it is estates like Morsgail continue to lie fallow, occasionally changing hands but contributing nothing to the well-being of the communities they overshadow and paralyse.

In September 1984 Morsgail changed hands once again. The syndicate of Irish businessmen whose company, Crannog Holdings, was registered in that tax haven the Isle of Man, sold Morsgail to Beaver Tool Ltd. They had previously disposed of the crofting estate of Uig to another syndicate. In all 40,000 acres changed hands again. In January 1985 Morsgail Lodge was gutted by a mysterious fire; the land remains idle. And so it goes.

There is not a road on the south-west coast of Lewis and Harris at all. To get from Brenish which lies beyond Uig Bay to Hushinish ten miles south you have to retrace your steps virtually all the way to Stornoway – a frustrating trek of 80 miles! On that journey you suddenly find yourself in Harris – the moors of Lewis wash up against a range of bony hills which reach their peak in the Clisham which is 2,622 feet above sea level. The soil is thin, the land largely infertile. The west is less barren. Much of that was converted into sheep farms in the nineteenth century and the people were removed summarily to the stony eastern coast. Here they built their elaborate lazybeds, *feannagan*, which give the lie to anyone who would suggest an islander is by temperament lazy.

'Nothing', wrote Fraser Darling in the early 1950s, 'can be more moving to the sensitive observer of Hebridean life than these lazybeds. Some are no bigger than a dining-table and possibly the same height from the rock, carefully built up with turves and the seaweed carried there in creels by the women and the girls. One of these tiny lazybeds will yield a sheaf of oats or a bucket of potatoes, a harvest no man should despise.'

Few of them are worked now but they lie there as a monument to determination in the face of adversity. In Scalpay alone there were 150 acres of these lazybeds – but that was before the rise of convenience food and the deep freeze.

I crossed on the ferry to spend a night on Scalpay. The small island is still heavily populated; it's difficult to believe that 450 people live here. Although the fishing is relatively good and Scalpay has one of the most prosperous communities in the Western Isles, the ferryman who sells me a ticket tells me that since Britain joined the Common Market things haven't been so good.

'It was on the herring that they used to depend; it was herring they were after all those years. Then they had to go to the white fish and the prawns. As soon as the Minch re-opened they went back to the herring but there was no demand for it. Right now four boats have gone to the prawn fishing, they're doing well at that – *very* well.'

The road down to the ferry slip from Tarbert had been a switchback of almost unrelieved grey rock. Ahead Scalpay in the evening sun looks fresh and green; the Shiants lie on the horizon bathed in light.

I'm the last car off and the skipper gives me directions to his brother's house, Suil-na-Mara, where I'm going to stay the night. Mrs MacSween is at church; the island is stolidly Wee Free with only one in ten adhering to the Church of Scotland.

When she returns I ask her about Murdo MacSween, a brilliant cook who was one of the founders of the Club of Seven British chefs. I wonder if she's any relation? 'He's a member of our family, Murdo, he's done very well down in London.'

Murdo's aunts Chrissie and Lily MacSween were both in turn married to Sir Compton Mackenzie. 'Yes, Chrissie and Lily are relatives of mine. Their father Calum lived in Tarbert. He was a great friend of Compton Mackenzie's of course.'

Mrs MacSween busies herself making tea. The house is spotless and gleams with care. The garden outside is as blooming as any garden in an English village. Had her family always lived on Scalpay?

'No, my great grandfather came from St Kilda.'

I have noted that islanders tend to gravitate to other islands.

'I think that's true. I have a cousin of my mother who's out in the Falklands. My son went out to the Falklands; altogether there were six Scalpay families who went to live out there.'

Scalpachs, I've been told, are very proud of their island.

'Yes,' said Mrs MacSween, 'my father coming back from Vancouver just rejoiced in meeting the stones themselves let alone the people.'

On the bookcase there are portraits of beautifully dressed children and a formal wedding with royalty in the group. Mrs MacSween tells me shyly that she was nanny to the Burtons of Dochfour. 'There were 600 guests at that wedding at St James's and the Queen Mother and the Duchess of Kent were there. You take milk?'

In the morning at eight o'clock she brings me a cup of tea and draws the curtains back to reveal a cascade of cardinal-red fuchsias growing on the slope behind the bungalow, a blaze of Romish colours in this Free Church island. A sheep is poised on a rock and its black face gazes down incuriously.

I get dressed and go for a walk. It has been raining in the night and the wind is fresh; what would pass for a brisk winter's day in the south of England. There are piles of coals beside each house and peatstacks. Although the skies are blue you need a thick sweater.

Scalpay is an island of surprises. A small patch of corn and potatoes waves beside a house where a plastic gnome, miles from Surbiton, stands nipped by the cold, his hands on a little empty barrow.

I return to the neat pebble-harled bungalow with its Cambridge blue paintwork and trim privet hedges. It stands like a suburban intrusion on this rocky stony ground.

'An aunt of Murdo's lives across the road,' says Mrs MacSween, bringing in porridge and oatcakes, 'I remembered to tell you after you'd gone to bed.' There is scrambled eggs and bacon and enough hot toast to feed a coach party.

I call on Scalpay's minister, the Rev. Alastair Smith. He, like many another islander, spent his early life at sea. It was when his father died at a comparatively early age that he got what is known in Gaelic as the *curam*. It is the anxiety for the future, the donning of the mantle of responsibility – the sudden act that changes one's life and brings one to Christ. This conversion can take many forms. It may be sparked off by reading the Bible, through hearing a particularly relevant sermon, or by contact with some devoutly religious person. Those who have had the *curam* turn over a new leaf. If they have been drinkers they will become rigid teetotallers. Dancing will be avoided and it will be seen by the rest of the community that the grace of God has descended and the recipient is born again.

In the Rev. Alastair's case the *curam* took him beyond communion and into the ministry. He is an easy man to talk to and we have a long discussion about that vexed question of hanging. He gives me the arguments for and against and we end up agreeing that it is a difficult thing.

How, I ask him, would he have addressed his congregation if he had been in the pulpit on the Sunday after the *Iolaire* had been lost? What words of consolation would he have extended to the bereaved?

'Well you would have to explain that there is a purpose in all God's actions – a Divine purpose which we here on earth can never fully comprehend. If we could we would be Divine ourselves. There are good reasons for all God's actions and with our limited vision how can we tell why such and such a thing occurs?'

I get the feeling that the Scalpachs are in good and moderate hands. I don't think the Rev. Alastair would willingly hang anyone.

Scalpay itself lies at the mouth of East Loch Tarbert where the ferry from Skye calls daily. I turn off before Tarbert and take the road along the coast to Hushinish and the island of Scarp. Halfway down the coast the road passes directly in front of Amhuinnsuidhe castle, built in 1868 by the Earl of Dunmore. It is an imposing pile and its most recent owner, a Swiss, lavished vast amounts of money on it, installing bidets in the twelve bedrooms and papering the walls with costly fabrics.

While staying in the castle, which he had rented for the summer just after

the Great War, Sir James Barrie, son of a Kirriemuir weaver, went fishing on
Loch Voshimid in the heart of the estate's unforested Forest of Harris. The
loch is dappled with islets and Barrie dubbed one of them The Isle that
Likes to be Visited and wove a fey drama called *Mary Rose* around it.

The castle is still for rent; the going rate is £5,500 a week which includes
the services of the three ghillies, Kenny, Roddie and Alcc, and the use of a
motor boat for sea-fishing trips. Tenants are expected to pay the wages of
the two cooks, three daily maids (Peggy, Dolly and Morag) and Ann-Marie
the continental living-in maid. Additional ghillies can be hired for £12 a day
and stalking can also be indulged in for an extra charge of £160 plus VAT for
every stag shot. It is not a cheap package as package holidays go but
Amhuinnsuidhe (pronounced Avven-*soo*-ey) is seldom empty, which is more
than can be said for the thousands of acres which surround it.

The road ends in an idyllic beach of cream sand and even creamier waves.
A track leads north to a pier once used by the islanders of Scarp. The island
was settled at the beginning of the nineteenth century but evacuated finally
in 1971. What few cottages remain are now used as holiday homes, but even
more exotic and ambitious plans are afoot. It has just been announced that
Rolf Rothmayer, who bought Scarp from a Mr Dewsbery, has sold it to a
hotel potentate called Nazmu Virani for £80,000.

Mr Virani, who runs the Virani Hotel Group, is planning a £3 million
holiday playground for the rich on windswept Scarp. It will have its own
airstrip and 150 Highland-style cottages. 'Inside', Mr Virani tells the *Caterer
and Hotelkeeper*, 'they will have coal or peat-burning fires as part of the
tradition but otherwise they will be to the highest international hotel
standards. It will not be anything like rows of chalets.'

There is to be a central luxury complex with a five-star international-class
restaurant and bars, swimming pools, saunas, solarium, squash courts and
all-weather tennis courts. That will be very necessary – Scarp is exposed to
the full force of the Atlantic gales – but Mr Virani sees no problem. 'What
we have in mind', he tells the *Caterer*, 'is the sort of development where if you
have to ask the prices you won't be coming.'

Perhaps Mr Virani could jet his trendsetting international guests in by
rocket; it would fit in perfectly with the rest of the fantasy plans which will
never come to fruition. And rockets would be nothing new. Old men in
Harris will still tell you about Gerhard Zucha who in July 1934 chose Scarp
as the scene of the world's first ever mail-by-rocket experiment.

He had already tested his rocket successfully in the Harz mountains and
on Brighton beach but this was to be the first inter-island experiment.

Accompanied by pressmen he arrived in Tarbert with his patron Herr Dombrowsky. So impressed was the GPO that they sent the postmaster from Lochmaddy to attend the trials.

The first apparatus was erected on a stretch of sand below the schoolhouse and the hollow rocket was loaded with letters and parcels. There were four addressed to King George V, a keen philatelist, and one from the Harris branch of the British Legion to the Prince of Wales. 'To test the inventor's claim that medicine could be carried if securely wrapped', reported the *Stornoway Gazette*, 'it was decided to send a bottle of cod liver oil to the twins at Scarp whose fame has gone abroad in many lands.' There was also an envelope with a 1½*d* rocket stamp addressed to Sir Godfrey Collins which carried two prime Scalpay herring and a note exhorting the Secretary of State to eat more herring and persuade the rest of Britain to do the same. Other rocket missives were addressed to Stanley Baldwin, the Prime Minister, and Lord Londonderry, Minister of Air.

Never had such excitement been generated. With Herr Dombrowsky and his assistant the inventor retired to a hollow below the huge boulders at the top of the beach and the three figures crouched dramatically over the firing switch.

'The crowd watched closely,' said the *Gazette*, 'eager to see the mail shoot forward on its journey to the mainland of Harris. The button was touched, there was a dull explosion and a flash of fire. For a second smoke obscured everything but when it cleared the firing apparatus was seen in ruins on the beach; the steel rocket in the midst torn and twisted and the letters strewn about the sand, many of them charred and burnt. Someone in the crowd laughed.'

Oh, the cruelty of the crofters!

Poor Herr Zucha tried to fire a second rocket but that didn't work either. On the following Monday the weather was unsuitable but on Tuesday the party repaired to Amhuinnsuidhe castle and had another go. There was a flash of fire, a burst of smoke and the letters were spread once again like confetti round the ruins of the rocket.

The Hebrides had to wait until the 1960s for rockets that worked but London was less fortunate. As the war clouds gathered Herr Zucha moved to Peenemunde and his peaceful postal rocket metamorphosed into the highly lethal V2.

South Harris begins at Tarbert. Its eastern coast is carved almost entirely out of rock. Here and there patches of green indicate the tenuous adhesion of soil, but the gneiss shows relentlessly through; so rocky is it that there is not a cemetery on that eastern coast at all – every corpse had to be carried to the west coast to be buried.

It was to South Harris that Lord Leverhulme came when the natives of Lewis resisted his plans to change their lives dramatically. He chose the township of Obbe to be his new Stornoway. Even after sixty years of decay and rust you marvel at the scale of his enterprise. Altogether he spent £525,000, a fortune in those days, building a pier, kippering sheds, roads and houses, but when he died in 1925 the enterprise died with him and most of his investment was sold as scrap.

There was no doubt at all that Leverhulme was a man of exceptional commercial genius. You can still see at Geocrab one of his brighter ideas – water turbines to run a tweed mill – but somehow his vision was inimical to the isles. The natives of Obbe did invite him to change the name of their village to Leverburgh and in return he built them a public hall – Hulme Hall it was called – but I wonder just how welcome and popular he was.

How welcome are the English now? They still suffer from the initial disadvantage of having very loud and assertive voices in this land of the soft-spoken. In the Tarbert Hotel one day when I was lurking in the bar having a half pint of McEwen's Export, not one of life's great treats, I had to put up with these Force 8 Oxbridge accents describing some absolutely super party at Magdalen and what Roger had done to Henrietta. 'No!' they brayed, 'Super!' all at the top of their alien voices.

Perhaps that was why Donald Stewart, MP for the Western Isles, tabled a Commons question to Edward Heath on 28 July 1971 asking him to negotiate with the governments of Australia and Canada 'with a view to assisting 20 million people to emigrate from England to these countries'.

Mr Stewart had been reading a report that said England would be bursting at the seams in the not far distant future and he was concerned that their excess population would overflow into Scotland. 'This purely English problem', he said, 'should be tackled on a large scale while there is still time. Otherwise the obliteration of the national identity of Scotland will arouse the greatest opposition and hostility.'

A decade later the English are still moving in; a lot of them doing good by stealth. None more so than that quiet couple Alison and Andrew Johnson, who have been running the old manse at Scarista since the mid-1970s. Andrew comes from Saltash; he took a degree in Natural Science at Cambridge and went on to a doctorate in metallurgy at Oxford. Alison read

English at Aberdeen, went south to Oxford and acquired a B.Phil. In 1973, yearning for the islands, they took a crash course at the teacher training college in Aberdeen and crossed the Minch to become teachers at the secondary school in Tarbert.

In December 1976 they bought the old derelict manse of Scarista, which had been built in 1827 by the Rev. Alexander Bethune. It looks over an incomparable vista of sands and across the Sound of Taransay to the hills of North Harris. Andrew re-slated the roof, put in central heating, re-plumbed and rewired. Alison relaid the flagged stone floors and created a fruit and vegetable garden out of a wilderness. Then they opened Scarista in June 1978 as a hotel. Since then it has won awards in all the guides for its hospitality and its food. 'This is the nicest hotel I've stayed in between here and Kathmandu,' enthused a *Good Hotel Guide* reader. In 1984 it won the *Guide*'s award for 'civilised living in the wilds'. It serves the best food in the Outer Hebrides, if not the whole of the Hebrides. Nothing comes out of a packet or a tin and the very little from the deep freeze is fresh food stored for later use.

When I called on the Johnsons Alison told me about a couple of catering food salesman who had been making their annual trip down the archipelago. 'When I told them I didn't use convenience food they wouldn't believe me. "Everyone else does." Well I don't, I said, we only use fresh food. They looked at each other and then one of them said, "Could we book for dinner tonight?"'

Dinner at Scarista – and people drive all the way from Stornoway for the experience – is unpretentious but unique in these parts. The Johnsons aren't making a fortune but I only wish more people would copy them. A few years ago Alison wrote me a letter describing just what the problems facing a hotelier in a remote region are. I print it because it shows how determined you have to be not to resort to the kind of over-processed food that most Hebridean hotels settle for as a miserable second best:

> The Hebrides [she said] teem with good natural ingredients: heather-and-seaweed-fed mutton, wild red-deer venison, a vast variety of fish from salmon to octopus, and superb shellfish.
>
> But putting your hands on all this stuff is a strenuous full-time business. Ask the estates for salmon, and you find it's all being blast-frozen and despatched south, though anonymous phone calls offer you fish by the hundredweight. Last winter I waited hopefully for my usual three prime hinds, only to find that our supplier couldn't get to his

shooting for heavy snow. Scallop divers get the bends, prawn fishers lose their gear in Atlantic storms, Calum who grows our potatoes shows an unshakeable faith in beastly Kerr's Pinks.

And what of exotica? Well, everything from cream to Kiwi fruit is exotic in Harris, and has to be organized by letter or telephone to make its way to the post van or the twice-weekly bus. People often ask if I plan my menus during the winter, that happy season of repose and meditation in which mainlanders envisage us. Not likely! Probably the turbot will arrive by 5 p.m. – if not I'll still have three hours to replace it – but the Stilton and grapes (to be served at 8.45) aren't scheduled to arrive till 8.15 (quick dash down the drive in the rain). I used to count on things, before the strawberry episode. They featured on the menu – the bus arrived – the cartons were there – but not the strawberries. They must have shared a back seat with one who couldn't resist temptation. Then there was the gentleman who came specially to enjoy our cheeseboard. I ordered £30 worth of the stuff from a reputable Edinburgh supplier. The cheese-loving gent came and went – no sign of the cheese. A Bank Holiday intervened, followed by a suppurating parcel of exploded Stilton and other horrors.

One learns to make other arrangements – never order from one firm when you could order from two. It's not economic, but it saves embarrassment. If we wanted to make a profit, I suppose we would do what many Highland hotels obviously feel forced to – rely on frozen, portion-controlled, utterly reliable, utterly boring supplies, and forget all about the halibut too small for Billingsgate, the half-boxes of prawns too few for market delivered at midnight for two hours of weary preparation, the egg that Henrietta looks as if she might lay any minute so that Mrs X needn't have a battery one in her scrambled.

We couldn't stand the boredom of it, though. All the enjoyment of our work comes from doing it as well as we possibly can, and better than anyone has a right to expect in such a far-flung locality.

We are becoming more and more obssessive about the freshness of our food. We like salmon from the sea not the river, lobster that hasn't been ponded, fish that hasn't languished on ice, venison (but it must be a first-rate beast) that has been hung for three days not three weeks. I won't start preparing food till the last possible minute and many are the scenes in the kitchen when some innocent diner takes too long eating his prawns, so that his vegetables go soggy. We don't have a *bain marie* any more than a microwave and class them as works of the devil. The porridge does not brew overnight in the Aga and we don't compose Crécy soup out of yesterday's left-over veg, *pace* the Stornoway diner who confidently so asserted. As for those dishes beloved of female cookery writers which 'keep well in a refrigerator for a week or in a freezer for three months', may they and their authors go to perdition. We don't believe in can't and are prepared to go on trying till we drop dead with the effort.

I only wish there were more Alison Johnsons in the Western Isles. Actually I found some fresh simple food earlier in the day at the Co-Chomunn no Hearadh, the Harris Co-operative in Leverburgh which is housed in a functional new building. Here again the immigrants were much in evidence. The Co-Chomunn and Craft Centre is run by Barry Dobson, a Geordie, and wielding the teapot in the café was June Macrae from Southsea.

I order a cup of tea and a homemade scone; the place is busy for Harris – three other people sitting at tables.

'Last week', says June, 'I took £304 and that's without coach parties. Barry said to me "You'll be busy on Monday" because it was Bank Holiday and he was thinking in the region of £50 to £55 and I took £78! And that's the highest ever taken on a Bank Holiday.'

On the counter are date loaf, fruit loaf, oatcakes, shortbread, all homemade. 'Next year,' says June, a pioneering look in her eye, 'I'll probably do a bigger variety, *torten* and things like that.'

June used to work at Stoke Mandeville hospital where she was in charge of the children's spinal unit. She has been in Harris for ten years; her husband was born on Taransay.

'There's nobody there now. Pabbay's uninhabited too and Scarp. They just go there for the shepherding.'

When June first came to Leverburgh in 1973 all the children spoke Gaelic before they went to school. 'Now they don't speak Gaelic at all. The parents don't teach it to them and to me that is very wrong. Somebody said to me once "I'd rather my children learnt French or German because it will do them more good when they leave the island".'

'Is it the incomers who are ruining things then?'

'It's the incomers who are keeping the Gaelic going I think – especially those with children; they're having their children taught Gaelic. We've got a girl who works here, she was educated in Stornoway and doesn't speak a word of Gaelic. Her children were taught Gaelic in school and won a prize at the Mod for the children of Tarbert – I mean that's lovely. I love the people keeping their dialects and language.'

I ask her how Leverburgh compares with Southsea?

'Oh, it's a much slower pace of life, not a rat race. Let's face it, anywhere on the mainland is a rat race.'

'Have you picked up Gaelic yourself?'

'I have a few words but my husband won't teach me, he says you're better off without it.'

'Why?'

'I don't know,' and June laughs, 'so that I can't understand what they're all saying I suppose!'

After my tea and scones I drive down to the south end of the island which has two star attractions: the finest church in the Hebrides and the most picturesque hotel.

The Macleods used to bury their chiefs in Rodel Church, which has been twice restored, first in the eighteenth century and then again in 1873 by the Countess of Dunmore. The Dunmores lived in Rodel House and afterwards it was occupied by Lord Leverhulme. In 1923 it became a hotel: Donnie Macdonald, grandson of the legendary Jock MacCallum, is running the hotel now and he tells me that there are big plans to renovate it. Don't, whatever you do, I implore him, destroy the character.

Rodel has most of the old furniture it had in the Dunmores' day and not much seems to have changed since Edwardian times. In a cupboard I find the *Cosmographic Atlas* for 1894 listing such Ruritanian extravagances as Moravia, Bohemia, Croatia, Bosnia and Montenegro.

As Donnie pours me a dram of Buchanan's 'Royal Household' he tells me that only 100 licencees were allowed to continue selling this whisky when it became the Buckingham Palace tipple. His grandfather was one of them.

The house has a decayed and lived-in air. I doubt it would survive a Board grant. Roddie says he'll keep the best pieces of the furniture. 'Keep the atlas too,' I urge him, 'it will be Rodel's last link with the Austro-Hungarian monarchy.'

The hotel stands on the edge of the sea confronting a most imposing stone harbour with steps and slips denoting an importance long since lost. It looked to me like a very early nineteenth-century construction but I was wildly out. Checking some references I found that it had been built in the late 1770s by a kinsman of General Norman Macleod of Macleod. This Captain Macleod, who was master of an East Indiaman called the *Mansfield*, bought Harris and St Kilda for £15,000 from the laird and decided, with good taste, that Rodel was the place to live in. It has one of the best sheltered small bays in the Hebrides. Captain Macleod deepened the south entrance and created what John Knox, who visited Rodel in 1786, described as as safe a basin as anything you could desire: 'Here the Captain has made an excellent graving bank and formed two keys, one at the edge of the basin, where ships may load or discharge afloat at all times of the tide.'

Macleod also built a store-house for salt, casks and meal and a manufacturing house for spinning woollen and linen thread and twine for herring nets. 'He has', recorded Knox, 'procured East Country fishers with Orkney yawls to teach the inhabitants; and has built a boat-house, sixty feet long by twenty wide, capable of containing nine boats with all their tackling.'

It was this Captain Macleod who repaired the church, made excellent cart roads throughout Harris, planted hazel and sycamore trees and built a corn and fulling mill. He did more. He fitted out a cutter, took soundings in the Minch, and found a bank half-way between Harris and Skye teeming with cod and ling. Macleod must have been the Leverhulme of his day.

'In the spring of 1786', says Knox, 'he proposed to try the fishery on the coast of Harris near his own house; but this generous design was ridiculed by his tenants who maintained that he would meet with no success and incur a useless expense. He persisted in the experiment and caught between the 10th of March and the 15th of April 4400 large cod and ling; 4 or 500 skate, innumerable quantities of dog fish, large eels and many boatloads of cuddies.'

I'm surprised that there is not a memorial to this splendid visionary. I think Donnie ought to put one up. Or maybe the Highlands and Islands Development Board could spring Rodel to a plaque in the Captain's honour – after all he anticipated them by nearly 200 years and his buildings and harbour are there to prove it.

5

MY GAELIC WENT INTO THE SEA

LOCHMADDY TO BERNERAY

There's no problem in getting from Harris to North Uist – a passenger ferry threads its way across the skerry-scattered Sound past Ensay, Killegray and Pabbay where in early Victorian times 340 people tilled the relatively fertile soil of what was known as 'the granary of Harris'. When Pabbay was cleared to make way for sheep some of the families moved to Killegray. Ensay had a small population of 15 at one time; it too is now left to the sheep.

The car ferry runs from Tarbert on Harris down to Lochmaddy. At the moment the triangular service between these two ports and Uig in Skye is operated by the 25-year-old *Hebrides*, now nearing the end of its life. As soon as the new piers are built there'll be a roll-on, roll-off floating cafeteria like the *Suilven*. Meanwhile the 2,000-ton *Hebrides* still serves its cups of tea in Royal Doulton mugs. It's a cold day as we make our way down to Lochmaddy, there's low cloud over the long line of the monochrome Uists, more like winter than August.

In the for'ard lounge is the polished brass bell of the old S.S. *Hebrides* presented by Lord Strathcona and Mount Royal. The earlier *Hebrides*, with its single funnel, two masts and triple-expansion engines was, like all the old West Coast boats, built strongly and built to endure. She had been in service for 57 years when she was finally broken up at Port Glasgow; if a car ferry lasts 20 years I'm told it's done well.

Loch Maddy, Loch nam Madadh or Loch of the Watch Dogs, takes its name from the scores of rocky reefs which stand like teeth from the water ready to rip your keel off if you make a wrong move. The loch itself is only ten square miles in area but its shore line, if you traverse every inlet and fjord, is 300 miles long.

Although Lochmaddy is the only place on North Uist you could describe as a town it is to my mind the ideal size – you could case the whole place and have plenty of time for a drink before the *Hebrides* unloaded its cars and sailed again. In the seventeenth century such was the abundance of fish in the Minch that 400 fishing boats used Lochmaddy; today there's only a French yacht in the harbour flying a lot of tri-coloured washing. One fifth of the island's population have migrated to Lochmaddy, lured perhaps by its amenities – a bank, a cottage hospital, a petrol station, the courthouse, a doctor and a famous fishing hotel which has the rights to over 150 brown and sea trout lochs.

Viewed from the air the north-east of the island is more water than land: a sieve of lochans and islands, treeless, rocky and low-lying. There is a thirty-six-mile circular road running round the coast with diversions in the north-east to the Sound of Berneray and Cheesebay and in the south to the causeway across to Benbecula. I've got an appointment with Margaret Maclennan, a young schoolteacher, in Cheesebay. Wendy MacInnes, whose family home is in Cheesebay, tells me that Margaret has begun to collect the history of those parts and she would be worth a visit.

'If I'm not at home myself,' says Wendy, 'I'll be in Berneray, I think Wednesday we'll be visiting relatives because we're off back to Edinburgh at the end of the week.'

On the way out of Lochmaddy I pass the Weehavitt shop. A challenge. Will they have a ribbon for my Olivetti 44? I pull into the parking space next door just as a burly figure in a tweed jacket and cavalry twill emerges from what turns out to be the Factor's Office. Weehavitt may well have it but I was never to find out – they were shut for lunch.

David Shaughnessy the factor is hospitable. 'Come in,' he says, unlocking the door of his office. The brass plate reads 'North Uist Estates'.

'Who owns the estate now?'

'Lord and Lady Granville,' says David and on cue the phone rings. David embarks on a long conversation about filler caps and the exact composition of petrol and oil needed in an outboard engine.

'. . . yes, Lord Granville. Certainly Lord Granville. I'll be up later Lord Granville. Thank you.'

I took it that he had been talking to Lord Granville.

'That was Lord Granville,' said David, 'having trouble with the outboard.'

For centuries North Uist had been part of the patrimony of the Macdonalds of the Isles. Then in 1856 Lord Macdonald, faced by mounting debts, was forced to sell the island to Sir John Powlett Orde; it passed then to his son Sir John Campbell Orde and then in 1889 to *his* son Sir Arthur Campbell Orde.

Lewis had been put up for commercial grabs much earlier when the Seaforths, who had held sway over the island for over two centuries, sold it to a Mr Stewart-Mackenzie for £160,000 and he in turn in 1844 sold it to James Sutherland Matheson for £190,000. That really was the beginning of the ruinous system of private ownership of land in the Outer Isles.

The Macleods of Harris sold their inheritance in 1834 for £60,210 to the Earl of Dunmore who in 1868 sold North Harris to the Scotts. In 1838 the last MacNeil of Barra sold his lands to Lieutenant-Colonel John Gordon of Cluny who by 1845 had acquired the whole of South Uist and Benbecula. His total outlay for his 100,000 acres was £163,799.

The stage was set for the gradual fragmentation of the Western Isles. It was a set up which led in the nineteenth century to the mismanagement of the land on a tragic scale. Thousands of acres lay empty while the people were packed together as tight as herrings in a barrel in unwanted and barren corners. It is arguable whether in such circumstances the absentee landowners were less of a burden than those with grand and often megalomaniac schemes of their own.

Matheson of Lewis and his successor Leverhulme, self-styled Lord of the Isles, were constantly dreaming up new enterprises, singleminded men who brooked neither discussion nor opposition. Lady Gordon Cathcart's autocratic and numbing reign in the southern isles lasted until 1935. Since then estates have changed hands as indiscriminately as counters in a casino – a contemptible display of avarice seldom tempered by any objective thought of the well-being of the people.

I find it farcical that private individuals should continue to hold almost unbridled power in what is officially a democracy. It is a power to obstruct development and hinder progress while all the time the land sits idle but increasing in paper value.

Given my views on the dead hand of landlordism it is perhaps merely a rhetorical question to inquire about Lord Granville's record as a landlord. Mr Shaughnessy is, as becomes a factor, wildly enthusiastic about his employer.

'They're absolutely marvellous people,' he says, 'full of ideas. Really keen on getting things going. Interested in anything that will make the estate go. They're delightful people to work for. Mind you, an estate like this can't run at a profit. There's a small income from croft rents, leasing buildings and things like that. We've just started scallop farming in the bay out there – we've got 15,000 of them.'

The phone rings again. 'That'll be Lord Granville,' says David. 'Yes,

Lord Granville . . . yes . . . well I think you'll find a catch inside the trap. I'll show you how it works when I come up, Lord Granville.'

David tells me that they are anticipating trouble with mink on the estate. They escaped from a now abandoned mink farm in Lewis and in the ensuing years have colonised Lewis, Harris and some of the smaller offshore islands; they are powerful swimmers and have been sighted on North Uist. Although these wild mink prey mainly on ground-nesting birds (redshank, snipe, curlew and lapwing), terns, oystercatchers, ringed plovers and anything sizeable are at risk. In an incident in 1984 they raided a commercial hatchery in Lewis and killed about 2,000 young salmon.

Later I hear a story that endears me to the Granvilles, Jaimie and Doon as they're known affectionately by the locals. There had been a meeting to discuss what should be done about the mink. Someone had seen a mink on Pabbay.

'Do we own that Jaimie?' asked the Countess.

'I really don't know. I think we do you know,' replied Jaimie. 'I'll go and have a look at the estate titles.' He disappears in the direction of the gunroom and comes back to announce that yes they do own Pabbay.

The story is of course apocryphal, woven by the locals to pad out their stereotyped view of the Granvilles. Just as professors are absent-minded so lords are seen to be unworldly and impractical, a bit vague but essentially kind. 'It would be like them not to know what they owned, they have so much anyway,' as one neighbour put it.

David Shaughnessy shows me a plan of the house the Granvilles built when they bought the North Uist estate twenty or so years ago. Like any traditional sporting lodge it has a gunroom, rooms for a nanny, nurseries, staff quarters. But the house is far from conventional. It is planned like a doughnut or a rubber ring used by those afflicted with haemorrhoids. The only circular house in Scotland, maybe in Europe. Perhaps the Granvilles' reputation for mild eccentricity stems from the building of this unusual home. The sort of place I'd love to have a look at.

'I'm sure Lord Granville would be very happy to see you.' Shaughnessy dials Bayhead 243 and I fix an appointment for eleven o'clock the following morning. 'Come and have a coffee,' says Lord Granville.

David tells me he lives in Cheesebay which is where I'm going. 'You can't get lost,' he says as we leave the office and he locks the door.

I follow the circular road round the island for about five miles and then turn on to the road for Cheesebay. On either side are small treacle-brown lochs. I pass a parked car; in the distance two figures in anoraks are fishing.

The landscape is flat and waterlogged. On my right now a few protuberances on the far side of Loch Portain but nothing higher than a few hundred feet – a ben in these parts is little more than a hillock.

You'd think it was impossible to get lost, but I forgot to ask Margaret where her parents' house was in Cheesebay. Is it the one on the main road or further down where the MacInneses live? Wendy said it was only a few doors away. Half-way down I see someone at her peatbank. This turns out to be Alice Mackillop and she asks me in. I'm glad I got lost, for staying with her for a few weeks is her brother Neil from Glasgow. Pushing 80, he is bright of eye and his mind is sharply focussed. Neil remembers vividly his childhood on the congested island of Berneray. 'When we were on Berneray the croft we lived on belonged to people called Macaskill. I believe there were about twenty houses on that one croft; we had nothing but the spot where the house was. We couldn't touch a blade of grass. It was leased then, the island, by a fellow called Fulton, he stayed in Newtonferry in that big lodge.'

After the war to build a land fit for heroes those who survived were all promised land, but it wasn't forthcoming.

'Wendy down the road, you know her, well her grandfather had a big piece of land at Sandhill in the north of Berneray and all the cottars were getting a bit of land to plant their potatoes and corn. We planted about five bags of potatoes on that piece of land we were getting from her grandfather Macleod. All the cottars had a cow but there were six of us in the family and we couldn't make a living.'

In February 1923 Neil and his father and twenty or so men from Berneray, all desperate for land, sailed across to North Uist.

'I don't remember whether we were in one boat or two but we came ashore up at Hoe Beg. I was with the old man and we all scattered about picking places and gathering stones. Some of the buildings were good; see that place where Wendy is, they hardly had to do anything with the building there, just square it up. There was two houses here and this is the one we picked. We were told that the people were a hundred years away from here, victims of the Highland Clearances, most of them went to Canada.'

Neil rises from his chair and draws me to the window. 'See that,' he says, pointing to tumbled walls on the hill. 'They must have been putting the cattle out there. See where your car is – oh, there were lovely stones there right down to the shore, a continuous wall.'

The Department of Agriculture gave the men loans to build. 'In the autumn the surveyors came to cut the land up into crofts. The Department took it over. There was no road here of course you carried everything on your back from cattle feed to bread. But we used the sea as a road. It was great for lobsters out here, this was where the Berneray men were doing their lobster fishing.'

'How did they get the lobsters to market?'

'They were all going across from Lochmaddy by the old *Plover* to Mallaig and down by train to Billingsgate. In those days she went across to Dunvegan in Skye and then she was coming back to Lochboisdale before she went to Mallaig – you would be crossing the Minch three times when you were going away from here.' And that in a 200-ton steamer in the winter gales was often an ordeal.

There was no work on North Uist in those days and Neil, like all the young men, was forced to leave home. 'I went away in 1929 to Glasgow to go to sea and I came back in 1931 and started herring fishing. Five of us had one of the old Zulus; we had an engine but those boats were built for sailing. The herrings we took to Scalpay, there were five curers on Scalpay in those days – or else we took them up to Stornoway. Most of it was going to Russia and America too.' The six of them worked thirty-five nets. 'With all the buoys and the nets and the drifters you could very nearly walk across the Minch to Skye. We would leave the net out for a couple of hours. If herring was scarce it would be up to £5 a cran.'

A cran was the traditional measure: four baskets with about a hundred-weight of fish in each basket. 'That was good money at the time but I saw us getting as far down as ten shilling a cran. Then they started with these ring nets and the fishing went down terrible.'

When Neil got married he took a croft on the coast at Hoe Beg and he and his wife raised six of a family. 'They're all scattered. There's one of the girls in Invergordon; she used to be a nurse but she's got a family just now. There's one in Glenrothes, she's a Sister in the Victoria. There's one out at Strathaven near Glasgow, she's married with a wee baby. One of the boys is an electrician and the other boy's with the Clyde Port Authority, he'll be there 20 years next February.'

Neil has twelve grandchildren but sadly just after he went down to live with his son in Glasgow in 1962 his wife died. Looking back on the hardships of Hoe Beg and Cheesebay and Berneray did he think people were better off now?

'In this place? Oh by a long way. They've got the road and electricity and everything now.'

'Are they happier?' Alice, who still lives in Cheesebay, shakes her head.

'No, I don't think they are. Every house was full when we were young, there wasn't an empty house. But see Hoe Beg now – there's only four families left and here I'm on my own now. John and Wendy only come for the holiday.'

Alice comes to the gate and points out young Margaret's house. It's a very lonely part of the world, this. Just a few scattered houses; little sign of cultivation.

Margaret is doing a teacher's degree at Jordanhill in Glasgow; her mother, a nurse, is on duty at the hospital in Lochmaddy. She puts the kettle on and tells me that her interest in the old days started when she gave a speech to the Gaelic Society of Glasgow. She fills in some of the details I didn't hear from Neil.

'There was only one family living here at Lochportain and he was Fulton's shepherd. When the raiders came they were sent packing and threatened with imprisonment but they came back and started marking out crofts and preparing peatbanks and getting the ground ready to sow corn. And then they were put off again.'

Margaret's family was one of six that came from Scalpay. There were others from Boreray, Berneray, Loch Eport and the mainland of Harris. They were all incomers; as Neil had said, the original population were long since scattered in Canada.

Twenty-one now, she remembers speaking only Gaelic as a child. 'I went to school at Lochportain first of all and I couldn't speak a word of English. Then after six months they closed the school down and we had to go to Lochmaddy and that's where I picked up my English.'

Margaret is buttering pancakes, cutting fruit cake. A sheepdog comes in wagging her tail, nuzzling up to my knee. 'She's just had eight puppies, she's very pleased with herself.' I ask Margaret what the language of the house is?

'My parents and I normally speak in Gaelic but my younger brother and sister, it's English they speak.'

Is Gaelic going then?

'It's definitely going. They're trying hard to keep it alive. But you go to Benbecula and you'll never hear a word of Gaelic. Ten years ago the Gaelic we had here was Harris Gaelic. We were very isolated; the main road didn't come here until about 1962. When you had isolated communities the Gaelic was very strong.'

I wondered why her brother and sister were not as passionate about history and language as she was?

'They don't just seem to realise what they're losing. They do Scottish history, Robert the Bruce and that, but there's so much they don't know about their own background. They have Gaelic, the two young ones, but they just don't use it very often. I see the difference between myself and my sister; she has no interest at all in Gaelic songs, old stories, things like that. I think it's the schooling, they just don't get it.'

Margaret hopes to return as a teacher to the Western Isles; to be part of the energetic Gaelic counterdrift. But will she be too late? How much will be left of the old ways?

'Well you hear so much about the good ceilidhs they used to have but now there's nothing at all. My mother, she probably hasn't been anywhere since New Year. She's called at her sister's and that, but that's not a proper ceilidh.'

I question Margaret about the old times when there were more families in Cheesebay, more young people.

'Where the pillar box is up there, they used to gather at night. Somebody would have an accordion, somebody a mouth organ and there used to be singing and dancing and they used to go to each other's houses all the time.'

She made it sound like a golden age.

'Well it seems it was a great time. It was more friendly. When dinner came on the table if you were there you stayed. Before,' and she means before TV came and cars and people driving to work in shops and offices in Benbecula, 'they used to go by the tide, they didn't go by time.'

I have just time to catch the six o'clock ferry to the island of Berneray where the raiders of Cheesebay came from. On the road to the boat at Newtonferry I see the first clump of trees since I left Lochmaddy; it stands beside the big house with a walled garden where Fulton the tenant used to live. The sands of North Uist are the colour of wholemeal flour; they rise out of the sea into dunes and roll on into the rich grass of the machair.

At the ferry slip there's another driver waiting. He turns out to be Ruaridh McVurich, the physiotherapist from the hospital, with some papers for the nurse on Berneray. To save him hanging about I offer to give the envelope to the ferryman. It's only half a mile, the stretch of sea between us and the island. At the beginning of the century Berneray was densely populated, over 500 people lived there. Today there's around 150 but Berneray is cited as one of the success stories of the Western Isles. Everyone lives in the south-east corner; the whole of the west coast is a huge and deserted beach, three miles of empty dunes.

The car ferry sets off from the island and when the ramp goes down Wendy drives off with her daughter. We have one minute to say hello and goodbye and thus does the new mobility inhibit conversation. What was it young Margaret said? We are driven by time now, not by the tide.

I'm the only car crossing over tonight and this time there is no chance of getting lost. I just follow the road along the shore until I come to a new bungalow with a red roof, past the council houses; so new it has, as yet, no garden, only a profusion of weeds.

Mrs Macleod is married to Dr Roddie Macleod, the Church of Scotland minister. She used to teach in the school. Tea is ready. Homemade tomato soup and to follow a taste of cockles, the first time, I tell Mrs Macleod, anyone in the Western Isles has ever offered me this free, delicious and nourishing bit of shellfish. Unfortunately the cockle has always been associated with famine in the Hebrides; a necessity you ate along with whelks when all else failed but better used to bait hooks for something really worth catching.

There is roast beef, mashed neeps and boiled potatoes and a lemon pie to follow, with grapes. In the visitors' book everyone seems to have fallen on their feet with Mrs Macleod. 'Heaven after camping for two weeks,' wrote the Sharp family of Carlisle. Jenny and Bob Ward of Cambridge noted their 'delicious drop scones which finished a good day on the island' and there were thank yous in German and French.

After supper I walked up the road to the manse and Dr Roddie came out to meet me. He'd been tapping out a sermon on a small and ancient typewriter. A Gaelic activist, Roddie had been a member of Comhairle nan Eilean and is at the eye of every political storm which blows over the island. Like many other parts of the Outer Hebrides, Berneray is still privately owned. When Lord Leverhulme died in 1925 his lands were divided into small parcels and disposed of at knockdown prices – Galson estate seven miles south of the Butt of Lewis went for 2½d an acre. In the currency of those days that was the equivalent of 57 acres for a bottle of 'Johnnie Walker'! Berneray was virtually given away as well.

'There was a man called Hitchcock at the sale,' Roddie tells me. 'He was owner or manager of the Lochmaddy hotel at the time. They asked for bids and there weren't any. So the auctioneer said in desperation will *anyone* make me an offer. A voice from the back, Hitchcock, said £500 and it was sold for £500 which I don't think he had at the time. He managed to borrow it from someone and the first time he collected the rents he paid it back.'

The rents have remained charitably low ever since; until recently they were the same as they had been in the 1930s. I asked Roddie if he had ever met the owner?

'No, he's dead now. Maybe his widow is still alive, but it's probably the son who owns the estate. He's a seed salesman in Essex or somewhere. We would prefer to have the island in community ownership operated by a committee elected by the community. People would feel they had more of a say in what was happening.'

Berneray is not much of an investment. There is, as in many other townships, an insoluble problem of unemployment. 'The boys can turn to fishing or crofting but there's nothing except marriage to keep the girls here. They tend to go into nursing or teaching so we have very few girls between the age of 15 and 30 on the island.'

But the emergence of Comhairle nan Eilean in 1975 put a spring in everyone's step. Even the replacement of a light bulb suddenly became simple and more logical. The bureaucracy of Inverness was replaced by common sense in Stornoway.

'We've got navigation lights', says Roddie, 'on the jetty. Now under Inverness, if the navigation lights went out I used to telephone to say they were out and they sent a man with a van from Inverness with a bulb! What happens now is that the Council leaves a supply of bulbs for a local man here to replace.'

Roddie talks about the mainland mentality and its obtuseness. 'When the new council houses were being built in Vatersay we discovered they were all-electric.' In a community where peat is free and hospitality around the fire is traditional it was like building a hospital without beds.

'It wasn't only that they ignored the need for fireplaces to burn peat in but the supply of electricity was a very fragile one anyway – it came by cable from Barra and Barra got its power from South Uist, so you had two chances of being cut off from your only source of heat! We tried to have fireplaces put in but they were at such an advanced stage of building it wasn't possible. That's the kind of thing that used to happen when your architects are sitting in Inverness; it was such a huge county they couldn't visualise what the needs of a remote island like Vatersay were.'

Central control weakened the enterprise of many a community and paralysed initiative. Now it's much easier to get things done.

'We have a community council here that meets once a month on a Saturday. On Monday all the things we've agreed on Saturday can be done. We operate a minibus that takes people to the post office and the shop and at that monthly meeting we decide who's going to arrange all the drivers for the next four weeks.'

For Roddie small is beautiful and above all practical. 'On North Uist they have a community council but there are sixteen people on it and they only meet every second month and then they disperse and may not see each other for eight weeks. Here where you're meeting each other every day you're much more likely to get things done.'

It's not only a new spirit that's abroad in Berneray but more money too. 'There was talk of a causeway at one time but it was going to be too expensive so we got the car ferry instead – that cost the best part of a million and we wouldn't have got that if we'd still been under Inverness. We've had six new council houses, they cost £200,000 and four more have just been completed along here at a cost of £170,000.'

Three township roads have been built too; that cost £300,000. Just past the passenger jetty a new harbour is to be built with the help of the EEC which will cost a million or so. It seems a lot of money to spend on 130 people – £3 million in the last ten years. But the minister does not believe that you can balance human lives against pounds and pence.

'The contribution of this island to Britain can't be measured like that. We've provided ministers and missionaries, scores of school teachers and doctors.' There's the record in two wars as well: the islands suffered losses in both wars more than twice as heavy, in proportion to their populations, as the rest of Britain. In the Great War out of a total population of 29,603, in Lewis alone 6,172 men were on active service; hundreds of women were away nursing and on war work, and of the men more than 1,100 lost their lives. The other aspect is that although money can help a community like the one on Berneray to survive no amount of money could rebuild that society elsewhere.

'There's something about a group of people like this and there aren't many of them left in Britain; it's like a big family. You might have an old person living alone; in other places they would cart him off to hospital. Here you might have two or three people working shifts to be with them all through the night rather than have them forced to leave the island. We had a funeral here not so long ago; a Berneray man who lived in Kyleakin on Skye. He was drowned when his dinghy capsized going out to his boat. A lot of people came from Skye for that funeral – there was a lady next door who with a friend provided lunch for 38 people! You can't buy that kind of generosity.'

So where does it spring from?

'It's got a lot to do with religion I think. This island is almost entirely Church of Scotland with just a few members of the Free Church – just the opposite of Scalpay which is mainly Free Church as you saw for yourself. Religion is part of the family atmosphere, it's one of the things that binds people together. Some of the strongest features of Highland society, like hospitality and kindliness and helping each other, are really Christian principles as well. In the old days when a bard praised a chief it was always his hospitality and kindness that were singled out.'

People on Berneray, then, were still ceilidhing with each other?

'No, they're not. TV has certainly spoiled all that. It tends to keep people in their homes a lot more.'

And the programmes they are exposed to all too often celebrate the urban values of a consumer society. Even more disturbing is the almost complete absence of enticing Gaelic programmes for young children. When Roddie came to Berneray eighteen years ago all the children were Gaelic-speaking and in the playground nothing but Gaelic was spoken. Now of the fifteen children in the school only about five have parents who are both Gaelic speakers.

'There was a little girl here who just started school, she was about four. Her parents speak nothing but Gaelic at home. After a while she stopped speaking Gaelic; she spoke only English. I would speak to her in Gaelic and she would answer in English. And I would say to her in Gaelic "Do you have any Gaelic?" and she would say "No!" One day I said, "What happened to your Gaelic?" and she said, "It went into the sea."'

We discuss the importance of language in the identity of a community. 'We've been talking about hospitality and generosity and friendship – all these things are bound up with the speaking of the language. They are part of the proverbs and part of the poetry of the language which must have its effect on people's outlook. Even work songs helped to keep people's spirits up when they were doing something mundane like rowing or using the quern. Whatever they were at there was a song that was particular to that kind of work and that must have helped.'

These days you Hoover with the rest of Britain to pop music; wash up to Culture Club while your own culture goes down the drain. I wondered if we might be producing rural communities with irrelevant and undesirable urban values?

'Probably in a place like this with a close connection to the land and the sea it's not that likely, but you'll notice it very strongly in Benbecula and the arrival of the military has influenced us even here. I remember when there was talk of the rocket range starting someone wrote to the papers to say that an advantage would be that the army would buy milk and eggs and so on from the local people, but the opposite has happened. The local people are buying milk and eggs from the NAAFI. If you go into the NAAFI you could be anywhere in Britain because all the accents around you are English.'

The erosion of the old language is not just a Hebridean phenomenon. Recently Roddie had been in Cape Breton on the east coast of Canada where many Hebrideans wound up at the time of the Clearances.

'I met scores of old people who spoke excellent Gaelic but the only people under forty who spoke it were two Americans who had gone there specifically to learn Gaelic. It was all right when the people were isolated but as soon as they got roads and close communication with the city Gaelic disappeared in one generation.'

In Ireland too Gaelic is on the wane. Roddie told me how he'd gone with Ron McIver the Secretary of Comhairle nan Eilean to the Gaelic theatre in Dublin. 'Everyone was talking Gaelic all the time in the box office but as soon as the audience had gone into the theatre all the Irish started talking English to each other,' he laughs. But the overweening ascendancy of English is obviously not a laughing matter. Money can bring ferries, roads, schools, jobs and material amenities but it seems to eradicate Gaelic as efficiently as Paraquat sprayed in a field of corn.

Back at Mrs Macleod's we have tea and biscuits and I look at her Gaelic library in the sitting room. They are closed books to me, incomprehensible. I feel a great sense of loss, a longing for something I never had – the language of my grandparents which would add so much to this journey.

'You have no Gaelic?' said somebody in Lewis.

'No,' I said.

'Well then you might just as well be wandering round the Western Isles like a blind man.'

I'm beginning to think he's right. Mind you, being blind wonderfully concentrates your sense of hearing.

6

THE STRONG IMPULSE OF UNTUTORED FEELING

NORTH UIST

In the morning I go across on the ferry for my appointment with the Granvilles. The sun shines, the sea is blue and Newton looks incandescently green after the evening's rain. A mile down the road I see a modern bungalow with flowers in the window, a trim lawn. Maybe they could tell me who lives in the big house these days. The door opens long before I can ring the bell. Even stopping a car in these parts is enough to awaken interest.

The house belongs to Mollie Macaskill and there appears to be a small morning ceilidh in progress. Tea and cigarettes are on the go.

'Come in and have a cup,' says Mollie, and before I know it I'm part of the room. Not having Gaelic does not debar you from this kind of hospitality but then this is not a Gaelic-speaking house. I'm just about to drink my second cup of tea when a large ginger-bearded man enters the sitting room. This is Mollie's son-in-law, as explosively intrusive a figure in this Hebridean scene as I will meet in the whole of my journey. Ideas start ricochetting round the room – Mike Russell is a media man, a fast talker. I can't focus on everything he says, there is a high-speed stream of ideas coming at me. We go out and stand in the garden so that I can concentrate as he hoses me down with his theories. A native of Ayrshire he came up here in 1977, two years after Comhairle nan Eilean was formed.

'It was in the great days of hope. I was appointed Director of Cinema Sgire.' *Sgire* in Gaelic means a parish or a district. So I suppose the rough translation might be Neighbourhood Cinema.

'I was the only outside, non-Gaelic speaker involved. We were financed by the Gulbenkian Foundation, the Scottish Film Council and the local council and the idea was to see if video could be used to help people validate their own past and to see if cinema would be useful socially. Video was a success but it was difficult to show, you could only have small groups. Cinema was quite successful.'

They started with no ideas at all, just a pile of equipment. The theory was that local people would play with video and meet each other. According to Mike Russell they had two good years and the highlight of their activities was the film they made about the Ministry of Defence rocket range on Benbecula.

'When they saw it, people were saying it was the first time they had heard their neighbours reveal what they felt about the rocket range in a formal context. All the interviews with local people were in Gaelic. The interview with the Brigadier commanding the base was in English. I suppose it was unfair but it counterpointed the very official way he viewed things with the very relaxed view of the locals. It was all summed up by one man at the end of the film who said that there had been nothing but loss. Although there were jobs, the people had been imposed on, made captives of another ideal. We were doing what the BBC should have been doing – they should have had a Gaelic film crew out here permanently!'

But then interest fizzled out. Mike sees it not as a failure on his part. He lacked backing, the money was withdrawn.

'By '79 Comhairle nan Eilean decided to go back to the safer options, traditional schooling and things like that. The Tories were in, money was short. In physical terms the islands may now be better than they were in 1975 but in terms of confidence, which is the key word, it's going backwards.'

Mike Russell, a committed supporter of the SNP, is now highly critical of Comhairle nan Eilean which in the beginning publicly committed itself to a bilingual policy. There was plenty of precedent in the Colonial Service. In the old days of Empire those recruited to the Malayan Civil Service, for instance, were required to learn Malay within three years otherwise neither salary increase nor promotion would come their way. The carrot of financial gain and personal advancement ensured that within a short space of time everyone learnt the language of the country. It has not happened in the Western Isles.

'There was no system', says Mike, 'whereby employees could have learnt Gaelic unless they were highly motivated – the bilingual policy became a farce.'

'You didn't do too well yourself,' I observe.

'No, I never came to grips with Gaelic when I was here but don't get me wrong. There is enormous hope here, this place will not die, can't die. What will happen is that after a few years people will try again in some other way. It's a pity that the renaissance fizzled out so soon.'

Looking around I see no signs of the land being cultivated. Mike married

Mollie's daughter; does he think there will be a live community here in ten or twenty years time?

'This community? I just don't see it surviving. The house up there is occupied by an incomer who hasn't any local roots. The house next to us is not occupied. Our household has four children and I don't see any of them coming back for good. If you look down there, that house at the end, the son may come back from time to time, he's at sea, he's related to us but I don't think he'll come back here permanently. There's another house, that's a holiday home. Then that house over there, they have a family of girls but I can't see the girls staying very long. What may happen is the same thing that's happened in Skye, people may retire here but I don't see a strong active, indigenous community surviving.'

He paints a depressing picture of a hollow community but I have no reason to believe it's not accurate. 'Mollie and Ian don't go out very much; the people down at the ferry don't go out very much. The car has also allowed people to choose their friends elsewhere. People can go to the pub and not just be confined to visiting each other, there don't seem to be the ceilidhs that people tell you happened in the old days.'

'You retired wounded then?'

'Yes, I retired wounded and somewhat cynical and a little bit depressed. We didn't realise what we were against here; that any change in an area like this is long, slow and very hard. We never realised that at the time.'

I drive up the road a bit depressed myself, but then the questions come flooding. Was Cinema Sgire all that worthwhile? Why give people expensive electronic video equipment when you could more practically present them with a notebook and a pencil? If they saw themselves on a TV monitor would that really make their existence more, what was the word, 'valid'? Did the locals fail Mike Russell, or were his schemes inappropriate to their needs?

I come to Sollas where the people are at the moment actively engaged in a bitter confrontation with the local police. A perfect scenario for the video camera. The police wait outside the local bar and follow people home. There is talk of harassment, victimisation. 'The sergeant in Lochmaddy is all right,' a youngster tells me, 'it's these f— constables. They've got nothing to do but make trouble.' I hear a long and involved story about a stag party that ended in a verbal punch-up with the police and someone being taken into custody. As in all such cases the tension seems self-generating, suspicion on both sides escalating into defiance by the locals and heavy-handed behaviour from the police.

Mind you the people of Sollas have no historic reason to feel an affinity for policemen. In 1849 thirty-three constables were sent from Oban to stand by while the population of 603 were evicted from their homes. They lived not only in Sollas but at Dunskellor, Middlequarter and Malaclete in a promontory bounded on both the east and west sides by sandy beaches which dried out at low tide, behind them the low-lying hills, to the north sand dunes. Although the land was relatively fertile the short summer was frequently too wet to ripen the corn and poverty was endemic.

For two years they had been living in destitution alleviated by the Highland Destitution Committee and meal provided by the proprietor, Lord Macdonald of Skye. The Committee had agreed to assist the emigration by giving 20s for each adult and 10s for each youngster under fourteen. Lord Macdonald had agreed to remit their £624 arrears of rent and take their crops and stock at valuation, to pay what extra was needed to get them to Canada and to send someone with them 'to see them comfortable.' Alas, the 110 families involved wilfully refused to leave. They said it was the wrong time of the year to be going to Canada.

When Sheriff-Substitute William Colquhoun arrived with his police force they were met with opposition. Four of the Sollas men were arrested before ten houses were unroofed and the people turned out. At this stage the parish minister, the Rev. Macrae, intervened and eventually all the heads of families signed a paper saying that they would emigrate to Canada the following year. This happened in August. On 13 September the four Sollas men were tried before Lord Cockburn at the Inverness Circuit Court.

The jury found them guilty but appealed to the court for the utmost leniency, 'in consideration of the cruel, though it may be legal proceedings, adopted in ejecting the whole people of Sollas from their houses and crofts without the prospect of shelter or a footing in their fatherland or even the means of expatriating them to a foreign one.' Lord Cockburn agreed that this was not a case requiring severe punishment and committed the men to prison for four months. 'Much sympathy', observed the editor of the *Inverness Courier*, 'was felt for the poor men – ignorant of law, ignorant of English, and acting from the strong impulse of untutored feeling.'

Their own feelings were that if their crofts were twice the size, if they were given leases and encouragement to improve their lot, they would be content to pay rent and would be able to survive. Lord Macdonald, overwhelmed with debt, was powerless to improve the lot of the people and eventually with the aid of the Perth Destitution Committee between 60 and 70 families, both crofters and cottars, were removed the following year to the south of the island and land even less hospitable. They didn't want to go and at this stage they said they would rather emigrate to Canada.

New Perth, as Langlash came to be called, was a failure from the start. The settlement was too far from the shore, and the first year was a disaster for the crops.

'Either', wrote a reporter from the *Courier*, 'the place is quite unsuited for the purpose or the nature of the soil has been entirely misunderstood by the person in charge of the affair; for such a display of failure in the first instance, I should think has never been witnessed anywhere.' The money, the writer thought, would have been better spent 'in sending the people to some of the colonies or in paying the arrears of their rent at Sollas and helping them to improve their stock and crofts.'

The outcome was equally unhappy. Shortly before Christmas 1852 the young and the healthy embarked on the emigrant ship *Hercules* bound for Australia leaving the old and the sick behind. The community of Sollas had been effectively destroyed.

Today you can still see the ruins and the outlines of lazybeds, but few people. It was, I suppose, a question of priorities. Had Lord Macdonald's affairs not been in the hands of trustees, had famine not prevailed, had the economic thinking of the time favoured a proper husbandry of the land rather than replacing people with sheep, Sollas might well be farmed to this day.

But the tide of emigration and eviction could no longer be held back. In Barra a third of the island was turned into sheep farms. Colonel Gordon despatched 2,715 of his tenants to Canada in the four years between 1848 and 1851. In February 1851, the year of the Great Exhibition when Britain's industrial and economic supremacy was put proudly on display to astonish the world, a party of beggars turned up in Inverness from Barra where they had been deprived of their crofts and crowded on to patches of stony ground impossible to till. Their condition, according to the *Courier*, 'called forth great compassion'. But apart from a charitable collection nothing was done. Gordon himself regarded the plight of his tenants as an unavoidable visitation of Providence.

It was the expulsion of the people, sometimes accomplished with their tacit agreement, sometimes achieved by a ruthless display of force, that has left so many of the islands uninhabited and the inhabited islands so depleted of people. And when people become thin on the ground they lack power. The cleared lands from Sollas to Malaclete overlook a strand flooded at high tide, which leads to the two-mile broad island of Valley. In 1967 the Board embarked on a bulb-growing experiment in North Uist; they had the help of soil experts from the Netherlands and maybe it was the Dutch who saw the possibility of reclaiming some of the low-lying beaches round North Uist. In the autumn of 1968 another 20 acres of bulbs were planted and a survey was commissioned to see how much tidal land could be reclaimed usefully. In 1969 eight tons of bulbs were marketed and the Board put up plans to the Scottish Office to reclaim and develop the Valley Strand. But tulip growing in North Uist didn't turn out to be feasible and the plan to reclaim 1,500 acres at a cost of £2½ million was withdrawn.

By 1972 the experimental bulb scheme was dropped. 'We were disappointed', said the Board, 'that this scheme could not be turned into a viable commercial enterprise. But, such setbacks will not discourage us from trying any new possibilities of fostering economic and social development in island areas.' There are those who believe that the Board was pressured into withdrawing its scheme. I stop to talk to a crofter with a dog and he waves to the broad and unproductive acres of the strand exposed now on the ebb of the tide.

'The bulbs did well, every bit as well as they grow them over in Holland, but they couldn't get the money to put it on a proper footing. That was in 1970 but it didn't stop them finding £20 million so that they could play at rockets. I'd rather see things growing – just think what a tourist attraction the bulb fields might have been in Spring too just when the weather is perfect. It's grand in the Spring.'

It's grand in August too and approaching eleven o'clock; time to turn off the road for Callernish House which is on the northern tip of the island; isolated with fine views of the sea.

The circular house has an archway in its southern side which forms an entrance to the gravelled courtyard. Once inside you are completely enclosed, protected from the winds which blow in the winter here with unbelievable force.

The Countess is keeping a weather eye on the window for signs of the Royal Yacht. This is the time of the year when the Queen and her family cruise round the north of Scotland on their way to Aberdeen and a summer in Balmoral; Lord Granville is a cousin of the Queen and now and again she likes to call. 'Last year *Britannia* anchored in Lochmaddy,' says the Countess, 'and they all came up for tea.' The royals were as always intrigued by the house and had a good peer round. 'We were in a bit of a mess and we just tidied up a lot of stuff and pushed it behind the curtains. Well Prince Andrew pulled a curtain and all sorts of things fell out.'

Although the Granvilles have a house in London they spend most of the year here at Callernish. Both of them are keen fishermen and birdwatchers. They have been known to take to the lochs when house guests become too much for them. Lord Granville went to Eton but he sent his children to the local school. He tells me about the scallop farming, the first in these parts, which seems to be going quite well. Doon admits that sometimes in the winter the wind becomes unbearable. 'It doesn't let up for weeks at a time and you get the most frightful headaches.' When they were trying to buy North Uist they were outbid by an American consortium but the owners, the Hamilton and Kinneil estate, decided that North Uist would be safer in Granville hands.

'I think they can't be coming,' says Doon, with the relief of the country hostess who might well be hard put to find enough uncracked cups to go round. If we did but know it, that day *Britannia* had anchored outside Stornoway harbour to pick up Princess Margaret who had arrived in the afternoon. This was obviously an event of some significance to local people. The *Stornoway Gazette* devoted half the front page to two photographs of the Princess ('dressed in a lovely orange two-piece suit') and half the back page as well. The radical *West Highland Free Press* had a sour headline: 'No expense spared on royal visit', noting that 'Princess Margaret paid a fleeting visit to Stornoway on Tuesday amidst the usual orgy of royal expense.' It described how three helicopters, a Hawker-Siddeley of the Queen's Flight and a frigate, HMS *Nottingham*, had all been involved in what they clearly saw as a gross abuse of public funds.

The *Free Press* attitude to the Granvilles would no doubt be equally acerbic. I should have asked Jaimie whether he thought North Uist would be better off under public ownership but that seems a bit unfair; I hear no unkind words about either of them. 'Very decent people' is what I'm told on all sides. And that's a flattering testimonial from islanders who have had more than their share of bad landlords.

The Granvilles are keen ornithologists; it was one of their interests which persuaded them to buy North Uist with its Balranald Nature Reserve, only five miles down the road from Callernish. My old friend Dr Desmond Nethersole-Thompson enthuses about these 1,500 acres of marsh, beach, dune and machair:

Dunlins rise and fall as if on silvery threads; mallard, teal, wigeon, shoveller, tufted duck and gadwell nest. In 1969 the rare scaup also bred. Dabchick, coot, moorhen, mute swan, water rail, snipe, redshank, twite, skylark and sedge warbler are all in these splendid marshes; and corn buntings, lapwings and corncrakes nest on the croftlands. (*Highland Birds*, HIDB, 1971.)

And that's not all. There are eider, red-breasted merganser and shelduck, ringed plover and oystercatcher, and common, arctic and little terns. 'With such a study area at your disposal', says Desmond, 'why travel further?' Except perhaps to get a boat out to the Monach islands which were turned into a Nature Reserve in 1966.

On the way south I call in to see George Jackson at Clachan whose peat-smoked salmon is air-mailed all round the world. He gives me a quick course in distinguishing between wild salmon and farmed salmon and inveighs against those who treat their salmon roughly.

'Look at the bruising here,' he says pointing to a dark area on the tail of a side of golden pink salmon, 'That could have come from a fish being thrown against the side of the boat. If people bring me a salmon for smoking I tell them I won't be responsible for the *way* it smokes because you don't see that sort of damage until the side is finished.'

George has got monkfish for sale at £1.80 a pound. That was the price it was when I left London the previous week. I suggest it's a bit high for a bit of fish locally caught with no transport costs.

'I see no reason why fishermen here shouldn't get a decent price. You get people going down to the pier and cadging fish, that's all wrong. If I'm not prepared to pay a good price then I just don't get the fish.'

A whole side of salmon weighing between 1¾ and 3 lbs costs £4.05 a pound from Jackson's Smoke House. I invest in a side for £11.25 – it'll be eaten when I get back to Skye with thin slices of lightly buttered beremeal bread. Beremeal bread? Read on.

I have an appointment further down the road with Donald Macdonald, a young crofter who farms with his father and uncle at Baleshare. I ring from a call box and am told he's at the hay. It's a good day for hay, dry with a breeze blowing off the dunes.

Baleshare is really an island joined to the mainland of North Uist by yet one more causeway. It was here in 1735 that Hugh Macdonald of Baleshare imported an Irishman to show his tenants how to manufacture kelp. The kelp boom spread all over the Hebrides.

It took 24 tons of seaweed to make 1 ton of kelp. The golden seaweed when dried and burnt and reduced to ash yielded alkali essential for the bleaching of linen, in the eighteenth century Scotland's greatest industry, and for the manufacture of soap and glass. At that time the only substitute was the calcined ash of barilla, a maritime plant found mainly in Spain and Sicily.

As the average cost of production was £5 a ton and kelp fetched up to £22 a ton, profits from the annual 5,000 and 6,000 tons produced in the boom years were prodigious. Little of this money filtered down from the proprietors who claimed sole ownership of the seaweed on their shores. Many tenants were obliged to collect seaweed as part of their tenure.

John Macculloch, the geologist who travelled extensively in the Hebrides every summer, described (*The Highlands and Western Isles of Scotland*, 1824) how a large proportion of the population were engaged in kelp-making between June and August when they could more profitably have been working the land. Seaweed was now too valuable to be used as a fertiliser. Cutting and burning, said Macculloch, was 'so laborious and severe as to have no parallel in this country . . . it may be considered a servitude.' North Uist was particularly rich in the seaweed that yielded alkali and its proprietor Lord Macdonald was receiving £14,000 a year from the labour of his tenants. Land prices rose, emigration was discouraged, and the population of the Outer Hebrides increased to 71,000 in 1821.

In 1822 the duty on imported barilla was reduced and in the following year the Leblanc process which produced soda cheaply from salt was perfected. Although the great days of kelp were over the birthrate continued to rise. In the 1830s the herring shoals mysteriously thinned and potato blight made its appearance. The population peaked in 1841 at 93,000 and there were too many mouths to feed. The drama of famine, destitution, eviction and emigration had begun.

It's difficult to believe that at the height of the kelp trade there were 5,000 people on North Uist, the majority of them, even the children, busy collecting and burning seaweed in the summer months. From afar off the Hebrides looked as if they had been set on fire; an acrid pall of smoke ran from Lewis down to Barra. 'The poet who indulges in visions of the days of old,' wrote Macculloch, 'may imagine the lighting of the war-fires and fancy that he sees the signals which communicated the news of a Danish descent through the warlike clans.'

On this hot August day of 1984 there's not a fire to be seen anywhere. I find Donald and Allan his father building a huge burial mound of silage. It's about twelve feet high already and they're having to haul the hay cart up to the top with a rope attached to a tractor. When it's finished they will drape it with black polythene and anchor it with lorry tyres. 'Last year', says Allan, 'we lost all the tyres one night in the gale. Now Donald says that in Norway they fill tyres with concrete; maybe we should do that here.'

In 1982 Donald spent two months in Norway and Denmark on a Churchill Fellowship. Why Scandinavia? 'Well,' says Donald, wiping the sweat off his forehead with the back of an arm, 'they have, particularly in Norway, as high a rainful as we do and I was really finding out how they manage their hay and silage.' He took a lot of slides while over there and has given some lectures to local groups of crofters in the Western Isles. His report has yet to be written up: 'You don't get much time for writing if you're trying to get the hay in.'

Donald nearly became part of the Hebridean brain drain and he'd be on the mainland still if he hadn't one day woken up and realised he was doing the wrong thing. 'When I left school I had nothing arranged so I went into the bank in Benbecula. I had five years there. I liked Benbecula but I didn't like the job so when I was transferred to Glasgow I knew the job wasn't for me. I didn't know what I wanted to do but I knew what I *didn't* so I just left and bought an Inter-Rail ticket.'

He made his way down through Europe and wound up in Israel. He was working on a kibbutz on the West Bank when he had a letter to say his father had taken ill so he packed his kitbag and came back to Baleshare. Since then he's been helping his father and uncle to run a unit of five crofts. They have 300 acres of which 100 is the sandy machair which stretches across to the shore. 'You can't do anything with it. If you cultivated it there's a danger the whole thing would blow away. It's very wet in wintertime; in summer it just dries out.'

The whole of this part of the North Uist coastline is very fragile and constantly moving. Baleshare itself means East Township. Way out beyond the island there was a West Township which was inundated by the same tide that cut off the Monach Isles and widened the Sound of Pabbay.

Last year they grew about 35 acres of oats and barley for silage and Donald is busy re-seeding and regenerating old land. 'We try to lay down five to ten acres of new grass every year; this year we laid down about fifteen.'

When Donald came back to help on the croft four years ago they had eighteen head of cattle; now there are 24 cows and five in calf. 'You hope your combined corn and grass silage will be adequate for winter feeding.' Besides the cattle there are 100 ewes and the Macdonalds are expanding. 'We're in the process of acquiring a 200-acre share of moorland, most of which could be re-seeded fairly well and we hope to build up the sheep numbers. But we want to avoid getting too big; if you have to buy in expensive feed, that's just pointless.'

'Can you make a living?'

Donald laughs. 'Well one man's living is not another man's living. There's a limit to what a croft can earn. It's not like being down south. If the price of sheep falls you can't just swap over to cereals and dairying.'

I say how impressed I've been in this corner of North Uist to see how much corn and grass is being grown.

'Oh yes, very often you can see land being used to the limit of its capacity; that frequently happens on smallholdings where they're very enthusiastic. Then you see a neighbouring croft just lying dormant.'

There's nothing dormant about the Macdonald crofts; beside the house a field of barley is waving. 'Not barley,' Donald says, pulling a few ears, 'it's bere.'

This is the first time in my life I've ever seen bere growing – anywhere. I tasted it first of all in Orkney in 1974 in the form of beremeal bannocks made with baking soda, cream of tartar, salt and buttermilk. The bere in those days was being ground by Scotland's only woman miller, Olive Flett. Now the mill has been taken over by a man from Berwick and in 1984 he ground some of the 25 tons of bere which were still being grown on Orkney mainland.

'Do you eat it?' I ask Donald.

'No, we just grow it for silage, a small quantity to keep up the seedstock for next year.'

In the eighteenth century nearly all the barley grown in the Highlands and Islands was bere. This primitive four-rowed barley, *Hordeum sativum vulgare*, flourished on thin soil and ripened early. It could withstand wind damage and was very good for you. Modern analysis has established that the small amounts of bere still being grown in Scotland have 31.5 per cent crude fibre compared with only 5 or 6 per cent in wheat.

Bere has a distinctively malty flavour. You can make bannocks from it or beremeal porridge. You could put it on your muesli for that matter, or bake your own high-fibre beremeal bread. Many distilleries used bere in the old days instead of barley for making their whisky; Highland Park on Orkney used bere exclusively until the end of the nineteenth century. It's a pity, like so many good flavours from the past, that you now have to seek it out. But there is a commercial expediency which no doubt proves it's no longer worth growing.

Donald has never tasted beremeal although he knows that in the old days his forebears used to thresh and hummel it, winnow and dry it, and then grind it in their querns. 'It was very susceptible to mildew and rust and those sort of diseases, things which are very detrimental to a cereal farmer – that's why the new strains of barley replaced it.'

Donald climbs back on the tractor, I climb back in my car clutching my ears of bere delighted to know that even though the tradition of eating bere has been lost, someone is still growing it.

And while my thoughts are on food I decide to go and have a look at one of the most profitable undertakings in the whole of the islands. Until 1960 you couldn't get from North Uist either to Grimsay or Benbecula with any degree of ease. In that year a causeway was opened; before then you had to cross four or five miles of sands at low tide, keeping to the cairns because quicksands on either side could trap you disastrously.

Contemplating the building of such a causeway in 1949 gave Alasdair Alpin MacGregor a splendid opportunity to inveigh against the fecklessness of the islanders. 'The cost of such an undertaking', he claimed, 'would be exorbitant, especially in these days of expensive materials and having regard to the ridiculously high rate of wages now being paid for dilatory and totally unskilled labour . . . one cannot see how the mass of the crofters inhabiting these islands would benefit at all.'

But the causeway has brought all manner of benefits to the Uists and Benbecula. Dramatically in the case of the group of Grimsay men whose livelihood depends on the road that now links them with Lochmaddy and the three-star restaurants of Paris and Brussels. The lozenge-shaped island of Grimsay lies between the southern end of North Uist and the northern shore of Benbecula and the waters around it swarm with lobsters, crabs and crawfish. In 1968 with a grant from the Board a big complex of lobster tanks was built at Kallin so that shellfish could be stored live to take advantage of high off-season prices. On this Saturday afternoon a fisherman is unloading a Ford Escort van full of lobsters. How many, I ask?

'There's 24 dozen there,' he says, 'that's a week's catch.' Already this week three loads of lobsters have gone out by road across to Skye, down to Kyle of Lochalsh to Wilson's of Holyhead who now lease the lobster tanks.

Inside the building there are hundreds of lobsters lying in the dark aerated waters, and crawfish too, ugly spiny-armoured beasts lacking the large claws of the lobster, reddish brown in colour with yellow and white markings.

Hector Stewart, I've been told, is the man to see; at 27 he is already a successful businessman although he describes himself modestly as 'just a crofter-fisherman'. He and his brother Donald have 400 creels which they work from a 37-foot boat bought nine years ago for £17,000 with a loan and a grant from the Board. Hector's father and his younger brother fish from another boat – lobsters are the priority, then crawfish and a long way behind are crabs.

In the garden of the cottage beside the loch at Baymore two young children are playing. Hector and his wife Anne have only just acquired the croft from a relative. Grimsay is one of the most attractive islands I've yet set foot on, a private place off the beaten track but in touch with the market forces of haute cuisine.

Anne and I listen as Hector gives me the background of the operation. The lobster ponds were set up by Minch Shellfish about 14 years ago. When they pulled out John Arrow of Selsey in Sussex took over but they didn't make a go of it, largely because the fishermen took to selling their catches for the highest price they could get – a lorry would arrive, outbid Arrow and walk off with the week's lobsters. Now Wilson's have the ponds but Hector and the other fishermen of Grimsay still have, in this luxury seller's market, the whip hand.

'We sell to the highest price. We have an agent in Loch Eport, Mike Branagan, and the people who want lobsters get their bids to him by Wednesday. He works for about 12 or 15 of the boats.'

When Wilson's were the sole buyer they had to take what Wilson's offered. Now it's different. 'Mike gets on the phone all over the UK and the man who can give us the best price on the Wednesday is guaranteed lobsters from our 12 or 15 boats regardless of whether Wilson's put their price up meantime or not – which they do try to and break us up.' Eventually Hector and the others plan to market their shellfish through the Uist Fisherman's Co-Operative; meanwhile they're going it alone and doing in the summer of 1984 very well.

'This week it was £2.75 a pound for select lobsters, £2.20 for large and second or cripples – you know the ones maybe with only one claw – and £2.60 for crawfish.'

Wilson's actually matched that price but the Grimsay men were not impressed, they stuck to their bargain with the buyers from down south. 'If you get people coming up here and going away with an empty wagon they won't do it again.'

It's two o'clock in the afternoon as we talk. The refrigerated lorry left an hour ago for Lochmaddy to catch the 5.30 car ferry for Uig on Skye. The 'viviers' lorry will be waiting there or on the mainland with its seawater tanks to transport the lobsters live straight through to France.

'How many went?' I ask.

'I would say something like seven to eight thousand pounds weight.'

I do a quick calculation.

'So that's maybe £20,000?'

'Well it would be over that. Last week it was about £23,000.'

'That's not bad for a week's work for ten people.'

'Oh, there's more men than that. There'll be about ten or twelve boats involved; most of them two-man boats.'

'Twenty-four people?'

'Possibly more.'

'Even so you're not exactly starving?'

'Not just now.'

In the winter they fish for crab. 'Crab has an overlap with the lobster season but lobster is more profitable. We're not getting rid of our crab just now.'

'Nobody wants it?'

'Well all the buyers are using crab as a lever to get the lobsters. They say "if you won't sell us your lobster we won't buy your crab".'

It strikes me that for a van and driver to come all the way from Selsey in Sussex as the lorry did today there must be big profits for the middleman?

'Well when Mike first did a deal with this man in Sussex they had no idea where Grimsay was. He got a map out down in his office and Mike had to guide him up through England and Scotland and out to the Western Isles. As for profit, well they're not doing it for nothing, that's one thing for sure.'

Hector and Anne are going to build a house for themselves on the croft. The future looks good?

Anne smiles. 'Well you could say that, yes.'

7

KEEPING A LOW PROFILE

BENBECULA

Benbecula (Beinn a'bh-faodhla, Mountain of the Fords) derives its name from its stepping-stone role between North and South Uist and the conical 410-foot eminence of Rueval, the only bit of high ground to raise the eyes. This is flat land, sandy on the west, rocky and peat-bogged on the east and sieved with freshwater lochs, rich in fish and birds.

Had it not been for Hitler Benbecula might be an island still. During the Second World War a vital RAF airfield was laid out on the flat machair of the north-west corner and in 1943 a causeway was built to link the airfield with Lochboisdale on South Uist. You could make out a case to say that everything of significance that has happened to Benbecula since then has come from war and the fear of war. Not all of it has been welcome.

The original 1941 runway was long enough to take Flying Fortresses. From the start the manner of its construction provoked strong protests. One man who took up the cause of the people of Benbecula was the influential island-loving Compton Mackenzie. From Barra he wrote to his old friend Sir Archibald Sinclair at the Air Ministry:

> It is impossible for me to keep silent while I contemplate the degradation inflicted upon the islanders of Benbecula and South Uist by the dumping upon them of the Ministry of Labour's human offal. Hogarth might have been perplexed to depict these phantoms of crime and disease who swarm upon every mail boat and are often sent back again immediately as too useless even among those dregs of labour being paid up to £10 a week.

Sir Archibald was no doubt diverted by this epistle from the west but the work went fitfully on.

The island is still dominated by the airport and the garrison of Balivanich with its NAAFI, its army quarters, messes and attendant workshops. It is an incongruous assemblage of largely systems-built offices and accommodation. In the centre of all this Comhairle nan Eilean has built its own modern offices and library. The prevailing colours of Balivanich are cement gray, porridge and all-bran, a tribute to the limited aesthetic horizons of army engineers and local government architects: a grim and institutional place even in the sunshine.

What struck me, walking round Balivanich, was the way in which the inhabitants didn't catch my eye. In the rest of the Western Isles people you pass on the road will greet you, maybe even stop and have a word. But Balivanich is a bit of army suburbia. Two garrison wives pushing babies pass me without a glance. A sergeant in a beret and big boots strides purposefully past eyes strictly to the front. I might be in Aldershot or Pirbright. I feel like an alien civilian.

The material benefits which the military presence has brought to Benbecula are striking. There's actually a chemist's shop here, the only one in the whole archipelago outside Stornoway. There's a swimming pool, not working at the moment, but maybe one day the leak will be patched. There are various clubs which locals can join and the spotless NAAFI has given the islanders a wider range of fresh fruit and vegetables than they ever had before. There's the excellent airlink with Stornoway and Glasgow. But on the debit side the local people have been swamped by an influx of 500 mainly English servicemen and their wives and children. It's a transient army-oriented population used to living a segregated life in other garrison towns. In a long career of foreign postings Benbecula isn't that much different from Hong Kong, Singapore or Cyprus.

'Well, it's colder,' says a sergeant I talk to in the NAAFI. His last posting had been in Germany. 'We don't see much of the locals. They keep themselves to themselves and we tend to keep ourselves to ourselves. I'm keen on birdwatching so I like it but I think most people don't really regard it as the best posting they've ever had. If you've done a winter here you'll know what I mean.'

Perhaps the most frustrating job in the whole of the island is performed by Alastair MacGillivray, headmaster of the local school, who lives at Muir of Aird a mile to the south east of Balivanich. He has a new bungalow and a garden full of flowers and, more to the point, vegetables. When I arrive he's mowing the lawn; a green-fingered man enjoying the last few days of his long summer holiday before the term starts again.

He is a Benbecula native; his wife is from Lewis – they both speak Gaelic but even when he went to Balivanich school as a child in the mid-1950s the language of the playground was already English.

'At home our wee boy spoke Gaelic with us but shortly after going to the nursery school he started using more English than Gaelic. To try and preserve what Gaelic there is the local children have been withdrawn into tutorial groups for a couple of hours a week and taught in Gaelic. In the playground the service children tend to stick together and the local children the same.'

With 75 per cent of the children coming from other parts of Britain, do they tend to swamp the Benbecula boys and girls?

'Well it's not so much their numbers that causes any problem, it's the turnover. It goes on throughout the year; half of your roll is going and you're taking in another half. Most years we would expect to admit 70 to 90 pupils and lose the same amount.'

Despite this constant turnover Alastair thinks he may stick it out until he retires, so it can't be that bad. But he does find the garrison mentality oppressive. 'They seem to have everything organised for themselves, everything laid on; transport for this and that. Very few of them seem to want to explore the area. You find that quite a few of the children haven't even been to the beach; if it was organised for them they would probably like to go to the beach. Quite often the parents ask why doesn't the school take the children out more to places round about – these are parents who all have cars themselves.'

Alastair and his wife have in the past responded to invitations to the officers' mess but he found that for him at least it wasn't very relaxing: 'More a parent-teachers meeting; they just wanted to know about their children. People living in Balivanich seem to manage very well with the army. I think the further you get away, the more the resentment becomes. But we've got to get on with it; there's no point in spending the rest of our lives resenting it.'

The rocket firing is suspended in August but for the rest of the year troops fly in every week from Germany and practice firing whatever it is they fire. The 500 men on Benbecula and at the rocket range on South Uist provide the technical and back-up support. It all costs vasts sums of money.

The original rocket range was set up on South Uist in 1961 to prove the Corporal missile. Three years earlier the army begun to build a tracking station forty miles west of the Uists on St Kilda. It cost £1 million; a further £6½ million was spent on Balivanich and, in 1972, £20 million more on the range. Small sums in terms of a total defence budget of billions but in an island like this where funds for essential public expenditure are often not forthcoming, it is a provocative display.

I am staying the night at Liniclate with Mrs Shepherd. Her guesthouse is a large double-storied house ('You can't miss it') in the south-west corner of the island. 'Heisker' has lots of hot water but by the time I get there it's a bit late for an evening meal. My fellow guests are civilians employed by the MOD up for a few weeks to see if economies can't be effected at the base.

At the Dark Island hotel down the road I have potato and leek soup and good haddock and fried potatoes. The bar is dark and full of taped music. There don't seem to be many army people about. 'It's cheaper for them in their own bars,' I'm told. I have a long conversation with a Benbecula man who now lives and works in Edinburgh. Could he ever see himself living here again?

'I don't think so. I've travelled all over the world and this place – well it's too small. Once you've been away, it's fine for a holiday but there you are. Could you live here yourself?'

I certainly wouldn't choose Benbecula to live in, with its constant reminder of NATO, the cold war and that aggressive daily firing of rockets.

'We try to keep a low profile,' an army officer explained to me earlier in the day, 'very low, very quiet. Not interfering. We're here as guests, we know that and we want to be polite and considerate guests.' A sensitive man, he was obviously worried by the anti-cruise propaganda and the anti-NATO movement in Stornoway.

A young couple on a cycling holiday join in the conversation. They live on an island too, at Cowes in the Isle of Wight. 'It's fantastic here,' the girl says, 'nobody about. We were in Harris this week and we had miles of beach all to ourselves, a real luxury after the Isle of Wight in August – there you can't move.'

She'd been in the NAAFI too to buy some sun oil. 'It must have made a fantastic difference to life up here; it's as good as the supermarket where we shop down home.'

'But supposing to get a shop like that you had to put up with an invading army; not just day trippers but a permanent garrison?'

She says, quite rightly, you could hardly have a rocket range in Cowes. 'It would ruin Cowes Week for a start,' says her boyfriend. They laugh. I don't see the people in the Isle of Wight putting up passively with the descent of 43,000 servicemen on their island – because in terms of relative populations that would be the number comparable to the present swamping of Benbecula.

Back at Heisker I sleep like a log and in the morning Mrs Shepherd fills me up with fruit juice, porridge, bacon, egg, sausage and liver and scones and oatcakes. She makes her own crowdie, butter and cheese when the cows are giving a good yield.

In the sitting room the Shepherd children and their cousins are watching Roland Rat on the box. It saddens the Shepherds, the all-pervasiveness of English culture and English language. When David Shepherd came here as a lad in 1947 and went to school at Torlum there was only one other totally English-speaking boy in the school.

'They all spoke Gaelic and I had to follow. It came naturally. Our eldest two before they went to school spoke nothing but Gaelic, now they have been more or less brainwashed into speaking English. When you say something to them in Gaelic and they answer in English, before you know where you are you're replying in English. You don't think about it, it just happens and then after about five minutes you say, "Oh gosh, you've got me speaking English again!"'

'Do you feel strongly then that they should be speaking to you in Gaelic?'

'I do. I do, yes. But it's not fashionable in the schools. There's so many incomers and they all speak English.'

The Shepherds have 20 acres, 2 cows, 2 breeding heifers and 30 breeding ewes. This year they have reseeded 6½ acres. I asked David whether he would describe himself as a full-time crofter?

'Oh, no! There's very few full-time crofters in Benbecula. There's no way even if a young man were given a croft that he could start with one sheep and build up and keep a family. You need to subsidise your crofting with a job. I collect seaweed – it's the oldest industry in the island. This is how crofting started; it was never meant to sustain a family. It was to give a man a place to build a house, keep a cow and grow a few potatoes so that he could survive and collect seaweed for the estates.'

Last year a professor came from Dundee University and gave a talk to the crofters. What he had to say made a deep impression on David. 'He showed us old records where it didn't matter how many tons of kelp a crofter produced he never got a penny for it. He maybe got three bags of meal in a year. And if he got £20 for his seaweed then the bags of meal cost £20. There was never a penny came back.'

He spends five or six days a fortnight gathering seaweed. It's easier than it was in the days of kelp; more worthwhile too. 'It's all done by hand; we cut it and tow it onto the beach and the firm's lorries come and collect it. Maybe you're earning £30 or £40 a day, it could be higher. Sometimes I have cut eight or ten tons in a day – it depends. In winter it's difficult, the days are shorter, the seas are rougher; you may only get three or four tons in a day.'

I ask what percentage of crofts are not being worked these days?

'There are very few *not* being worked, it's the *level* at which they're being worked. What's happened is that the older people get, the less they can do. When they get to 60 they sell a couple of cows; when they get to 65 they sell the rest of the cows. Then they carry on with the sheep until they're 70 or 80 if they last to that age span. Then they'll take an illness and maybe sublet. The person who it's sublet to isn't going to improve it because he doesn't know how long he's going to have it.' Such temporary arrangements, and there are many all over the islands, contribute to the running down of a croft.

John, the eldest son, comes into the room. What is his future going to be? David shrugs.

'When I left school the done thing was Glasgow first stop, get a job. But that's not easy these days. With the army being here there's more work and more people coming back. I hope he'd get more schooling than I did. There's quite a lot of apprenticeships with the army; he's very useful with his hands, repairing tractors and that, very quick on the uptake like. I'd like him to at least have a trade of some sort.'

Again David stresses the croft as only a foundation for a way of life, not a way of life in itself. 'To live in these islands you've got to diversify. We both sustain the croft but we're getting the benefit of it in potatoes, fresh milk and our own meat and all the rest of it – I don't know if you can put a price on the likes of these commodities.'

Nor for that matter a price on the environment itself. 'It's just a Mecca for the children. They go out and disappear at sunrise and you don't see them till sunset; even then you have to pull them in by the ear to get them to go to bed. They've got the beaches, the open fields. Everything costs more but then by working that bit harder it's worth it. A croft can give you great satisfaction.'

What it cannot give you, of course, is complete independence. As the Rev. Donald Mackinnon pointed out in 1884, 'crofters were not intended or expected to be self-supporting farmers but working men with allotments.' In 1984 there were 17,792 registered crofts in the north of Scotland of which a third, 5,972, were in the Western Isles. Historically, if land was any good it was grabbed by the proprietor and turned into a farm, so a high proportion of crofts are sited on some of the poorest agricultural land in Europe. That is one of the reasons why the EEC devised its Integrated Development Programme to improve both stock and land.

On 1 September 1982 the EEC's five-year plan 'to improve working and living conditions in the Western Isles' got under way. A project team was set up to handle applications, meetings were held from Ness right down the Long Island to Barra, and ideas soon began to emerge – to optimists it seemed to be the most stimulating thing that had happened to the crofting community since the arrival of the Napier Commission.

Not everyone greeted IDP as the saviour of the crofting race. Professor Lodge, principal of the North of Scotland College of Agriculture, outlined three points of concern. If the objective was to sustain the indigenous population in this high-cost region the very first thing that should have been done was to survey 'the capacity of the population to engage in productive activity.' He claimed that it was illogical to 'distribute scarce financial resources . . . towards these parts of the agricultural industry which are least productive and most likely to involve continuing high costs.'

Perhaps his most damaging contention was that, judging on past form, efforts to stimulate technical development would be unrewarding: 'The basic agricultural problems of the Western Isles are climate, soil and markets and no amount of money can change any of these. Such proposals as liming, fertilising, reseeding and fencing can only afford temporary improvements at best and I find it difficult, if not impossible to envisage any form of expenditure on agriculture which can be expected to have a lasting effect.'

Dr Alistair Fraser, who was at that time a part-time member of the Crofters Commission, refused to accept this defeatist line. If Professor Lodge had his way, he said, everyone might just as well pack up and leave the Hebrides: 'There is no point bemoaning the conditions that the islands are up against. We've got to accept them and try to make the best of them.'

Later this conflict of interests was cleared up. It turned out that the Professor thought mistakenly that it was the British government which was going to spend £20 million on agriculture in the Western Isles not the EEC. But the college continued to point out the difficulties of farming in the Western Isles. Dr Graham Dalton, writing in the economic journal of the college, *Farm Management Review*, argued that the entire output of every farm and croft in the Western Isles was probably less valuable than any *one* of the larger farms in eastern Scotland. He worked out that the average annual receipts per head of the population of the Western Isles came to only £90 each, or £137 if you added the subsidies.

And crofting has never lacked subsidies. A cynic once said a croft was a small area of land surrounded by regulations; it might be more rightly described as a small area of land supported by grants and loans. There are grants for land reclamation and regeneration, draining, fencing, installing cattle grids, planting shelter belts of trees, digging silage pits, erecting farm buildings and making roads to improve access. These vary from 60 to 85 per cent of the cost of materials and labour.

There are other grants available for building and renovating crofthouses, and improving livestock. Money has recently been set aside to carry out research into using wave energy in the Western Isles. The IDP programme has been seen by most islanders as a lifeline for crofting and there is a growing awareness that the idea of crofting as a way of life must be canvassed more enthusiastically among young people. Angus Macleod, a former Director of Education for the Western Isles, has called for a percentage of school time to be set aside for instruction in crofting and fishing. 'It is imperative', he has said, 'that we should take a new and very hard look at our available resources – land, fishing, peat, alternative forms of energy, crafts – in fact anything and everything that will help to attain a greater degree of self-sufficiency, to obtain additional income and employment and to retain our native population on these islands.'

The Highlands and Islands Development Board over the years has been deeply involved in doing just that. But the obstacles often seem dauntingly insuperable.

As I journey down this empty archipelago, basking now under the summer sun, I begin to wonder whether any scheme, however adventurous, will ever come to full fruition. How long before it would be washed out by rain, bankrupted by the sheer distance from markets? In the ten years up to the end of 1983 the Board invested over £23 million in the Western Isles in the form of grants and loans in an effort to create 2,219 new jobs. Of those 2,219 jobs only 1,090 survived until 1983. In the last decade, 6,404 jobs in farming, horticulture, fishing, fish farming, fish processing, boat building and marine engineering, crafts, hotels, catering and tourism were created in the Highlands and Islands, of which the Western Isles had its due fair share. Each job, in grants, loans and shares, cost £274,000.

Many of the enterprises set up with wildly generous grants from the Board have collapsed after a few years. Public money squandered, the locals will tell you, especially if they have seen a neighbour dip his hands into the public purse.

'A very common thing', a crofter told me, 'is to apply for a grant or a loan or both to extend your house. You just say your wife is going to run a guesthouse. Well maybe she is and maybe she isn't, who can tell? So you add a couple of bedrooms and a new bathroom and then that summer you do bed and breakfast and then maybe the next year your wife takes ill and she's not up to it. What's to stop you? There's plenty have had grants for that.'

There's one thing for sure, if all crofters had the energy and enterprise of David Shepherd, and for all I know they have, then even the most adverse conditions would be turned to advantage. David toils tirelessly; no sooner have I finished talking to him than he's off out of the door into his car and up the road to St Peter's Port for a morning's seaweed gathering. There are only two roads leading to the skerries on the east side of Benbecula. One winds down to Loch Uiskevagh, the other ends at the pier at St Peter's Port facing the island of Wiay, now a bird sanctuary.

By the time I've dawdled down the winding road to the pier David has already joined another cutter and they are making their way in a small boat with an outboard motor round the island of Fodragay. *This Pier is dangerous. No Admittance. Signed G. Macleod, Director of Eng. Services* reads a notice just as you are about to step onto a rickety-looking structure with missing planks. This is the famous pier which was never used by anyone. There wasn't even a road to it.

I'm carrying in the car with me, just to compare the new with the old, a 2*s* *Bartholomew's New Reduced Survey Map for Tourists and Cyclists* probably printed just after the Great War. The road in those days came to a halt at the small clachan of Hacklett – across the water lay Grimsay and then more open water before you reached Eilean na Cille on which the pier had been built in 1896.

Not only was the pier unapproachable from the west, more to public bewilderment it was only navigable by the foolhardy from the open sea and Hebridean mariners are no fools. Evidently at the end of the century it was felt that as North Uist had a major pier at Lochmaddy and South Uist was served by Lochboisdale, Benbecula too should have a pier. There could not have been a more useless place chosen than Eilean na Cille; nobody lived there, nobody could get there. It was the perfect bureaucrat's decision; ideally placed on the map, in practice useless. And used it never was. Causeways and a road to join the pier to the road at Hacklett were built later, but no ship's master could be persuaded to risk a vessel anywhere in those waters.

The seaweed industry in which David works part-time has had a more successful history. It only dates from the Second World War when a firm began to process seaweed on the mainland in Kintyre. In 1957 a factory was opened at Sponish near Lochmaddy to process the weed which is cut from rocks at low tide. The seaweed is dried and milled and is used for a variety of products from food to cosmetics and pharmaceuticals.

On the road back my eye falls on a bit of fallout from the last war – a Nissen hut converted with great ingenuity to look like a traditional crofthouse. It has been faced with breeze blocks painted black and white, an incongruous folly amid the lily lochans and the moorhens.

8

THE HUNTING INSTINCT
IS STRONG

SOUTH UIST 1

South Uist is shaped, if you will pardon the simile, like a foetus. Its back, down which runs the main road with small veins shooting off to the shore, is 25 miles long, sandy and smooth. The feet push out into the sea below Loch Boisdale and the head lies above, almost separated from the body as Loch Skipport pushes it away west to the freshwater Loch Bee. Where the eyes might be is Loch Carnan which, had the authorities been a bit brighter in Victorian times, might have been the most effective harbour for Benbecula. It is now used by the army as a base for the landing craft which services the military garrison on St Kilda.

South Uist wasn't connected to Benbecula by road until 1943 when the causeway-bridge joining Creagorry to Carnan was opened. It was a shorter link than the one which would join Cramisdale in Benbecula with Carinish in North Uist in 1960 but it was a vital wartime connection between the new airfield at Balivanich and the main cargo and passenger port of Lochbois-dale. The crossing of these fords was hazardous and only possible at low tide. Although the North Ford looked more daunting, it was the South Ford which took more lives.

Lying like obstacles in the mile of wet sand were two separate channels. 'A man might cross one,' wrote Frederick Rea, 'but by the time he reached the other the tide had turned and was running like a mill-race in the channel which, of course, was then much deeper and wider, so that he was caught between the two channels of the tide' (*A School in South Uist*, p. 203).

'Faothill mhath dhuibh', 'a good ford to you', was the parting benison bestowed on those crossing the sands. I had a good ford, not another car on the road, as I crossed to go down to Lochcarnan to meet Neil Macpherson, the spokesman of the fishermen of the Western Isles.

Although his office is in Stornoway, he weekends whenever he can with his wife and children in South Uist. They have extended the old crofthouse and it symbolises much of the Western Isles today. The original walls are there firmly planted in the rock but the improvements are very 1980s; new materials and design, trendy even. Future-conscious, as admen might say, a Now house for Now people.

Neil is very much in the thick of anticipating future tastes and is constantly on the phone to people who talk about optimising market receptability and the interface of product and packaging. He worked for the Western Isles Council as a development officer and is currently wearing two sou'westers: he is Secretary of the Western Isles Fishermen's Association, the body which speaks for everyone engaged in fishing in the Outer Hebrides, and he is also the man in charge of marketing at the Stornoway Fishermen's Co-operative Ltd. He is, a contact told me, messianic about fishing.

I asked him whether he thought that maybe the failure of the Board's enterprise at Breasclete was partly due to a too conservative attitude among fishermen. He leaps in his seat, stung by the thought.

'I totally reject that. Apathy! That's absolute nonsense, it's just trotted out by people who don't know what they're talking about. At the same time that Breasclete was collapsing I couldn't count on the fingers of my hand the new species the fishermen turned to. Scallop dredging was introduced, prawn creeling, crab fishing, crawfish fishing, velvet crab fishing; some went to shellfish cultivation – mussels, clams. Sand eel fishing started, pair trawling started.' He bangs his fist gently on the table. 'To try and paint the fishing community as people who just won't change is absolute nonsense. But having said that there are still big potentials for exploited species. There are big, unsatisfied markets for squid in Spain, Portugal and France. We don't have the expertise but no problem – the Japanese could teach us that!'

I mention monkfish, the bizarre-looking fish which the French call *lotte* and whose flesh is so firm and delicate that unscrupulous restaurants use it as an analogue for lobster.

'There again there's a tremendous demand for monkfish in Europe. On Thursday night the monkfish in Stornoway were going to be dumped because there's no local market for them; there was no transport going across the following morning and I knew that on the other side of the Minch monkfish were fetching £60 a box – goodness knows what it would be fetching in ports in the north of France! If you could chill it, get the transport organised, you could send it down there and get the French price less the transport . . . if the effort was put in.'

If effort is needed Neil's the man. But getting things done takes time. One breakthrough the Western Isles has had is in getting its farmed mussels accepted by Marks & Spencer. 'Growing mussels on rafts is an ideal project for multi-strategied crofters – you don't have to look after them, you don't have to feed them and we've got about 30 pilot schemes going at the moment. They're good mussels, grit-free, the shell is pleasing to the eye. Above all M & S were able to prove to themselves that our mussels were absolutely safe – they'll never take mussels from Spain or Holland because of pollution risks.'

How big was the enterprise?

'Well in 1983 we sold 30, 40, 50 tons, maybe in 1985 that could rise to 300 tons. We had a bad year last year; the ropes on which the mussels grow became fouled with sea squirts, small jellylike things, but that's only a temporary setback.' If the waters were to withdraw from the Hebrides entirely I can see Neil discussing it as a temporary setback. But if the prospects are that bright why has fishing been in the doldrums for so long?

'Well we had a poor reputation in the past, the other thing is that we are a long way from markets, there's been no encouragement for the fishermen to improve and very little attention has been paid to marketing and presentation. Because we haven't been getting the prices the fleet's under-capitalised.'

One of the things the island fishermen lack is the technology of the east-coast boats. 'They can swim their fish inside the purse-nets, it gets rid of fat, cleans the gut out; our small boats can't do that.'

The forty or so boats fishing out of Stornoway are small and confined to inshore waters. 'Their staple is the prawn, the *nephrops*, which they catch in trawls. In the winter they fish for cod, haddock, whiting, monkfish and so on.'

Neil's current enthusiasm is for aquaculture and he sees only the capacity of the market limiting production. The small lochs of the east coast of the Long Island are ideal for growing fish and in particular salmon. The returns can be spectacular.

'Imagine a reasonably successful fishing boat for this part of the world with a five-man crew grossing, say, £100,000, perhaps £120,000. Now a salmon cage eight metres by eight metres by twenty feet deep will produce between £35,000 and £40,000 worth of salmon – so that's just one wee corner of seawater. Extrapolate that out to what seawater is available and you can see the potential.'

'You mean people will be leaving their boats to become fish farmers?'

'That *has* happened to a certain extent in Norway but I don't see it happening here. You see it's *farming*, there's no way it can be disguised as *fishing*, and the hunting instinct is strong here: the cultural sociological stimulus for a Hebridean to fish is very deep-rooted. The crofter or person who's going to go for fish farming isn't going to come from generations of fishermen.'

He may well not even come from the Hebrides. I finish my coffee and leave Neil to go back to his pocket calculator. Living in the old schoolhouse at Lochcarnan are Jane and Eric Twelves from Pontefract. Both in different ways have capitalised on the ecological amenities of the island. Jane runs Uist Wildlife Holidays. In her brochure she offers 'waders and seabirds galore, otters, seals, red deer, corncrakes and raptors'.

'It's a package tour really. For £240 you get the return ferry fare across from Oban to Lochboisdale, full accommodation at Grogarry Lodge, minibus transport round the islands, boat trips, sea fishing, evening talks – what else? We arrange a trip to St Kilda if they want.'

'And what sort of people come?'

'Obviously it's very much the birdwatchers and the people who want to unwind in peace and quiet and of course this summer it's been absolutely glorious, week after week of uninterrupted sunshine – they all go back as burnt as if they've been to the Costa del Sol. But I think they've seen a lot more than you'd see on the beaches down there.'

She's taking a Scandinavian naturalist out in the boat to wander round the skerries and islets at the entrance to Loch Carnan otter watching and she leaves me to have a look at Eric's salmon farm.

Since 1965 the Board, literally, has sunk over £11 million into fish farming, and private enterprise has put in another £18 million. In 1983 ten farms in the Western Isles were given £661,000 worth of assistance and another ten were in the pipeline. Word has been getting around that if it's not a licence to print money, with all the financial help from the Board and the EEC, it could be a non-losing gamble.

Eric Twelves came to Lochcarnan to work for one of the big operators, a subsidiary of Booker McConnell. Eric's Booker Prize was to escape and do his own thing a few miles down the road.

The McConnell operation is one of the largest and most successful in Scotland – lorries, cranes, stock-rearing and a sizeable payroll. Eric is still beholden to McConnell. He buys his smolts from them and he sells his full-grown salmon to them. McConnell have two sites in the Uists and two in Lewis and they have the marketing muscle to get the best prices.

'Come and see what we do,' says Eric and introduces me to Peter Crook, a professional engineer who's been mixed up with fish farming since the late

1960s. Peter got involved when he was working for Unilever Research Laboratories as a project engineer, and he now supplies equipment and technical advice to fish farmers.

'In February 1969 I was told that one cold night the cages and everything holding Unilever's experimental fish farm in Lochailort had sunk without trace. I volunteered to try and put things right.'

He did and he went on to develop the hardware needed for fish farming, first with Unilever then with Marine Harvest. He reorganised the North of Scotland Hydro Board's hatchery at Invergarry, built a £350,000 salmon smolt farm in Glen Moriston, and took Marine Harvest to the stage where they have 200 farm units moored in the sea lochs of west Scotland. He supplied Eric with his hardware too.

We hop in the rubber boat and Eric takes us down the loch to where his investment is maturing. Peter tells me that Eric is in well on course. 'He's only had the farm for just over a year and it's already produced 14 tons of fish.'

The 'farm' comes into view: four caged tanks, heavily netted to prevent poaching from herons and kingfishers. 'The beauty of a thing like this,' says Peter, 'is that one man can manage it in his spare time.'

An electric buzzer burrs softly for a few seconds. 'That's the automatic feeder, it releases exactly the right amount of food pellets into the water. The fish swipe them and hopefully get fatter every day.'

It sounded simple.

'Well it is. A farm like this would cost about £14,000, that's with all the moorings and nets. A chap can finish up with a grant of 70 per cent of his first two years' investment from the IDP which he doesn't have to repay as long as he stays in it for five years. If he makes it work he's got off to a very good start.'

Eric undoes the netting and we jump on board the catwalk between the cages. The salmon are swimming up and down restlessly and occasionally leaping out of the water. Eric surveys them with some pride.

'We had 9,400 surviving this year in two cages; that was out of a potential of 10,000.' I ask about the tie-up with McConnell, which sounds a bit restrictive.

'Well it is and it isn't. They encourage us to buy the smolts from them because they don't want to introduce exotic diseases into the place. We sell through McConnell, so we don't want to annoy them – to be quite honest the quality of their smolts is better than you'd get on the mainland.'

In May and June he put in 15,000 post-smolts and he also has 1,700 salmon left from last year. 'All these here are going to get zapped at the end of April. What happens in the salmon game is that it's economic to send a load of six or eight tons away from here on a Monday or Friday and that salmon is sold through all the major cities in the country. I shouldn't be telling you this but McConnell make as much as they can in the provincial cities and the rest goes to Billingsgate to one or other of the big dealers who move it round the South East.'

The advantage of farmed salmon is its regular availability. 'A buyer may want 20 boxes of salmon a week. He may get 20 boxes of wild salmon in May, June and July but what's he going to do for the rest of the year? That's where farmed salmon comes in. This week down south they're hunting for salmon, they can't get enough of it; last week they had lots of wild stuff.'

From 1985 it is estimated that the Western Isles will be producing 1,000 of the annual 5,000 ton grown throughout Scotland.

And can you tell the difference? I went to a blind tasting of wild and farmed salmon on the west coast a few years ago and couldn't. When you cut salmon open the body cavity on a wild salmon is much smaller than on a farmed salmon; there is a difference in the colour of the gills too, and because the wild salmon burns up a great deal of its fat making its way upstream to spawn, the farmed salmon tends to have more body fat and therefore be oilier. But it would take someone in the trade to tell the difference. Taste very much depends on the formula of the concentrate which the captive fish are fed. They're getting better at it.

'Is it money for old rope?' I ask Eric.

'Not really. You go out with a pair of binoculars in January after a gale just to see if there's anything left of your investment. We don't live on the salmon. I fish for velvet crab as a main occupation; they're really tasty.'

Driving back up the road I count on the fingers of one hand the really tasty meals I've had on this trip. Where was all that monkfish left on the quay at Stornoway? It never appeared on my plate. Why haven't I been served velvet crab, which according to Eric is the kind of delicacy which lifts crab into the gourmet class? And why hasn't anyone offered me mussels or oysters? They're all being farmed successfully.

I turn back on to the main road and give the matter some thought. Here I am on an island surrounded by fish with prime lobsters being ferried out all over Europe and there's not a seafood restaurant in the whole of the Western Isles. I remember a friend of mine who settled in Skye after teaching at the Sorbonne for fifteen years. 'I hadn't been on the island for a day before I saw all these mussels on the shore, cockles too. I asked someone where there was a good fish restaurant and he laughed in my face. Of course I laugh too now but I'd been used to France where if you had a village on the coast you had fish restaurants. Not here you don't.'

Gastronomically this is a deprived region where convenience food not fresh food seems to be, if not preferred, then at least accepted quite happily. South Uist has always been noted for its cattle but where is all the local milk, cream, butter and cheese? If it does exist then it hasn't been put on my plate. My milk has come largely from the mainland and not infrequently it is the metallic-tasting UHT.

On my travels I've encountered Michael Daw of the North of Scotland College of Agriculture in Aberdeen. He's been doing a survey for the Board to see if more milk could be produced locally. In the Uists and Barra most of the fresh milk is pasteurised and imported from Oban and Uig. The milk from Nairn and Inverness comes by lorry to Uig in Skye and is then ferried to Lochmaddy three or four times a week. The researchers only found three crofters who were interested in becoming milk producers in the Uists and Benbecula and none at all in Barra. The people of Barra, because of the frequency with which milk turns up from Oban almost on the verge of going sour, have moved bodily over to UHT; a whole new generation is being reared who have never tasted fresh milk. The only place producing any significant amount of fresh milk is Stornoway. Although 70 per cent of the milk is imported one producer keeps 160 cows. No milk is sold by private crofters.

And yet within living memory there was plenty about. Finlay J. Macdonald wrote a highly evocative book called *Crowdie and Cream* (Macdonald, 1982), memoirs of his Harris childhood. If his grandchildren were to write theirs they might well have to call it *Chedda-plus and UHT*. The fare may have been simple in Finlay J.'s day – brose, potatoes, herrings and the occasional piece of mutton – but at least it was real food, not the heavily processed junk that has spread all over the Outer Isles. In the old days a crofting family with a cow could keep itself in milk for much of the year. Today there are only 26 dairy cows and heifers in milk or in calf in North Uist, 68 in South Uist and 8 in Barra.

As with so many other essentials, the islanders depend heavily on the mainland to keep them going. So if you're looking for crowdie and cream the Western Isles is not the place to find it; unless it's crowdie from a mainland creamery or some kind of longlife substitute for Finlay J.'s thick rich Harris cream of the past. Here is his tribute to Daisy who in her prime and when the summer machair was at its most lush could produce four gallons a day:

First there was of course the milk itself for drinking. The balance was set out in large flat basins to yield enough cream to keep the family in fresh butter for immediate use, leaving pounds over each week for salting for winter. Once the cream had been removed gallons of thick sour cream were stood on the warm fire, converted into crowdie which floated to the surface of tangy refreshing whey – the ideal drink for hot days of peat-cutting or hay-making.

And then Finlay J. remembers the greatest delicacy of all which gave him the title for his book:

the crumbly crowdie mixed with fresh cream which piled high on a fresh oatcake spread with fresh butter combined into a flavour with an inbuilt memory. Crowdie and cream! The bitter and the sweet blending as they so often do, is an experience for which there isn't one single word that I know of, whether relishing the dream or the reality.

It would be nice to think that the tourists who come in the summer months to the Western Isles could also taste such crowdie and cream or even occasionally a herring grilled in oatmeal or anything which had any local relevance. More often than not the evening meal is rich not in the taste of the Hebrides but in additives and preservatives.

Five years ago on one of these islands I was doing B & B in the house of a fisherman. In the early afternoon I encountered the husband down at the jetty taking fish off the boat: fresh haddies, flatfish, a skate, some lythe. My expectations were aroused and at 6.30 that evening dashed. Our evening meal was Heinz canned tomato soup, instant Smash potatoes, Findus frozen peas and a boiled frozen chicken served with packet gravy and Paxo stuffing. It was followed by tinned fruit salad and Angel Whip Dessert. I can taste it still.

I have already enthused about the Johnsons of Scarista and their refusal to use convenience food; despite their success in the hotel guides nobody appears to have realised that not everyone who comes to the Hebrides is happy to be forcibly fed on over-processed rubbish. I sat one evening in the front room of a crofthouse gazing out on a scene of incomparable grandeur. The sea, like molten gold shot with crimson, was foaming on the shell-white sands; on the horizon the sun was descending like an enlarged blood orange. I could hear a corncrake in the machair. Where else would I rather be? My hostess bustled in with the supper and I realised that actually I'd rather have been in some country where there was a possibility of eating fresh food.

There was tinned spaghetti in tomato sauce, frozen sprouts, a fried hamburger and McCain oven chips. I spread it about the plate, managed to palm the meat into the dog's mouth and moved on to tinned mandarin oranges, and raspberry ice cream made in a factory in the suburbs of London largely from palm oil which left a taste of soap in my mouth. I went for a walk along that ravishingly beautiful beach and I longed to be in Greece or Italy or Spain where even the poorest of the poor have not lost their taste for real food or their skill in cooking. The following morning I had English-made cornflakes for breakfast, Danish bacon, New Zealand butter, Dutch tomatoes, cottonwool sliced bread from Inverness – and of course UHT milk. The food was alien, only the warmth of the hospitality was genuine and real.

It's sad that in such a place of beauty where people are so welcoming and considerate they should inflict such grievous bodily harm on your palate. I aired these views with a couple who gave me a lift from Ludag to Lochmaddy on one of my trips when I'd left my own car in Skye.

Joanne and Gary Gunn have a guest house in Stornoway. She specialises in the teaching of geriatric nursing and he runs the guest house and is also Chairman of the Outer Hebrides Tourist Board. As we bowled up the road to Kilpheder he told me he'd taken a few days off to run down the Long Island to meet as many members of the association as possible and persuade people connected with tourism who hadn't so far joined to cough up a subscription.

'People don't reply to letters but if you actually stand on the doorstep they can't refuse can they?' He told me he'd enrolled Donald Campbell, the boatman who runs the ferry to Barra. 'I swapped the fare for his next year's membership!' I asked him why they called themselves the Outer Hebrides Tourist Board when the official designation was Western Isles.

'I think lots of people are confused. When we're advertising the Western Isles people think of everything from Mull to Skye but "Outer Hebrides" can't mean anything other than Lewis to Barra can it?'

Doesn't he think it strange that an Englishman should be the driving force behind tourism in the heart of the Gaeltacht?'

'Well it often happens, doesn't it? They'll put up an outsider rather than seem to be pushing themselves. I think English people are more brash, pushy if you like. I mean I don't mind being seen to be organising whereas if a Lewisman did it his friends might say he was getting too big for his boots, showing off, and they might well be less keen to co-operate; at least that's the way I see it.'

It's also the way Dr Judith Ennew observed it when she spent her two years researching in Lewis and Harris. She pointed out that an outsider was very often chosen as a spokesman rather like a lightning conductor: 'If their activity as public figures meets with local criticism this does not damage the fabric of family and neighbourhood relationships.'

This is one of the reasons why arrivals from the mainland, or 'white settlers' as they are pejoratively described, frequently find themselves thrust into the thick of some local controversy where the wise and the careful keep a diplomatically low profile. Incoming teachers, bank managers, doctors, priests and ministers find that they are being edged on to committees to represent the community. The overt explanation is that such people are used to speaking their mind and coping with officialdom but deep down there is a reticence and a suspicion of the egregious activist.

What, I ask Joanne, do they do with their guests on Sunday in Stornoway? That is a problem, she admits: 'We warn them that they won't be able to get a drink in the town and a lot of people think it's silly but you've got to live with that.'

'When I get some time,' says Gary, turning off for South Boisdale, 'I'm going to write to the Lord's Day Observance people and just ask them what their attitude is. If they say they have no objection to Sunday opening then the Council can make available amenities for visitors. I mean it is really a bit of a disservice to get people to come here and then withdraw all facilities on Sundays. The tea room opposite Scarista House is the only place open in Lewis on Sunday where you can get a cup of tea.'

Joanne tells me that Helen Macintyre whom they are going to see is also a nurse and she is the Tourist Council member for South Uist and Benbecula and Gary's Deputy Chairman.

As Gary parks outside the Macintyres' house a van pulls up and a chap leaps out with a screwtop whisky bottle of milk. This turns out to be Roddie Steele giving the lie to my slanders about lack of local enterprise. He supplies 40 families with fresh milk and very good milk it is too, but before I can ask him if he's into crowdie and cream he's off down the road.

Helen's husband Norman works for Telecom but he's got the morning off. There's a croft to run as well and Helen does B & B and can take three people a night. While Gary transacts his business with Helen, Norman tells me that he was brought up as a child in Glasgow; like so many other people, his father had to go south to find work. As a child he spent every summer with his grandparents in South Uist. 'It was a six-week crash course in Gaelic really so when I came back here I was speaking it very well.'

We talk about the Council's bilingual policy and the harmony of the islands. Helen joins in: 'It often seems to me that they haven't got their priorities right. They've just been having a long debate in Stornoway about whether their proceedings should be in Gaelic or English when there's a great problem to be solved with Daliburgh school.'

Norman tells me that South Uist has a more relaxed attitude to the Sabbath than North Uist. 'During the stormy weather last winter I was out on Sundays repairing lines, now you wouldn't get them working that way in North Uist.'

We say goodbye to the Macintyres and a few miles down the road I leave the Gunns to make their way back to Lochmaddy and the boat for Stornoway.

South Uist is the first stronghold of Catholicism you reach as you work your way south. You notice that as soon as you cross the causeway. There on the left of the road is a shrine: *Failte Dhut A Mhoire* says a legend in faded lettering and inside the Virgin stands with the Christ child, a source no doubt of great scandal to Calvinists and those who equate mariolatry with heathen practices. When the good people of Iochdar parish erected a thirty-foot high statue of Our Lady of the Isles on the slopes of Rueval in 1957 to commemorate Marian Year there was a predictable outcry from the Free Church in Stornoway. A malign influence on the landscape, they thought it.

Our Lady's granite eyes look out unseeing at the rocket range and looking down on her from the top of Rueval is a space-age military complex one of whose functions is to monitor the firing on the sands below. The range is not active in August and the gateway on to the dunes is locked. 'Leave immediately when red flags are hoisted or red beacon is lit,' says an MOD notice.

The machair is lush and fertile. Cattle graze peacefully, the hay is being harvested, there is the occasional cry of a bird. To the south of Loch Rueval is the famous 4,000 acres of Loch Druidibeg nature reserve where formidable squadrons of waterfowl and in particular the greylag geese breed. The crofting community is currently locked in a verbal battle with the pro-conservationist lobby. They claim that with two UNESCO Biosphere Reserves, four National Nature Reserves and 35 other areas designated as Sites of Special Scientific Interest they can't move without an ornithologist waving his binoculars angrily and writing to the *Scotsman* about the infringement of the rights of some wretched bird.

On the other hand you could equally make out a case to prove that the small-scale and largely unmechanised activities of the crofter have preserved the Hebrides as a last haunt of the corncrake and the red-necked phalarope. No money has been set aside to explain the conservationist case to the crofting community either in English or, more to the point, in Gaelic. If the Western Isles is such a unique ecological area why is this national resource not being properly funded, as national parks are, for example, in England? And if it is national policy to try and preserve the islands so that man can exist in harmony with nature then man ought to be compensated for any economic hardship which he suffers as a consequence. One is constantly reading about landowners in England being compensated financially for not draining some ecologically valuable marsh or not cutting down a vital woodland, why shouldn't such inducements be extended to the crofting community?

Wandering in a relaxed way towards the south of the island I pass an unusual cameo. Beside what looks like the roofless remains of a chapel a crofter is standing talking to two youngsters. They are fresh-cheeked, their hair cut short-back-and-sides. They might be selling insurance or conducting a survey. They both have slim briefcases under their arms.

I park the car and walk back. The crofter tells me that the building is indeed a chapel. 'It was built in the 1890s by a Seceder from Mull. It was never used and the roof blew off in a storm in 1921 or somewhere then. They used the slates to roof a house.'

I said I found it strange that a Free Presbyterian should come all the way from Mull to try and proselytise in the stony and no doubt unreceptive ground of this predominantly Catholic island.'

'Well there are funnier things than that I suppose,' says the crofter and his glance embraces the two well-scrubbed lads.

'You wouldn't be Mormons by any chance,' I say to the eager youngsters in their clerical suits, for I have seen it is not the pursuit of Mammon which is brightening their eyes but evangelical zeal.

'No, we are Jehovah's Witnesses – from Leeds. We're partly on holiday, partly on a sponsored mission.' They introduce themselves. 'I'm Michael Hodgson and . . .' '. . . I'm Andrew Shillitoe.'

I wonder why on this baking hot day they're wearing jackets and throttling themselves with neckties.

'We obviously wear suits, shirts, collars and ties because it's nice to make a good impression,' says Andrew. Michael says that they do know South Uist is staunchly Catholic but they have had a good reception.

'They've got very firm ideas, but we've had a few nice chats with people. We've found some people who have moved here, Anglicans and so on; the response has been good, better than down in Yorkshire,' and they both laugh, hardened doorstep salesman for Jesus inured to rebuffs and insults.

'At least', says Michael, 'the people up here are very religious and you've got a basic to talk to people on. Where we come from half the people don't have a faith.'

So what can they offer the people of South Uist?

'Basically we talk to people about hope for the future.'

'Surely Catholics have a great hope for the future?'

'We believe that man was made to live basically on the earth. We've had diffuse scriptural discussion on that with a few Catholics.'

'You mean you don't believe in Heaven and Hell?'

'No, the Bible says clearly that when you die you're dead; conscious of nothing. It also speaks of a class of people who do go to Heaven but it numbers them among the elect.'

Andrew tells me it's very complicated but the Apostles were a classic example of people who were destined for better things.

'Are you elect?'

'No, we're in the class that stays on earth and one day the earth will be a paradise all over.'

'But you'll be gone?'

'No, we'll be here.'

'But what happens after you die?'

'We don't die. The Bible promises that man can live for ever.'

'What with ginger hair and so on?'

'Yes, but without the infirmities,' Andrew points to the back of his hand, 'like these warts.'

The crofter has drifted away during this confusing and somewhat pragmatic exegesis and I am left to puzzle it out on my own.

'So you will keep the same body then?'

'No, not the same body but God remembers every single one of us and we'll have the same memories that we've had in this life.'

'So you'll remember your unproductive visit to South Uist?'

'Well we didn't really plan to make converts did we?' says Michael appealing to his fellow disciple of Good News.

Michael and Andrew, whom at this stage I couldn't help feeling some degree of sympathy for – much as one might sympathise with gas fire salesmen in the Sahara – said they were on their way to Benbecula where there was (as there might have been a coven of early Christians in the catacombs of Rome) a family of beleaguered Witnesses. Andrew told me he had rung them and the fatted calf was about to be killed or whatever might be the right and proper post-Biblical welcome for these missionaries from Leeds. They head north and I get back in the car and follow the road south.

9

VERY LITTLE LAND IN HAND AT ALL

SOUTH UIST 2

You've got to know your way round South Uist; there are few helping signposts to point you in the direction of historic or archaeological curiosities – chambered cairns, standing stones, menhirs, duns and brochs are found all over the Western Isles but only if you know where to look. I've noted one or two places in advance and just as well; if I hadn't armed myself with the Ordnance Survey map I would have missed Ormiclate Castle altogether.

It lies in ruins nine miles to the north-west of Lochboisdale. Built in 1701 for the chief of Clan Ranald, it was burnt at the time of the Jacobite rising, some say by a careless scullion. Others put it down to vengeful Hanoverians. A more emotive ruin and another Jacobite relic is what the map marks as 'Flora Macdonald's Birthplace'. But where is it? Nothing indicates that the woman who is remembered in legend for helping Prince Charlie escape in drag to Skye took her first breath anywhere here. Flora subsequently met Johnson and Boswell when they were staying in her house in Skye in 1773. 'She is a little woman', wrote Boswell, 'of genteel appearance, mighty soft and well bred.'

I turn the car round and go back to a pebble-dashed bungalow at the top of a cart track which may well lead to the home of this gallant woman of whom Dr Johnson said, 'Her name will be mentioned in history, and if courage and fidelity be virtues, mentioned with honour.'

There is a vase of bright artificial flowers in the window, floral curtains, a TV aerial and several wheel-less vehicles and an old bus surrounding the house. Miss Walker who comes to the door tells me that, yes, I am on the right track.

'Go down the road there,' she says, 'and you'll see the cairn inside the walls. There's only the walls left now.' She tells me she was born in the house facing Flora's which is now itself just a crumbling ruin used as a byre. 'Some say she wasn't born in that house at all.'

So there are doubts. I walk down and there on a knoll are low walls and a memorial cairn raised by the Clan Donald. She wasn't born here, it says, but she lived in the house which once stood on this site. It couldn't have been much more than a cottage with three rooms and a kitchen but the site was well chosen. It faces out to the sea and behind it on the far side of the road rise the slopes of Sheaval.

At Askernish, a couple of miles south of the Birthplace, is the only golf course in the Western Isles outside Stornoway. You get a ticket to play there from the Estates Office. The factor for the South Uist Estates is a youngish man from East Lothian called David Allan. He's at home when I call, working at his desk.

In the pinewood entrance hall is a framed address to the Victorian proprietors which, with Mr Allan's permission, I copy out. It is so faded by the sun, it's almost on the verge of being undecipherable. I suggest that he might get it photographed before it fades away altogether. It's certainly worth preserving, if only as a testament to the unfailing courtesy of the peasantry whom the Cathcarts ruled over with such imperious disdain. Lady Gordon Cathcart had inherited from her first husband, John Gordon of Cluny, roughly 100,000 acres of the Western Isles and she survived, a remarkable example of the tenacity of the wealthy, until 1935. In 1942 her executors sold the north end of Benbecula to the Air Ministry and two years later the remainder of the estates went to a wealthy banker called Herman Andreae for some £75,000. Thus ended what can only be described as ten disastrous decades in which one-seventh of the Outer Hebrides was held to ransom by a family who kept their profits up and their tenants down. Their record from Colonel Gordon's evictions to his daughter's autocratic patronage represents a well chronicled document of the unacceptable face of private proprietorship in the islands.

But to return to Askernish. There on the wall is this pathetic tribute to the naive belief of the peasantry that patience is a virtue and that obsequious deference will eventually be rewarded. It was hand-indited on 26 August 1882 by a Charles Maclean at the request of the tenants and other inhabitants of Benbecula and South Uist and this is what it says:

> This being the first time your ladyship has visited your estates of Benbecula and South Uist since the late important decision in the House of Lords put an end to the tedious and vexatious law plea in

which your interests were so seriously challenged and now that that decision has fully and finally confirmed your title to the possession of your extensive and valuable properties both here and on the mainland we have unanimously resolved to offer to your ladyship and to Sir Reginald our most sincere congratulations on the most auspicious termination of the law suit and to express our warmest desire that you may both be long spared to continue the kindness and generosity which have been manifested by your Ladyship in the management of your Ladyship's Long Island estates since your Ladyship came into possession of it and of which we have had such happy and pleasant experience. We have only to add that it would afford us the greatest pleasure if your Ladyship and Sir Reginald could find it convenient to spend a portion of each year amongst us.

What makes this distressing piece of sycophancy even more poignant is the hand-painted Arcadian scenes which adorn the text. There are vignettes of island life and bagpipe playing all wreathed in thistle leaves and crowned with the dictum: Health and Happiness.

'She really was', a friend of mine tells me, 'a prize bitch. There was this occasion when she was asked if she would build a hospital in South Uist, and after much persuasion she agreed to give the land to do this. What she gave them was nothing more than a quagmire and she made it a condition that the hospital had to be built between the first of November and the last day of January and be all ready for use in that time. It so happened that there was an appallingly hard frost and the whole thing froze over. It meant that they could bring carts from all points of the compass with the stone and it was up! The money came from the Marquess of Bute I think and the nuns came in and staffed it and there it was!'

The other story of Lady Cathcart's hard-hearted approach concerned the raiders of Vatersay who believed that there was an ancient right that if you could build a house between sunrise and sunset the ground on which the house stood became yours. Lady Cathcart was not amused; ten of the raiders were imprisoned for two months.

Her successors in South Uist, a syndicate of businessmen who bought the estate in 1959 from Herman Andreae, tread more warily. Their 90,000 acres stretch from the northern tip of Benbecula to the tail of Eriskay. On the estates are 840 crofts.

'Virtually all the land', David Allan tells me, 'is subject to crofting tenure. We really have very little land in hand at all.'

'Why did they buy it then?'

'Just for the fishing and the shooting. The estate in itself is quite viable because there is other income from sites, from quarries, it's quite a reasonable business.'

'And the shooting?'

'Snipe, duck, a few geese, one or two woodcock.'

There's the Howmore river which many people believe to be the best fishing river in the Outer Hebrides, yielding trout up to 14 lb in weight. Then there's the scores of brown trout hill lochs. There's salmon fishing and sea trout.

'We let just one lodge, that's Grogarry. We can accommodate up to twenty there but we really need a minimum party of seven, it's not worth opening it up for less. We get all sorts – birdwatchers, people who fish, people who in the winter come to shoot.'

There's additional income from land which they can sell to the Council or privately to people who want to build a house. Considering that Herman Andreae, the speculator who bought the estate in 1944, paid only 83 pence an acre for it, the present price of £5,000 an acre seems, well, cheeky?

'Well the District Valuer drives a hard bargain, we wouldn't *always* get £5,000 an acre.' Mr Allan is reluctant to tell me what they would get and he points out that if a crofter buys land from the Estate, in law he is entitled to 50 per cent compensation.

David Allan used to work for an estate owned by the Stirling family. 'But it was bought by an Arab syndicate and I didn't see eye to eye with them.'

'There's nothing to prevent this syndicate selling to Arabs or Japanese or Moonies?'

'Nothing to prevent anybody selling to anybody, no.'

'Do you think that's right? That land should be sold over people's heads to strangers, possibly international fiddlers and crooks?'

'Nothing wrong with it as long as they take care of it and develop it.'

'Do these people, the present owners, take care of it?'

'The estate doesn't see itself as entrepreneurial. They might go into holiday cottages, salmon fishing perhaps, but we're not losing money at the moment and that can't be said for all estates.'

The true nature and the long-term effect of the private ownership of so vulnerable an area as the Western Isles was pointed out in the evidence which the Federation of Crofters' Unions gave to the House of Commons Committee on Scottish Affairs when it was looking into the working of the Highlands and Islands Development Board. 'The present system', they claimed, 'is a dismal failure after a trial period of about 200 years. In the past it produced a very great deal of human suffering and misery. In the present it frustrates the development of the area and restricts the activities of crofters as it always has done.'

Their submission went on to assert that private landownership was not geared to the economic well-being of the resident population. From what I have seen of private estates in the Long Island on this trip it seems to be a very mild statement of the obvious and one that no economist could question.

Even Donald Peteranna, 'The Godfather' of South Uist, seems depressed by the lack of opportunities that present themselves in South Uist for a man like himself consumed with entrepreneurial zeal. Mr Peteranna, like my cousin in Stornoway, possesses a rather splendid Mercedes – it is the glittering symbol of the successful Hebridean businessman. Like my cousin he also owns two hotels and a building company, Uist Builders, with offices in Daliburgh.

I find Mr Peteranna in his office; behind him a large traditional clarsach. Can he be a practising harpist?

'No,' he says modestly, 'it was made on Eriskay by Michael MacNeill of Northbay. I bought it two years ago. I thought I'd put it in the Dark Island Hotel for decoration but I never got around to it.'

Mr Peteranna tells me that his family have been five generations on South Uist. 'I found some papers the other day and they were going back to 1760 and there was a reference to a John Peteranna. I think my family were off a Spanish-Italian boat. Their name was Pedrana.'

I ask how business is going?

'This end is absolutely desperate, South Uist. Absolutely desperate. We have done more work in Barra in the last five years than here.'

Apart from the council and the army he is the biggest single employer of labour in the southern isles. There are more than a hundred on the pay roll: 'Sixty on the building sites, fairly steadily and 25 to 30 in the Dark Isle counting part-timers.'

If he thinks the council isn't doing enough to stimulate development why doesn't he stand for the council himself?

'Well I'd be outside the door most of the time; there are quite a lot of other corners we're involved in.'

'What ought to be done then?'

'I wish I knew the answer – I wish I knew the answer to that one.' He looks at the harp in the corner, and scrutinises the ceiling, and then he goes and shuts the door. Is there to be a revelation?

'They made a survey of housing in South Uist and found damned near a hundred caravans being used.' It is the natural outrage of a builder of homes. 'They've spent a lot of money on Barra.'

'Why Barra particularly?'

'Perhaps they have good councillors there.'

I ask Mr Peteranna whether or not he thinks the syndicate which runs South Uist helps or hinders development, but he doesn't feel he can comment on that.

I repair down the road to Lochboisdale for a snack. The pier was once the centre of a busy herring fishing trade but at one o'clock in the afternoon it's deserted. There are a couple of cars outside the Lochboisdale Hotel which is run by South Uist Estates. The flag of St Andrew flutters from a staff beside a rather touching memorial cairn erected 'by their friends in memory of Major Finlay Simon Mackenzie who was host at Lochboisdale Hotel from 1928 to 1960. And his wife Millicent Duff Mackenzie.' A long stewardship and many a big brown trout brought back in those thirty-two years. The Major died on 7 December 1963 and touchingly, Millicent followed him on 24 January.

A new manager has just taken over and he's hoping the syndicate which owns the South Uist Estate, will find some money for refurbishing. He tells me that his employer, Mrs Smiley, went off on the ferry that morning on her way down to London to have a big meeting with the other syndicate members to raise more money: 'The hotel is getting very tatty it needs a bit of money spending on it.' From the loudspeaker on the wall comes the voice of John Lennon, 'Let it be,' he sings, 'let it be, let it be.' Let it be for much longer and it won't be there at all. On to the granite hotel have been added the usual flat-roofed extensions: a dining room on one end, a lounge bar on the other. There are bar snacks.

'Funny you should ask,' says the manager, 'we had monkfish all the week but we've just run out. I think there's fresh haddock though.' I have a tasty plate of haddock and the ubiquitous chips and a pint of McEwen's Heavy. The music is fairly relentless. I escape to the residents' lounge where on a table are all the fishing records dating back to Victorian times and the proprietorial days of Sir John Powlett Orde who bought the estate from Lord Macdonald in 1885. It was Sir John who built the pier from which the cattle are taken to the mainland and from where at 0630 on weekday mornings in summer the *Claymore* slips away to Castlebay and Oban.

The old fishing books conjure up days of sportsmen in ulsters and knickerbockers, attentive ghillies pulling Oxford dons and clergymen over the surface of peat-brown lochs. The hotel still has exclusive rights to all the freshwater lochs on the island and some of the guests have been coming for decades to fish for brown trout and try their hand at sea trout.

After lunch I drive down to the south end of the island; there's more haymaking in the crofts of North and South Boisdale and on the edge of the sea by the inn at Pollachar, which means Bay of the Standing Stone, there is indeed a standing stone, a prism nearly six feet high. A sign says it was thrown down and re-erected and possibly dates to the third millennium BC. Does it have sepulchral significance? If not, for what purpose did it stand there? Nobody seems to know.

The inn is closed and I drive on down to East Kilbride and the jetty at Ludag where the new car ferry goes to Eriskay. The only person in sight is a girl with a scarlet anorak, pigtails, and a Shetland tourie. 'Hi,' she says. I 'Hi' her back. She is from Baltimore by way of Katmandu and Findhorn.

'That's Eriskay,' she tells me, nodding her head across the water, 'don't you think it's somehow special?' I agree.

'I think this whole place is just magic,' she says, 'did you see that *STONE*? My Guard, just think how long it's BEEN there.'

'You mean the Standing Stone?'

'Well I mean still STANDING after all these years! Don't you feel you're on the edge of the WORLD here?' Her conversation is rhetorically interrogative; the questions seeking support rather than comment.

'Have you been to Findhorn? That is really SOMETHING OTHER.' I have been to Findhorn and it's very Something Other. An international spiritual community of some 200 members, it was founded on the shores of the Moray Firth in 1962 by Peter and Eileen Caddy and Dorothy Maclean.

The story has been gushingly told by Paul Hawken, an American journalist who lived in Findhorn for a year (*The Magic of Findhorn*, Souvenir Press, 1975). It goes like this. Hotel manager Peter Caddy is thrown out of his job; he moves to a caravan park at Findhorn with his wife Eileen who gets messages from outer space. Peter had progressed through Methodism, the Rosicrucian movement and Tibet and was ready for anything. Their chum Dorothy, who moved to Findhorn with them, had been into Sufism and she Heard Voices. One day she was talking to a Landscape Angel, a kind of celestial chatelaine of Findhorn, who told her to start planting fruit and veg. The marrows and the dwarf beans and the tomatoes all talked to 'Dottie', as she was known, and she talked to them and they grew to gigantic size.

Lady Mary and Lady Eve Balfour, nieces of a former Prime Minister, sped north and as expert gardeners pronounced that something very strange was going on. There was Magic and Power in the air. 'The plants', proclaimed Marcel Vogel, an IBM research scientist, 'are fed by the consciousness of the community,' for by then all manner of unusual people had made their way to Findhorn.

They came in their ponchos and their homespun dirndls – failed clairvoyants, believers in Strange Forces, yoga instructors from Los Angeles, drop-outs from all over. They were eager for miracles and sat attentive at the feet of ex-Squadron Leader Caddy, 'clean-cut, fiftyish with three children and a lovely silver-permed wife', as one magazine put it.

The silver perm was not the most unusual thing about Eileen. One day she was out collecting seaweed with Dottie when she gashed her palm with a knife. Ordinary folk might have leapt for the Elastoplast. Eileen quickly closed her hands and prayed in a whisper, 'I affirm wholeness.' 'Finally,' according to Paul Hawken, 'she opened her hand and it was clean and unblemished. There was not even a mark.'

Today the community flourishes. There is gardening, dancing, singing, reflection, prayer and parenting. Warm, welcoming, firm in their belief that what they have embraced is far more uplifting and rewarding than what they have left behind, the present-day Findhorners are a happy and busy bunch.

'Where else in the countryside', asked Virginia Lloyd-Davis who showed me round Findhorn some years back, 'would you find 200 people who have the same sort of education, people whom you can talk with on the same level?'

Where indeed? The IQ at Findhorn is daunting, the conversation on a rarefied level. Although Peter Caddy now spends his time on global lecture tours, the 'core group' of twelve focalisers who run the Findhorn Foundation believe actively in the Founder's Caddychism: co-creation with Nature, holistic ecology, the dynamics of group life, spiritual self-discovery, inner knowing, the transmutation of karma, the dynamics of soul unfoldment and more.

'Is there anything like that out here?' the girl asks, and is astonished when I tell her that there isn't.

'But this is a perfect place for some kind of meaningful commune.' I tell her about the peninsula of Scoraig near Ullapool where about sixty people have settled in an old ruined crofting clachan. Most of the buildings are now restored, fields are being cultivated, food produced, wind-power harnessed; an alternative community more earthy than Findhorn and more interested in brewing good beer than exploring soul consciousness.

'I wonder', she says, 'why nobody thought of coming here to settle?'

17 The drawing room, Rodel Hotel, Harris

18 Tomb of Alasdair Crotach, 8th Chief of Clan Macleod, St Clement's Church, Rodel, Harris

19 White house, near Carinish, Harris

20 Foreshore and sheep, Baleshare, North Uist

21 The military presence, Balivanich, Benbecula

22 Mermaid Fish Supplies, Clachan, Locheport, North Uist

23 New fencing, Bornish, South Uist

24 Child and peat stack, Bornish, South Uist

25 Grave, Eriskay

26 Iain Ruaridh MacInnes, manager of the Co-Chomunn, Eriskay

27 Calum and Morag Macaulay in their garden, Castlebay, Barra
28 Polly and Jack Huntington in their sitting room, Cuithir House, Barra

29 Compton Mackenzie's house, Traigh Mor, Barra

30 After mass, Vatersay

31 Sheep being ferried from Pabbay for auction on the mainland

32 The deserted village, Mingulay

I wonder too; the Outer Hebrides has got its share of candle-makers, potters, painters, recycled hippies and misfits but it has not yet been invaded by an organised group fleeing from urban pressures. And yet the place is perfect for such mild eccentricity; plenty of fish in the lochs, peat for the cutting, and grants by the score for any enterprise you care to name. The more I think about it the more I warm to the idea of perhaps replacing the rocket range with one of these caring peaceful communes. Far better for huge carrots to sprout from the sand than rockets. Better to have what they call a planetary village on the machair than a tracking station; better guided meditation than guided missiles.

I offer the girl from Baltimore a lift back to Daliburgh and she tells me about unconditional loving and personal transformation. Out of the corner of my eye as we enter the unlovely outskirts of Daliburgh I glimpse a bespectacled and suited African disappearing into a caravan. But nothing any longer surprises me; maybe there is ju-ju as well as magic in the air. I have a strong suspicion that the African is a medical man. There is a high incidence of Afro-oriental practitioners in the islands. The community health specialist in Stornoway is a Dr Amidi, the local Daliburgh GP is a Dr Abdul Khaliq, and my caravan-dwelling African turns out to be Dr A. V. Afewu who has replaced a Dr David Chatterjee who recently suffered a heart attack.

Dr Chatterjee had been conducting a long correspondence in the *Stornoway Gazette* complaining about a wide range of matters from the inadequacy of the Daliburgh hospital and its equipment and staff to the small size of his salary. With their customary gift for conjuring appropriate nicknames out of the air the unfortunate Dr Chatterjee has come to be known as Dr Chatterbox.

I wondered why these exotic medical man had been recruited from tropical climes to work in this predominantly Gaelic-speaking area. I called on Dr Afewu and he invited me into his caravan for coffee. He came, he told me, from Ghana and had done his medical training in Poland. I suggested it was a bit like *Sanders of the River*, an interesting role reversal.

'What do you mean by that?' he asks.

'Well once it was the white man bringing medicine to the underprivileged Africans. And now here you are, a black man ministering to the disadvantaged in South Uist. What made you shoulder the black man's burden so cheerfully?'

Dr Afewu tells me that he had tried to start a practice in London but was defeated by the Catch 22 system of the medical establishment. 'You have to

have a list of patients before you can become a GP but to have patients you
have to be a GP. I had to go on national assistance. And then I was offered a
locum here.'

'Surely there must be hundreds of thousands of people in Ghana in need
of medical attention? Plenty of jobs there?'

Dr Afewu gives me the impression that doctoring in Ghana, although very
rewarding spiritually, is not attractive financially. 'I have a duty to my family
to earn as much money as I can.'

He is only in this rented caravan for the summer; when the visitors have
gone he will be able to go back into a house which is now being let to
holidaymakers; yes it does get a bit lonely at times. There is a book of
Christian meditation beside the portable TV set. He seems resigned to his
exile, much perhaps as a District Officer with a box of bandages and a bottle
of quinine might have felt on the Gold Coast in the days of Empire.

By now it's raining rather hard and I decide to book into the nearest hotel.
It turns out to be, according to the remnants of its mural lettering, the
B RODA E OTEL, a dislocation of identity more attributable to the
force of the winter gales than Mr Peteranna's building skills. Inside the
Borodale Hotel is warm and darkly lit, a cross between a Holiday Inn and a
night club in Lytham St Annes. What, I found myself wondering, was it
modelled on? Nothing to do with the Hebrides – there had never been an
inn like this in these parts. I think its decor must owe some eccentric debt to
Crossroads. But the staff transcend the building; in these inimical surroundings they retain their Uist identity.

The food doesn't. Like food in so many other Hebridean hotels it is
largely processed and lacking in joy. The evening is redeemed by the arrival
in the bar of Martin and Caitriona Macdonald. I foresee an evening of high
conversation. One of Martin's more recent achievements was the preparation of a survey for An Comunn Gaidhealach on Gaelic and Broadcasting;
Caitriona is a great storyteller. Martin's survey oscillates between the
bleakest prospects for the future of Gaelic and the most optimistic. The most
pessimistic was posited by Professor W. B. Lockwood in his *Language of the
British Isles Past and Present* (Andre Deutsch, 1975). 'We think', he wrote, 'that
Scots Gaelic will most likely be extinct by about the beginning of the last
quarter of the next century.'

On the other hand Professor Derick Thomson is more hopeful. 'It is
possible now to predict', he wrote in 1976, 'that the Gaelic revival is only in
its early stages, and will continue strongly for the remaining quarter of the
century. There can be little doubt now that the figures of Gaelic-speakers

will by then have surged well over the 100,000 mark.' Even so, out of a Scottish population of way over 5 million it is a minimal number on which to build either a political or an economic power base.

These are points I am eager to discuss with Martin, but by the time I come back from the bar with drams the cabaret has begun. A local singer reinforced with power-packs and electronic backing is belting out Gaelic songs at such high decibels that only mouthing words is possible. The noise is paramount, conversation impossible except every now and again when the singer pauses for refreshment.

'If this is Gaelic culture,' I mime in Martin's direction, 'I can't hear your answer.' But Martin is looking elsewhere, equally overwhelmed by this massive assault on the eardrum. A dilemma this. How do you reconcile a very traditional language and culture to the ephemeral influences of pop culture?

All the way down the islands I've been talking to people about the survival of Gaelic. Is it on the wane, is it gaining a stronger foothold? One man who knows the answers better than most is Dr Kenneth Mackinnon, Reader in the Sociology of Language at Hatfield Polytechnic. He tells me that in the last decade there has been a measurable increase in Gaelic literacy in the Western Isles; it is most marked among school children. 'Gaelic literacy', he says, 'is highest in the Calvinist areas of rural Lewis, Harris and North Uist, where ability to read the scriptures is a traditional feature of the religious culture. Literacy is less in Catholic South Uist and Barra and less still in Benbecula whose population is of mixed religious culture and whose incidence of Gaelic is lower owing to the presence of the military.'

Sadly Dr Mackinnon's long-term forecast for the survival of Gaelic is not hopeful. He reckons that younger women in the Gaelic communities are the least supportive group of all when it comes to traditional Gaelic culture. 'The efficiency', he says, 'of cultural transmission would appear to be weakening.'

It is likely that the next few decades will see an increase in self-conscious Gaelic literacy and a decrease in the traditional use of the language as a binding force in the family. Today only 1 in 60 Scots speaks Gaelic – that's merely a Census figure. Martin Macdonald would argue that these figures are distorting: 'The parent who addresses his children in Gaelic and is replied to in English is a well-attested phenomenon. So the number of people who understand the language in the Gaelic areas must far exceed the number of speakers.'

Even more important than who speaks the language now is the growing emotional awareness of what would be lost were the Gaelic to disappear through lack of concern and interest. Dr Mackinnon reports that in Barra 96 per cent of respondents, and in Harris 94 per cent, describe themselves as 'feeling in favour of Gaelic'. Since those opinions were gathered there has been an increase in Gaelic radio and television output. To the outsider like myself replacing English road signs with signs in Gaelic would seem to be merely a cosmetic exercise. What perhaps is ominous in Dr Mackinnon's research, ominous for the survival of the language, is that it was those who were most fluent in Gaelic who were most desirous that it should survive. 'Those', recorded Dr Mackinnon, 'with the highest loyalty scores were older, highly fluent, had no further education and followed traditionally regular church attendance patterns' (Kenneth Mackinnon and Morag MacDonald, *Ethnic Communities: The Transmission of Language and Culture in Harris and Barra*, School of Social Sciences, Hatfield Polytechnic, 1980).

Not a promising prognosis.

10

A SENSE OF BALANCE AND
A GOOD EAR

ERISKAY

Eriskay lies like a stepping stone between South Uist and Barra. Its historical claims to fame are two – the arrival on what is now known as Coilleag a' Phrionnsa of Charles Edward Stuart in July 1745, and the foundering in February 1941 on a rock called Hartamul near Eriskay of the *Politician*.

Prince Charles had set off from Nantes on 22 June accompanied by three Scots, three Irishmen and an Englishman to overthrow the Hanoverian dynasty. Alexander MacDonald of Boisdale who met the prince on Eriskay is said to have tried to persuade Charles that his scheme was bound to fail, as indeed it did. The prince was not impressed but he was hungry.

According to the posthumous account of the Jacobite rebellion in *The Lyon in Mourning*, when they landed 'they could not find a grain of meal or one inch of bread. But they catched some flounders which they roasted upon the bare coals in a mean low hut they had gone into near the shore and Duncan Cameron stood cook. The Prince sat at the cheek of the little ingle and he laughed heartily at Duncan's cookery.'

A romantic picture, but is that what really happened? The Gaels are compulsive story-tellers, masterly improvers on the truth. According to John Macculloch, who began travelling widely in the Hebrides in 1811, the Prince 'found some women roasting shell-fish on a fire in the open air' and he partook of their fare. Yet another account claims that as soon as Charles landed he was taken to the house of the tacksman of the island, Angus MacDonald, where he passed the night.

The circumstances of the arrival of the *Politician* are more reliably chronicled. The 12,000-ton ship, connoisseurs of the island scene will remember, was making its way from Glasgow to New York in February 1941 when she ran aground on a reef to the east of the island of Calvay which lies between Eriskay and South Uist.

On board she had a mixed cargo which included bicycles, perfume, toothpaste, fur coats and 20,300 cases of whisky. According to Alasdair Alpin MacGregor, 'people arrived on the scene from as far north as Lewis, from as far south as Mull. They came armed with rods, ropes, hooks and all manner of ingenious contraptions for the fishing out of the ship's interior as much as possible of the whisky she carried.'

The hilarious events of the following months when the police and excisemen came to try and restore sobriety and retrieve what they could, have become a part of Hebridean folklore. Compton Mackenzie turned the story of those spirited wartime days into the best-selling comedy *Whisky Galore*.

The *Politician* did for the Sound of Eriskay what Krakatoa did for the Sunda Strait: the fallout is around still. Hardly a year passes but the film version of *Whisky Galore* isn't shown in some art cinema or on television. The story had all the elements of fiction: undreamt-of treasure brought by fate to the very doorstep of islands parched with wartime thirst; the first tentative forays to save the cargo; the spread of the news; the start of a ceilidh that seemed endless, and the embellishing of stories and songs which rival any tales from the past and which have become part of the Hebridean oral tradition.

In *Tales from Barra told by the Coddy* (Morrison & Gibb, 1973), John Lorne Campbell, who prepared the stories of John Macpherson of Northbay on Barra for print, grouped them into various sections – tales of the MacNeils of Barra and other lairds, tale of treasure, tales of local characters, stories of sea monsters, fairies, second sight, ghosts and witchcraft. Stories of the *Politician* had a section to themselves.

You'll be told folk tales of the *Polly* to this day but the official story has never been published. When I was researching a book on whisky in 1978 I spent some time in the library of the Customs and Excise headquarters in London where I was given a great deal of help by the librarian Graham Smith. One day I was sitting in his office chatting when I noticed a hefty file on the corner of his desk. He saw my eye trying to read the title upside down.

'That's a collection of papers that would interest you,' he said. It was the complete Customs and Excise archive of the *Politician*. I asked if I could borrow it. I gathered it still came under the Official Secrets Act and was not yet for public consumption.

What is now largely forgotten is that several of the islanders did time in Inverness for 'being in possession' of what was, according to the law, not theirs to have taken. It won't be long before the file will be opened and then no doubt the story of the *Polly* will be retold in more documentary detail than it was by Compton Mackenzie. I'm sure it won't be half such fun.

Maybe there's something about Eriskay that makes it news. A couple of weeks before I resumed my journey down the Long Island I was lying back in London watching something undemanding on the box, a panel game, when a very Hebridean-looking figure hove into view and sat down beside the quizmaster. He was dressed as a priest and the team were invited to guess what he did. This was Father John Archie Macmillan and it was not for being a priest that he was on the 'It's My Secret' Show.

'What part of Scotland do you come from?' said the quizmaster.

'I live in the island of Eriskay in the Outer Hebrides.'

'Right. Coming up on the screen is Father Macmillan's secret now.'

There was a gale of laughter from the audience but that was nothing unexpected. The whole point of the game was that the 'secret' of the guest should be as incongruous as possible.

'I'll give you a clue,' said the quizmaster. 'The Father's particular skill requires a sense of balance and a good ear.'

What Father John Archie did, and I was happy to see that he baffled the panel of celebrities, was play the bagpipes while water-skiing to raise money for charity. His total to date was £2,000. The panel beamed and clapped, the audience roared with delight, and Father John left the studio to return to his cure of 188 souls on Eriskay.

Donald Campbell, the Ludag boatman, took me there on a cold, wet day with the rain almost horizontal. When I first went to Eriskay in 1975 it had one of the most interesting shops in the west. Kept by an old man unmotivated by thoughts of profit, it seemed to be a repository for tins of Ambrosia rice pudding and knicker elastic. As a result of the old shopkeeper's eccentric attitude to stock control the women in self-defence did their weekly shopping at the Co-op in Daliburgh and got their consumer durables by mail order.

I had gone to write a film about the famous Eriskay ponies; it was the only programme I ever assayed which never got on the air. The small-eared ponies were there all right but apart from looking cuddly there didn't seem to be much happening to them. An island vet has since suggested to me that the famous Eriskay breed of ponies is a figment of romantic imagination and they are no different to other ponies in those parts. It's interesting that John M. Macdonald, a Barra man himself who studied Highland ponies all his life and was accounted to be one of the finest judges of live-stock in Scotland, failed to mention them at all in his definitive book on the subject (*Highland Ponies*, Eneas Mackay, 1937).

If there ever had been a strain of ponies native only to Eriskay what, I wonder, happened to them in the 1890s? When Frederick Rea, the Birmingham schoolmaster who was at the time headmaster of Garrynamonie School in South Uist, went with Father Allan to Eriskay he explored the island in detail. Far up on the hillside he could see small dark heaps – stacks of peat: 'There were no horses or ponies on the island so the women went up and carried down supplies on their back in creels, or baskets slung from their shoulders.' Where then had all the Eriskay ponies gone? Did they really exist as a separate breed?

The island itself it only 2½ miles from north to south and no more than a mile and a half wide. Its shores, apart from the strand where Prince Charlie landed and the beach below the burial ground, are rocky and the soil unrewarding. When Eriskay was sold to Colonel Gordon in 1838 he cleared the people to make way for sheep but a few of the evicted families from South Uist and the island of Hellisay, three miles south of Eriskay, were allowed to scratch a living there and the lazybeds on which they grew oats, rye, barley and potatoes can still be seen.

Although Prince Charlie's name is associated with Eriskay in the history books, the most formative figure in the island's story was the scholar-priest Father Allan MacDonald. Trained at Blairs College in Aberdeenshire and at the Scots College in Valladolid he was appointed to the 40 square-mile parish of South Uist in 1884 and from then until his early death at the age of 46 he devoted his life to his 2,300 parishioners including the 300 who lived at that time on Eriskay.

A tireless collector of stories, songs and folklore, Father Allan suffered a breakdown in health after ten years in Daliburgh and in 1894 the Bishop translated him to the relatively restful shores of Eriskay. Here he replaced the old thatched roof church with the gaunt granite building which now commands the height of Cnoc nan Sgrath, facing across to South Uist. The church itself, dedicated to St Michael, has a strong feel of the sea about it.

Eriskay's sole wealth lies in the fishing grounds which surround it and one of Father Allan's first innovations when he came to settle on the island was to say Mass every May on board the small Eriskay fishing fleet. To this day most of the boats bear names which witness to the Faith, *Ave Maria*, *Regina Maria*, and *Santa Maria*. Outside the church is the angelus bell rescued from the German battleship *Derflinger*, scuttled at Scapa Flow in 1919. The base of the altar rises now from the bow of a lifeboat which once hung in davits on the Second World War aircraft carrier *Hermes*. The sea surrounds Eriskay, it provides Eriskay with its main source of income, and in its day it has widowed many a woman.

Before I went up to the church to meet Father John Archie I whipped in out of the rain to the brand new co-operative which has become the secular centre of island life. When I was last here in 1979 it was a crucial day for the entire island. They were choosing the man who would manage the co-operative. These co-operatives are one of the best ideas the Board has sponsored. The scheme was launched in the Western Isles in November 1977 and the idea was that as many people as possible in the community served by the co-operative would buy shares in the venture; they would elect a board of directors on a one man, one vote basis.

No limit was seen to the activities of a co-operative; it could be shop, marketing agent, bulk buyer, café, anything which was deemed most suitable. Current projects include sheepskin curing, a bakery, peat cutting, a slaughterhouse, agricultural machinery hire, knitwear; running hostels, guesthouses, package tours and self-catering cottages; refuse collection; fuel supply; fish processing and farming – nothing which could benefit a community and create jobs would be rejected. Today there are co-operatives at Ness and Park in Lewis, at Leverburgh in Harris, on Scalpay, at Iochdar in South Uist, on Barra, Vatersay, Great Bernera and Eriskay. The Gaelic word for them is *Co-Chomunn* pronounced K'Home-'n.

These things of course take time to organise. On Eriskay, for instance, the steering committee was appointed with the help of the Board in July 1978; in November of that year a public meeting was held to thrash out the details and in March 1979 the management committee was elected. None of the candidates who attended the selection board on the day I was in Eriskay got the job. It finally went to a man who was at the time working on a North Sea oil rig; he had to finish his fortnight's stint before he could get back to meet the committee and they decided that he was the man they wanted: Iain Ruaridh MacInnes.

I threaded my way past the shelves of convenience food in the Co-Chomunn and found Iain at his desk at the rear of the shop. He is no stranger to the island.

'My father's from Eriskay but like many another he went off to work in Glasgow. It's the usual story; when school closed in Glasgow we were all shipped up here and when it re-opened they dragged us back. I had aunties and uncles and cousins galore.'

Iain took up the post in June 1979. The 98 shareholders in Eriskay had subscribed £7,500; the Board had matched it with another £7,500.

'In the old days, as you probably remember, the women used to bring their orders for weekly shopping down to the village hall and one or two of them would go over to South Uist to buy everything they needed and then when they got back all the shopping was parcelled out. Really that was a co-operative enterprise in itself so the Co-Chomunn is just a more highly organised and logical extension of that. The strange thing is the women rarely go to South Uist now.'

Although Eriskay now has a £1,000,000 car ferry and getting on and off the island by car is no longer a problem, loyalty to the Co-Chomunn is steadfast. The first thing that had to be done was to design the shop; it was opened on 7 March 1980 – not bad going.

'How do you stock it?' I asked.

'Sometimes with great difficulty. We have an associated membership with the CWS but apart from that we're a normal retail operation competing for stock with other retail outlets.'

Iain told me that half his salary is paid by the Board who, in order to get the Co-Chomunn set up, agreed to provide administrative costs for the first three years in full and after that half the cost, in the hope that by year five the members would have built up enough resources to employ their own manager with no help from the Board at all.

'At the moment we have four full-time employees and we've taken three girls on who've just left school – they're financed on the government scheme.'

In November 1982 the old wooden village hall, rotted by rain and weakened over the years, blew down in a storm and a new hall was going up next door. 'Last year we made about £4,000 profit and that's why we can afford to build this new hall which is going to have a cafeteria.' Even so without the Board's funding they would have made a trading loss last year of £3,500.

'True,' says Iain with one hand on his computer, 'but this year we are geared to break even. We're in competition with the shop in Uist so we've got to run our margins pretty tight but of course we've got the additional charges of bringing all the stuff from Lochboisdale so we're walking a tightrope all the time.'

They have their own van but when they go to South Uist for stores it costs £7 return on the ferry. What other enterprises has he got up his sleeve? Couldn't he use all those ponies to attract tourists?

'I don't want to know about the ponies, they're still running around. It's an area I've never wanted to get involved in. Ponies are owned by families and you either have to take the whole thing over and run it as a horse ranch or not at all.'

But they have established a diesel station to save Eriskay's five big fishing boats and the three or four smaller lobster boats having to go to Mallaig or Barra for fuel. And there's the famous Eriskay jumpers and sweaters.

'We get orders for jerseys and things like that from America, France, Germany and Canada. What we do is supply the wood to the knitters and they get £35 for making a jersey. The selling price at the moment is about £55. We realised that women were being exploited – they were getting £12 for a jersey. Now we've increased the price other buyers have had to put their price up too.'

And that is what a co-operative is all about, I suppose, preventing exploitation and increasing amenities. While I'd been talking to Iain the children had come out of school across the way and were playing in shrill gull-like voices. There are 40 of them on the island now between the ages of 5 and 14, another dozen at secondary school in Daliburgh and 4 more at the Nicolson in Stornoway.

The headmaster is a new arrival since I was last here. John Harrison himself has no island connections at all. He is surprisingly young and when he arrived on Eriskay, two years ago, he was only 26 and a bit wet behind the ears. Educated by the monks at the Benedictine public school at Fort Augustus, he speaks with Oxbridge vowels although it was at Glasgow University that he read History, French and English. His previous teaching job had been in the relatively sophisticated town of Fort William.

'I thought when I came here I'd have the same kind of friends I had in London or Fort William but these people didn't exist at all. It was a huge shock and what kept me going was just work – work, work, work. It was fun because it was totally new. You look at people in a different way; I never thought I'd be pally with a fisherman – I'd never met these kind of people before.'

Now he's a bit more adjusted. He's become friendly with fisherman Angus Mackenzie, there's Father John Archie and Iain in the shop, and he has lots of friends in South Uist, 'mainly teachers but that's inevitable I suppose.'

I asked him if he had leaned heavily on the experience of his predecessor Mr Macdonald who lives in retirement in his cottage by the pier?

'No. I think I wanted to make my own mistakes. Luckily the headteacher in Daliburgh had only been here six months or so before I arrived so I picked his brain; he was very helpful and the people in Stornoway were very kind. You pick it up very quickly.'

147

Recently one family left Eriskay and the roll call dipped strikingly. 'We lost five of school age and there were two others and that brought us down. But it's not too bad, the projections are quite healthy. In primary one and primary two it's not going to be dramatically different to what it is now.'

There are, besides himself, two full-time teachers in the primary department and one other full-time teacher in secondary. Seven itinerant part-time teachers come across on the ferry for half a day or a day depending on their contracts.

'One's terribly dependent on ferries and the weather. Sometimes one expects staff and they don't turn up through no fault of their own. What's nice though is that although we have such a small secondary department we can offer all or most of the subjects you'd get in a larger school.'

Does he feel out of things not speaking Gaelic?

'I don't speak Gaelic but I do understand it. Half our teaching is in Gaelic in primary. Until recently of course the problem was that Gaelic was treated as a foreign language, now people speak Gaelic in a more relaxed way, they chit-chat in Gaelic.'

The record of academic achievement in the islands has always astonished those who believe that a remote rural environment leads to a remote if not permanently diminished rural mind.

'I couldn't agree more,' says John, 'you would imagine that because of lack of opportunities out here they wouldn't be as bright but it hasn't turned out that way. Some of the brightest kids I've ever taught are in this school.'

According to John the children of Eriskay think far more laterally than children on the mainland. 'They operate not as children but as mini-adults. They're very philosophical about certain things. I still get very upset about the weather, they just take it for granted, they laugh when they see me getting irritated. They're hugely patient children; they don't fly off the handle or that sort of thing; they don't get hysterical like some children do. . . . I'm impressed by their manners and by their thoughtfulness.'

But had John got onto their wavelength; cracked the code?

'You can't *really* get to know them. The first year was kind of trying. It took a whole year for us to begin to get to know one another, then the barriers were dropped.' John told me about their trip to the mainland last May, a school party to Glasgow and Edinburgh. 'We were just falling about with laughter at some of their attitudes to things we took for granted – things like roundabouts and traffic lights. I made a long list of all the sights we were going to see and we did all those things but they learnt so much more by just looking at what was happening around them. They couldn't believe it.

They'd never seen crowds before and they were really inhibited and worried by the masses of people in Princes Street. They were alarmed. It's very difficult to conceptualise what a town is going to look like if you've never been off Eriskay.'

I left John Harrison to continue his task; preparing young minds for the shock of traffic lights and the dubious values of the mainland. Although 70 per cent of the children in that school, he thought, would stay on Eriskay, the rest would go off and lead very different lives elsewhere. Would the simple disciplines of Eriskay stand them in good stead? Was this a better base from which to conquer the world than a high-rise flat in Glasgow?

There is a popular belief that those who are short of this life's material assets are in some way enhanced by their lack of advantages. The noble crofter theory, you might call it. I went up the hill to St Michael's to explore these thoughts with Father John Archie.

He was on the 'phone when I got there and he motioned me through the varnished pine door into the sitting room. A fire burned in the grate and over the mantelpiece was a sombre relic of his famous predecessor, an ormolu and marble timepiece with a brass inscription in gothic lettering: 'Presented to Father Allan McDonald by the general public on the occasion of his leaving Dalibrog, South Uist for the island of Eriskay, 2nd February 1894.'

The room is very much a bachelor's pad; no softening feminine touches of the mother or the wife. There have been housekeepers in the past I know. I was told some years ago how the Eriskay priest lost his housekeeper and advertised for a replacement in the *Tablet*. Shortly thereafter a very well-spoken Catholic lady appeared at the door of the presbytery on the hill and duly took up her duties. Entering the kitchen she saw what looked like a black feather boa hanging bedraggled from the hook behind the larder door. It had a beak, wings and webbed feet but was not something she had encountered previously in her *cordon bleu* career. It was definitely a bird of sorts and it smelt strongly of the sea. There didn't appear to be anything else in the cupboard so plucking up her courage she plucked it and carried it through to this very sitting room.

'Ah,' said the father, 'you've found the cormorant then? Perhaps you'd like to cook it for our tea.'

'Certainly,' said the housekeeper with great poise, 'do you like it braised, plainly roasted or *à l'orange*?'

Father John Archie breezes into the room and turns off the cassette which lies alongside the TV set and the video. Most people have this sort of gadgetry these days, but not everyone appears on the box. I couldn't imagine Free Church ministers, for instance, popping up on an ITV quiz show or playing the bagpipes on skis for that matter. What would *they* make of such a worldly attitude in a man of God? Father John Archie roared with laughter.

'Wait until they hear about the article in *Titbits*! There was a reporter on the telephone last Tuesday,' he says choking with the thought of it, 'he wanted to know about the piping and skiing and why not? If it's good and in aid of a good cause it's worth broadcasting the news. I told the panel my next move was to play the harp while hang-gliding!'

He stirs the peats in the fire and tells me about a Fleet Street reporter who was here earlier in the year. 'I found it very difficult really, he only wanted to talk about sex. What was it like being celibate and that sort of thing? He helped himself to the whisky while I was out,' again John Archie laughs, 'oh, it's very difficult.'

'Surely', I said, 'you're in the prime of life, thirty-seven, you must have a lot of time on your hands?'

'Oh I have a number of hobbies.'

'What do you do?'

'Practically anything. I tinker about with cars; if anyone needs something doing, I can usually put an engine right. I have a fishing boat which two men are working for me. They're working the crabs, it's organised as a Trust.'

I ask if he feels that the islanders set him up on a pillar; use him as a standard of their own morality?

'Oh I'm not a pillar. I am just the messenger who brings the strength. No way do I want people to imitate me or rely on me. I'm as weak as them. It's not only my faith that's carrying me through, it's their faith as well.'

I recalled talking to Father John Archie's predecessor on Eriskay who described the tightrope he had to tread to avoid giving offence by cultivating cronies or making too many close friendships with this faction or that. For in islands, as in all communities, there are rivalries and jealousies.

'It's difficult on a small island not to be involved more with some people than others. I go for a Protestant!' And again Father John Archie laughs the argument away. 'No, it's true! I'm very friendly with the only Protestant on the island, the skipper of the ferry. Calum Macleod and I are very friendly but I do find I stay more to myself and of course I suffer consequently. I have a priest friend in Glasgow and I make fairly regular trips to the mainland and I stay with him and we put the Church to rights. I also have a priest friend in England whom I phone regularly. Like last week, I was feeling a bit lonely and fed-up and tired and I talked with them both on the phone.'

He paused. Outside it had begun to rain again. 'It's a hard one. I *am* gregarious.'

Because he is fond of company and could easily succumb to the pleasures of socialising I get the feeling that he consciously holds himself back.

'I try to see what's needed but not to go pushing at things. If people want help they have to show the first sign of wanting that help.'

I said that was very different to the approach of some priests who were always in the thick of things, organising piers and protests and flying off to grab a slice of County Council cake for their flocks.

'I do that too, but I need a sign at the beginning. You have to be adaptable.'

And adaptable to the weather too?

'Oh yes. You want to do something one day and the gales blow and you can't get out of the door let alone go over to South Uist. You have to find something else to do.'

I asked him whether that kind of frustration was not diminishing? Or was it, perhaps paraxodically, ennobling?

'I find it ennobling. It gives me the opportunity of looking more at myself and not being content with one's own personal limitations or the materials you have to work with. The important thing is how you cope with adversity. The summer months are so short of course, you don't have much time to get the harvest in. It's my own belief that it affects people's religion and funnily enough the further north you go in the islands the stricter it is. Even the Catholics in the islands are dour compared to continental Catholics. I'm not making a moral judgment whether they're worse or better Catholics – it's their attitude which is stricter.'

I asked him, as I had asked the minister on Scalpay, just how he would have explained the tragedy of the *Iolaire* to his congregation. What would he have said in the pulpit on that January Sunday after the *Iolaire* had been wrecked with such a catastrophic loss of life?

'I couldn't explain it. My theory is that we are given an allotted span of life in this world; we are given different circumstances and we are asked to do with them what we can. I don't know if when God cuts somebody's life short whether it was planned for all time for them. I think it is you know.'

What then, to bring it nearer, would he say if four youngsters had gone from Eriskay and been killed in a senseless car crash on South Uist?

'I would just express my own sorrow, that's as far as I can go. I would talk about our belief in an eternity which is our consolation. It needs tremendous faith to accept such a thing. And I think most people in the islands have that faith which sustains them through it. Hardships and tragedies have to be borne as readily as the joys of life. I found one time that a woman whose husband had died came to see me and said, "Why, why, why?" and I said, "I don't know." And that comforted her more than me trying to give explanations. I was always impressed with that. How can I explain what I don't understand myself?'

On the way down to the slip to take the ferry back to Ludag I remembered the island priest who had told me how he had defused a potentially difficult situation by committing a legal wrong which added up in his eyes to a moral right. He had been called to administer extreme unction to an old man who had been involved in a tractor accident. Had the young crofter driving the tractor been perfectly sober maybe the accident would not have occurred.

'There was no hope for the old man and we made him as comfortable as we could. Then the police arrived and they had the bag and they wanted to breathalyse the youngster. "You can put that away for a start," I said, "things are quite bad enough without that." Just imagine the anguish that would have caused to the old man's relatives, the boy's family, the boy himself. Fortunately they saw what I was driving at.'

Small communities are far more open to breakdown than large ones. There are times to stand back, times to act. As Father John Archie said, 'I try to see what's needed.'

As the ferry left the slip the sun came out and varnished the brightly-coloured roofs of the Eriskay houses in a light verging on the apocalyptic. A rainbow hooped across the modest eminence of Ben Scrien. For all I know there were angels on the celestial soundtrack. I couldn't help thinking that there might be worse places to await the holocaust in – 'beautiful island of whitest strands, the whiteness of the wavetops around thy edge, winter storm cannot hurt thee, thou art like the Holy Church of God, the everlasting rock is thy foundation.'*

*Translated from an unpublished poem of Fr Allan McDonald by John Lorne Campbell.

EYES THAT WERE DEEP AS A CALM

BARRA 1

On the last day of September of that glorious summer I met up with Gus Wylie at Glasgow airport and along with Father Calum Maclellan the priest of Castlebay and one or two returning islanders and a visitor we climbed into the Loganair plane for Barra.

'A holiday?' asked Father Calum.

'We're hoping to get to Mingulay.'

'Mingulay, that's a great place.'

It was pretty blowy when we taxied out on to the runway. We took off and headed west across Loch Fyne and the northern tip of Jura. The waters were choppy down in the Firth of Lorne, small toy-like white crests of foam ruffling the slate blue sea. Over Ross of Mull and Iona and, within 25 minutes of leaving Glasgow, we're touching down on Tiree. It is a flat and sandy island remarkable for its record of sunshine; but not today. I get out of the plane to stretch my legs and walk about on the machair, but I'm almost blown away by the wind. You can understand on a day like this why the island has been compared to the deck of an aircraft carrier. There's nothing but open sea to the west and winds of a hundred miles an hour are not uncommon. As we take off and head north-west for Barra and I peer with an apprehensive eye at even choppier white horses, I'm beginning to have grave doubts about the next few days.

'A bit rough down there,' I shout to Wylie, who has the professional photographer's resignation in the face of marginal weather. Somewhere on those waters if all is going according to plan a sixty-foot yacht ought to be on its way to Castlebay to uplift us south to Mingulay. Will it get too rough for the yacht to get there or too rough for us to make a landing on Mingulay itself?

The plan for the last lap of this journey was hatched earlier in the year.

with Douglas Lindsay and his wife Mary who live on Kerrera and charter their yacht *Corryvreckan* for summer cruising in Hebridean waters. When the handsome and elegant green-hulled *Corryvreckan* came into Portree in July the Lindsays had been complaining about the lack of wind. 'We're burning a fortune in fuel. Either that or you just lay becalmed and that's not what people expect when they've booked for a cruise.' The Lindsays had offered to take Gus and myself to Mingulay at the end of the season 'just for the trip' and they weren't going to complain if a picture of the *Corryvreckan* in full sail Mingulay-bound appeared in the book. We compared diaries. 'What about the first weekend of October?' suggests Douglas. 'If we leave it any later it'll be too late, besides we'll be laying the boat up for the winter after that.' Walking back down to the pier in Portree where the *Corryvreckan* was taking on water I couldn't wait for that first weekend in October to come. And now it was here and we were coming down through low cloud in a sharp bank to land on the cockle beach on the north-east shore of Barra.

This is our second visit together to Barra and Gus says, looking at the great skies, 'Hope we have better luck than last time.' Last time I'd prefer to forget. I'd been asked to write a piece about the new hotel which the Board had built on a superb site at Halaman Bay; a folly if ever there was one. It cost £300,000 and it seemed to me at the time that with its wall-to-wall carpeting it had little to commend it to anyone searching for a real taste of Barra.

It rained the whole time we were on the island and when we came to leave there was a torrential downpour just as the plane was about to leave Glasgow. Was it worth coming, they radioed the legendary Katie Macpherson who ran the airstrip? She didn't think it was; there was too much water lying on the beach.

Eventually there was a lull in the rain, the tide was right, the beach fairly dry, and the plane came in. This time we weren't going to stay in the hotel. It had closed for the winter anyway. The Glasgow chain which had tried to run it had pulled out, defeated by the heating bills, and the Board had sold it for a small sum to the owner of the Castlebay Hotel who had quite wisely decided to close it early. Why keep all those empty bedrooms heated when there were plenty of rooms back in Castlebay?

On the strand to meet us is Reg Allan, himself a keen photographer and a local councillor. I had rung him earlier in the week and asked him to find us somewhere to stay. Preferably, I said, in Castlebay, where we can keep an eye on the pier so that we'd be ready to leap on board the *Corryvreckan* as soon as it came alongside.

We piled into the postbus and drove round the shore to Northbay, one of the two small Barra townships where the people have polarised themselves. Roughly circular in shape, Barra is encircled by a road thirteen miles in circumference. If 12 o'clock is north Castlebay, the nub of the island which looks out to Vatersay and the southern isles, sits at 7 o'clock. Northbay, facing Eriskay and South Uist, is at 1 o'clock and there's not much in between. From Northbay the road runs up to the cockle beach of Traigh Mhor and a couple of miles further on to Eoligarry and the jetty for Ludag on South Uist. The interior of Barra, which rises to 1260 feet at the summit of Heaval, is untouched. There are two roads running a mile or so inland at 9 o'clock but the cultivated ground is mainly alongside the road and that's where all the crofthouses are too. The eastern coastline is rocky and punctuated by skerries and reefs; the west is a shoreline of dunes and sandy bays and it was on the most beautiful of these at about 8 o'clock that the Board put up its expensive new hotel. As we pass Reg points out the blotches on the sloping chalet roof where new tiles have replaced those blown off in winter gales. It's only eight years since it went up but already the building is showing signs of distress. Too flimsy for that exposed position perhaps?

Too big it certainly was – forty bedrooms, each with its own television set – far beyond the financial resources of any local man to run. As a result it was initially handed over at advantageous terms to Scottish Highland Hotels Limited which was already running the Board's equally lavish hotel on Mull. The hope that it would remain open all year round, an attraction for visitors and local people alike, was a fanciful notion. The hotel never filled in summer and was ghostly in the winter. Few of the locals were tempted to leave Castlebay or Northbay on a wet and windy night to drive to the modern bar of the Board's brave new hotel. The English manager and his wife in her ankle-length tartan skirt went south again and yet one more enterprising Barra venture put together from the outside had run itself into the ground.

'It should prove a useful addition to the economic and social life of the island,' said the Board in their annual report for 1974.

'It should never have been built,' says the old man sitting next to me in the bus, 'a waste of money.' Money is being more usefully employed at the moment, a million pounds of it on renovating the old Swedish-style wooden council houses in Castlebay. They are being reclad and modernised. On the left of the road as we enter Castlebay is the exciting new school nearing completion. Later in the day Reg takes me round it; fully carpeted, imaginatively designed, it's more like a swish suite of executive offices than a traditional school. If you couldn't learn here you couldn't anywhere. But even with this new educational tool the older and more ambitious students will still have to go the Nicolson in Stornoway if they want higher education. And the bright ones will take wing from Barra to marry and raise families somewhere else.

We drive a little way up the east coast road and everywhere there seem to be new signs of affluence. Old stone croft houses are having their roofs raised and receiving picture windows. People are planting gardens, doorbells chime, there are vases of artificial roses on windowsills. Is suburban blight descending on Barra along with double glazing and oil-fired central heating?

There are more young wives entering and leaving the Co-op in Castlebay, more prams, than there were eight years ago. Or has the sun brought them out in a dash before the next squall? The main street hasn't changed at all. The one row of shops descends solidly to the pier. In this, the safest western anchorage, if not the only anchorage between Oban and Stornoway, there are only a handful of small boats. Nothing remains of the Victorian herring boom that filled the bay with five hundred sails in the summer months.

Reg drops me off at Clachan Beag and I meet Don MacNeill and his wife Elizabeth who run what turns out to be one of the most hospitable guesthouses I've ever set foot in. Elizabeth cooks and looks after the rooms and the food; Don looks after the guests. From the glass-fronted sun porch of the Clachan you can see the whole of the harbour, the pier, the castle of Kisimul and in the distance the island of Vatersay. It is here that Don spends a lot of his time. A Merchant Navy Officer, he had a nasty accident which left him with a 100 per cent disability pension, a recurring bad back, and medical advice to take things easy. That hasn't turned out to be possible. The man is a great organiser; a prize fixer, as I am to find out. Not only that, I reckon he has probably the best weather eye in Barra. Don's father was a pilot on the Irrawaddy in Burma and that's how Don got his nickname of 'Rangoon'. The sea in his veins goes back many generations.

'My grandfather had an eighty-six-foot Zulu and he followed the herring. They used to arrive on Barra in May, the Zulus, and then they followed the shoals around the coast right down to the North Sea. In the early days it was all sail, then steam came.'

Don Rangoon points right along the length of the bay, 'There were scores of curing stations in Barra. Boats came from Scandinavia, Germany, Holland, even Canada and the States. You can see the remains of the jetties sticking out of the water all round the bay. The women followed the fleet. I never saw it myself but I've heard the old men say that you could walk across the bay to Vatersay on the decks of the boats.'

It is the conventional image which conjures up past prosperity and plenty. I've heard it before from the lips of old men in Portree. There it was not so much fishing boats as the white-hulled, brass-funnelled yachts that sailed north to Hebridean waters after Cowes week: 'You could walk from the pier here right across to the Black Rock on their decks without wetting a foot!'

I could never quite believe that, but the herring boats in Castlebay – yes. There are photographs enough of the sea of masts, the quays full of barrels, and the herring girls at work with lightning hands, 'their laughter', in Derick Thomson's words, 'like a sprinking of salt showered from their lips, brine and pickle on their tongues and the stubby short fingers that could handle fish, or lift a child gently, neatly, safely, wholesomely, unerringly and the eyes that were as deep as a calm' (*Eadar Samradh is Foghar*, 1967).

The stench of fish oil and rotting guts and roes that hung over Castlebay would have turned all but the toughest stomachs but it was a smell, while it lasted, of money. From early May to the end of June when the fishing fleet departed for the east coast ports there were 3000 or so extra souls in Castlebay. In waterproof aprons and gumboots teams of girls gutted and packed. The herring were thrown fresh from the boats into wooden troughs and sprinkled with coarse salt. With a sharp knife the belly was split open, the guts fell into a tub to be sold as fish manure and the fish was thrown, depending on its size, into one of three barrels. When each barrel was full it was emptied into tubs and stirred in more salt. The fish, now thoroughly salted inside and out, was ready for its final packing in yet another barrel. This was lined with salt at the bottom and then layers of herring were packed in belly up, each layer covered with more salt. Working a ten-hour day a girl could fill 30 barrels each with 750 herrings.

After standing for a week or so the moisture of the fish converted all the salt into brine and a hole was drilled two-thirds way up the barrel to drain off as much as possible. After that another 250 herrings layered in more salt could be packed in and the barrel would then be secured, turned on its side, and filled to the bung with brine.

The heyday of the herring was in the period before the Great War when freighters came from Hamburg, Danzig and the Russian ports to take back the barrels. In those days Scotland provided northern Europe with half a million barrels of pickled herrings a year and 6000 fisher girls followed the shoals from the Hebrides down to Yarmouth in the summer months. The silver darlings were as important to the economy then as North Sea oil is today.

The boom lasted into the 1920s when the weekly wage for a girl was 25*s* subsistence and one shilling for every barrel packed. By then the Moray Firth Zulus had been replaced by steam drifters and over-trawling had destroyed the spawning beds. The herring bonanza was over. That night I found myself talking to John Allan Macneil who runs the ferry to Vatersay. He told me that when his father, Calum, was a boy there were 42 curing stations lining the shore in Castlebay. But he saw no hope for a revival of the herring fishery. 'The way things are at the moment it's not very easy for the herring to survive.' John told me that every year for the last twenty years a fleet of Dutch trawlers has ravaged the traditional herring grounds.

'They come up round the west of Ireland and they go right up as far as St Kilda. It's big ships they have. They've even got a hospital ship along with them, she was in the bay this year. Every Sunday they anchor somewhere, maybe Mingulay Bay or Village Bay in St Kilda. They have a church session in the evening and anyone who wants to see the doctor, goes to the hospital ship they call the *De Hoop*.'

One year the Barra fishermen counted 27 boats in the Dutch fleet but they reckon it can, as the season goes on, rise to 40 or more. It is a story of skill, cunning and stealth.

'What happened,' says John, 'is that, unnoticed by the west coast British fleet, the Dutch found the herring tracks coming into the Minch 15 to 20 miles west of St Kilda.' It was conveniently outside the twelve-mile limit.

'They are there all summer slaughtering herring at the source of supply and that's why we no longer get any concentration of herring in the Minch. When Mallaig and the north west mapped out a conservation area in the Minch there was nothing there to conserve. You don't see it in the *Fishing News*, you don't see it in any of the papers. We've been telling them about it year after year and it's only now they're beginning to realise there's something wrong.'

It wasn't until October 1984 that an internal EEC Commission report was made public revealing that the Dutch were employing a clandestine system of double book-keeping which enabled them to conceal their over-fishing of the North Sea and the Atlantic waters. This might explain why the Dutch fleet has expanded in the last three or four years while the British and other EEC fleets have been forced to cut back by quota limits imposed to protect threatened fish stocks. Legal action against the Dutch government which tolerated the 'grey market' in undeclared landings was expected to be taken in the European Court of Justice.

From the beginning of June until the end of August the lethal Dutchmen are flying up and down the western waters taking anything that swims and especially the herring. John talks about the 1950s and 60s when the herring catch fell by half but even those days he sees as far better than the present diminished state of the Minch.

'We used to have the Klondykers here and we did a good trade with Germany, Holland, Belgium and Norway but then they closed us as a herring port about seventeen or eighteen years ago and they did the same thing with Stornoway this year which never should have been allowed. That's why there are no Klondykers going into Stornoway any more; they're all going to Ullapool and taking the trade away from the islands.'

We talk about the old days and I tell John I've got this urge to go to Mingulay. 'Well my grandfather stayed on Mingulay, he was a fisherman. It was hard rowing in from there, a twelve-mile haul. They were living on the birds and that's what kept them going along with the few sheep they had, but like the people on St Kilda you don't hear of them killing their own sheep, it was all the birds – puffins and guillemots that was the staple diet.'

John's grandfather and his mother were born on Mingulay. He tells me how his grandfather used to sail down as far as Colonsay and Islay in the summer to fish for lobsters. 'They would be sold in London, they weren't getting a lot for them, there'd be a lot dead on arrival.' He himself joined the Merchant Navy when he was fifteen. He came back in 1961 and since then he's run the Vatersay ferry, the Barra lifeboat, and he's been a member of the fire brigade; he also makes the run up to Barra Head to service the lighthouse every now and then. 'When I look at Mingulay Bay going up to Barra Head it looks like a haven, there's no telephone to bother you, no contact with the outside world, there might have been a lot to say for it after all. Although it was hard living in the winter it must have had some benefits.'

Why did they stick it, I wondered?

'I just think it was a question of survival; their domain was Mingulay and that was it.'

In the sitting room John's four children are watching television. Is there a future for them on Barra? 'I hope so, but I think if they stay they'll have to follow the traditional lines of fishing and crofting. There'll be jobs for the girls in the fish factories. Living in Barra is a healthy way of life if nothing else. We seem to have a bit more freedom than you have in the city.'

John tells me there is a new spirit of optimism and prosperity abroad in the island. There are now maybe 60 men working at the fishing with 22 boats operating out of Northbay, Castlebay and Vatersay. 'Most of the houses you see being done up and the new ones, come from the fishing, the remainder

159

of the money comes from oil; there's about thirty Barra men still working in North Sea Oil.'

Barra has had a fish factory for some years now, Barratlantic, which processes white fish. An even bigger plant is planned at Ardveenish. Behind it is the Board whose plans are every bit as enterprising as they were at Breasclete in Lewis.

'It's one of these joint plans designed to create jobs but there's not a penny of local money in it.' John is not pouring cold water on the idea but like many Barra people he wonders if it's going to be a re-run of the Isle of Barra Hotel, lots of money spent to no long-term purpose.

'I'll say this for the Board they've really done well with their fishing boats, that's brought a lot of money into the island which wouldn't be there otherwise, but I'm keen that there should be local shares in this new factory. Everything that was started here with the Board that had local commitment is still going strong. Anything that has just come in hasn't been so successful, I just can't tell you why.'

The new complex is going to be built near the pier at Ardveenish just north of Northbay. The Board sees it as a partnership between themselves, the Hull Fish Meal and Oil Company, and the fishermen of the southern isles. It will create 30 jobs at a cost of £80,000 a job. Not much perhaps when you consider it costs the state £5,000 a year to keep a person unemployed.

The Board have been doing their homework for some time. They have surveyed the waters of the south Minch for sand eel and pout, the raw material of fishmeal, and the auguries look good. But opinion in Barra is divided. Everybody wants the factory, building it will create work, and once it's working there will be five part-time jobs as well as the projected thirty full-time posts. But there is a caution abroad; the spectre of Breasclete hangs over the project. What happens, cautious voices want to know, when the sand eels disappear the way the herring and the white fish have. All sorts of foreigners will be coming in; what guarantee is there that they won't be fishing for white fish as well?

Back at Clachan Beag the fishing has been good. Gus and I have peat-smoked salmon as a starter and a plump local plaice with chips to follow. I'm a bit late for an appointment I've made with Father Calum. He's moved out of his presbytery, which is being done up, and I find him in an empty holiday flat nearby.

The southern isles are noted for their priests. I don't know what it is, but they are men of singular personality. The last time I was in Barra the ebullient Father Angus McQueen was priest-in-charge. Small, built like a boxer, he ran the place. Maybe that was why the Bishop removed him to exile in Ballachulish. Since then he has been further displaced to Rothesay. For a dedicated isleman like Angus it must be a refined form of purgatory. But of course all for the good of the Church, and no doubt good for the soul too.

'Angus?' says Father Calum, 'Oh, I came here the same day as Angus McQueen. This is my second time in Barra, I was seven years in Northbay. The thing that used to depress us both was none of the young people wanted to stay, they were marking time at school until they went away.'

Then in 1965 the Highlands and Islands Board was created. 'With their financial help people got interested in fishing, so you had youngish men with young families earning their living here. At the same time life was getting very uncomfortable on the mainland. A lot of people in Glasgow were housed in new high-rise blocks and life became pretty grim for them; they really were desperate to come home.'

At that time the pattern of employment in the Merchant Navy was changing. 'With jet flights, instead of being away for nine months or a year, men were coming home every second month. That affected the birth rate. In between the last two censuses we've had 300 more people coming to live on Barra.'

The Board, with its aggressive policy of Counterdrift, must have its full share of praise in persuading young people that they can make a go of things north of Inverness. People in the islands began to think more deeply about their peripheral problems; the *West Highland Free Press* played its part in creating a new mood of belligerence and confidence.

Father Calum was for a time Vice-Convenor of the new Comhairle nan Eilean, before that he had served on the old Inverness County Council. 'I used to get fed up with the fact that we were the Tail End Charlies out here. I used to fly regularly from Benbecula to Stornoway and I flew over all these deserted islands – Taransay, Scarp, Pabbay and all the rest of them. If we can't do anything to repopulate them, at least, I felt, we can see that no more islands become deserted. When the new council came into being there was always a fear that Stornoway would overwhelm us all. They had more fluent councillors and all the expertise. Allegedly the intellectual elite, but really the new council has to be praised because they have paid attention to outlying areas. It's been a great shot in the arm.'

But what about the brain drain; the bright youngsters going off to the Nicolson and on to universities and never coming back? 'Oh, well,' says my host, switching on a bar of the electric fire, 'I'm part of the brain drain. I'm from Eriskay and I went to Rome to study and it wasn't until my late thirties that I came back to the islands. It didn't take me long to pick up the old ways. I stopped writing letters in three weeks and I haven't written any since!'

It is a joke, a stance, but I see what he means. Life here is different, the preoccupations of Westminster and Brussels seem gloriously irrelevant. I wonder what he thinks of the fish factory and the other schemes to provide jobs like the ill-fated spectacle-frame factory?

'Well the spectacle-frame factory proved that if a small firm offered semi-skilled work young girls would be prepared to stay at home and it's only a pity that it didn't survive. I still think we're missing our opportunities here. Fishing for shellfish is lucrative but the young men aren't investing their money in it, not buying a new boat or whatever. The Council is convinced that there are enormous quantities of squid in these waters, maybe one day we'll be fishing with lights as they do in the Mediterranean, but that hasn't come about yet.'

He thinks it's sad that for the last two years fifteen boats have been making a small fortune taking scallops from the shores around Barra but only one boat from Barra has joined in this lucrative enterprise. 'They haven't got around to thinking of storing lobsters so that they can benefit from the winter prices and not some entrepreneur on the mainland.'

He is worldly for his parishioners not himself, worried about fancy schemes that may go disastrously wrong. 'Take Barratlantic. Now that was set up originally for the American market and there was a boat going to come and take all the stuff away to America. By the time it was ready the bottom had fallen out of the market. There was supposed to be a pier but it wasn't built until ten years later so there was no encouragement for boats to come in.' He feels there's not enough thinking ahead, seizing opportunities. 'As soon as the Integrated Development Programme was announced I said we should be drawing up our plans for development. The Council hasn't got a development department to this day – it's lumped in with planning. So what are we getting out of IDP? Nothing but fencing and drainage!'

We discuss Mingulay for a bit and its empty future. Father Calum doesn't entirely agree. 'I could easily see people going to live there again with improved conditions. If they had built a modest breakwater people might still be there. It's the right use of money at the right time that's important.'

As the sun goes down beyond Vatersay and Mingulay I ask him how he reconciles the simplicities of island life with the sophistication of the mainland. After all he, who has lived in a city as rich as Rome is in culture, history, and artistic achievement must find Barra a bit visually and aesthetically deprived?

'It's a strange life, but I don't feel I'm missing out all that much. In Eriskay where I was born we were happy, we didn't yearn for what we hadn't got. We had a little stunted tree and I used to go and look at it from time to time. It wasn't all that pretty. In the summer we worked all the hours of the daylight. That was why we loved the winter: you stopped when the sun went down. My father had a small seventeen-foot boat, he was a lobster fisherman, a merchant seaman. He didn't want what he couldn't have. Maybe that's our future. We should stop looking to the mainland for everything, perhaps we've got it all here.'

Back to Clachan Beag for a late-night cup of tea. Gus is marshalling his cameras. Tomorrow the *Corryvreckan* will arrive. Or will it?

Don Rangoon is not all that confident. 'It's beginning to blow,' he says, 'and you just don't know in these waters what may happen. Maybe it'll blow itself out by morning, maybe not.' If it doesn't get better then, even though the yacht makes Castlebay there's no guarantee that we can land on Mingulay.

12

THE MAINLAND PEOPLE
ARE DIFFERENT

BARRA 2

Sunday morning. I haven't slept at all well. It was wild in the night. I draw the curtains. Vatersay is veiled in cloud; there are brisk white horses in the bay. Down for a big breakfast: porridge, bacon, egg, sausage and lots of tea. Gus has decided he'll go to Vatersay with Father Calum who will be celebrating his second mass of the day in the corrugated iron church there.

It's windy out, nobody about. Everyone who is up is now at mass in the church of Our Lady Star of the Sea with its castellated clock tower and restrained interior. I steal into the back of the church and am surprised to find Father Calum saying mass in English. But there's a good reason – like Latin, Gaelic is no longer universal, English has ousted them both. Outside the church I fall into conversation with a young teacher. She has the Gaelic and I ask her why, in this most Gaelic of all the islands mass should be in the foreigner's English?

'Oh well, a third of the congregation here this morning wouldn't just have the Gaelic. Lots of people have come back whose husband or wife isn't from the island. Their children understand it but won't speak it. There's an awful lot of families where the mother speaks Gaelic and the father doesn't. Maybe the children were brought up in Fort William or Glasgow until they were nine and they won't have a word of it.'

She tells me that all the children are taught Gaelic in primary and secondary school; both Gaelic and French are compulsory in the first and second year but there are subtle cultural differences. 'In the primary school we talk in Gaelic in the staff room. In the secondary school most of the teachers are from the mainland so the language is English. It's two different cultures – island and mainland. I just don't think they mix.'

What, I wonder, makes the difference?

'Nice as the mainland people are, they're *different*. It's in their values, what they think is important.'

And what does she think is important?

'Well, I don't know but it's definitely different. It's not your religion, it's to do with Gaelic culture; the way of life. Ours is just as different today as it was a hundred years ago.'

Altogether she tells me there are now 370 children at school in the island, of whom 260 are being taught in Castlebay. And the school roll is rising.

'My father was at sea and my mother was working in the Castlebay Hotel. It was their generation that had to go away to get work in Glasgow. My father got a job in the shipyards – now that's a typical family and the same pattern was followed by every one of my cousins and relatives. Everyone went away and got married away because there was work away. But in the last ten years the number of children in school has practically doubled because all the families started coming back.'

The return to the islands in the late 1970s and 80s is one positive measure of Mrs Thatcher's urgent mission to streamline industry and weed out the non-essential and the expendable.

'Unemployment on the mainland, that's what brought people back. But there was the hotel and the fish factory, building those created a bit of work. In the next ten years it could intensify and the more people who come back the more jobs are created. I think Barra is one of the few places on the up and up when everywhere else is on the down.'

She is particularly enthusiastic about the couples coming back with young families. Are they returning to an environment of isolation?

'Oh no, you'd be just as isolated, perhaps more so if you lived in a rural community in Aberdeen or Perth. I certainly wouldn't go back. I *live* more here; in Glasgow I just existed. Community-wise there's more to do. In Glasgow you just go to work and sleep. Yesterday was the first day I've had in the house since May probably. You see there are two communities here, the community of summer and the community of winter. After October the winter activities start.'

We part, she to start her busy winter, me to walk down the east shore of the bay to see if I can catch a distant sight of *Corryvreckan* scudding before the wind towards Castlebay and our rendezvous for Mingulay.

Not a sign of anything. Not a sail, not a hull anywhere in sight. It is bitterly cold and horribly rough out there. Nobody in their right mind would want to venture out to Mingulay on a day like this.

Unlike Lewis and Harris where nobody but churchgoers are seen to move on Sunday, all sorts of things are happening here. Youngsters are playing football, sheep are being moved and penned in a fank. I go back and engage Don Rangoon in exploratory conversation. Does he think the *Corryvreckan* will come? He lights yet another cigarette and peers out of the picture window of Clachan Beag's sun parlour.

'Very doubtful,' he pronounces, 'it's really dirty out there. And besides even if you got to Mingulay I doubt if you could land with the tide like this.' That adds an even more depressing note to the proceedings. Mingulay is receding into the mist.

'When the ferry gets back from Vatersay we'll call up the coastguard in Oban and see if they have any news of the *Corryvreckan*. They may be trying to get a message to you.'

I decide to take another turn up the road. I'm told there's a new GP on Barra. Bik-something his name is. Biku could it be, or Beeko? Another African like my doctor in Daliburgh or might he be some Nepalese refugee or a dhoti'd Tamil from Madras? I knock on the doctor's surgery door and am greeted by a very English-looking young doctor called David Bickle who instantly invites me in for tea. He and his wife Kim are from Swindon. He'd wanted to come to the Western Isles for as long as he could remember.

'My wife saw the advertisement and by the time the day came for the interview everyone else had dropped out. So I got the job.'

Since coming to the island they have had a baby daughter. 'Actually the population as you've probably heard has been going up. When Dr Hill left there were 1,493 patients on the books, now there are 1,517, well 1,518 with Sophie.'

At that moment the phone rings. It's the police station down the road. David listens, nods, and says he'll be along in a minute or two. It turns out two cars have collided head-on, a seemingly impossible feat on a Sunday afternoon on Barra. One of the drivers is the leader of the Brownie Pack. 'I won't have to breathalyse her anyway,' says David, collecting a bag and leaving his tea in the cup.

Kim was in advertising and public relations in Swindon. Does she find this an alien community?

'Well David was so keen and as long as he's happy, and he is, then that's OK by me. I just wish everyone wasn't so demanding, he really gets no time to himself. I don't mind when people are really ill but when he gets called out in the night to treat someone who's the victim of their own excesses. . . .'

David is fairly young to be handling a practice like this on his own. Is that a strain?

'Well he may be, but he really is a highly competent doctor, I don't think he'd have taken the job if he wasn't confident he could do it. And if anything really serious happens he can always ring for an air ambulance, that's a great help knowing you can get someone to Glasgow if they need major surgery.'

David comes back, finishes his tea, and the phone rings again. Again he nods. 'I'll be up in half an hour,' he says and turns to me: 'All go on Barra as you can see.'

Two priests, two nuns, two policemen, one doctor, a handful of teachers – that's about the extent of the official classes in the island. Didn't David and Kim long for a few kindred spirits, media folk for her, fellow practitioners for him?

On my journeys through the islands I have been impressed by the passionate defence which exiles from the cities put up for the simple life.

'Don't miss it at all,' says a potter whose urban life revolved round opera, ballet, theatre, cinema, good food and wine and the sharpening of intellect with his peers. His most stimulating conversations now are with his crofter neighbour next door who reads the *Press & Journal* and borrows large-print westerns from the travelling library once a week.

'I get all the books I need, people come to stay, there's the phone, I go down to Edinburgh at least three times a year but I'm always glad to be back. Things are more *real* here. And where in a New Town would you get a view like that? He points to a vision of moor and beach slightly impaired by a kit bungalow, an abandoned chassis of a Ford Popular and an electric blue caravan in the foreground. You can't argue with that level of enthusiasm.

But Kim and David, they have no Gaelic, who do *they* talk to?

'Well,' says Kim, 'we see a lot of the Huntingtons, Jack and Polly. You ought to call on them, I'm sure they'd love to see you.' I make a note to do that.

Back at the Clachan there's bad news.

'Someone on the phone from Kerrera,' says Don, 'they're not going to make it, I'm afraid. Seemingly, they just can't get out for the wind.'

'What's the forecast?'

'Well that's not good either. You never can tell, but', and Don points to the bay and the angry water, 'you can see for yourself.'

When I ring the Lindsays I find it wasn't for want of trying that they didn't set off. 'There's no pier on Mingulay, as you know,' says Douglas, 'and even if we could have got out there, which would have been pretty unpleasant, I doubt if we could have got ashore with any degree of safety. Sorry but I'm afraid that's it.'

It looks then as if we're not going to get to Mingulay this year. 'A pity', says Don, 'after coming all this way but the weather in October, I mean you just never know what it's going to be like. Maybe if we got a break in the weather someone would take you out. . . .'

All highly disappointing. I think I've blown it. Waited too long when all summer on almost any day it would have been simple to reach Mingulay in the smallest motor boat.

Monday is no better; wet, cold and miserable. In the morning I go across on the ferry to Vatersay with John Allan MacNeil. It's a fibre-glass boat like the one that plies between Ludag and Barra, open amidships with a wheelhouse and for'ard cabin. Jetty to jetty it's less than two miles, a journey of ten minutes or so from Castlebay to Vatersay but the northern shores of Vatersay just below Ben Orosay are much closer to mainland Barra. Just a few hundred yards separates the two islands. The sort of distance you could easily bridge?

'Yes or you could throw a causeway across. You'd have to build a mile of road on the Barra side to join up with the existing township road at Nask but if a causeway were built you could drive from Vatersay to Castlebay in ten minutes.'

In Stornoway drastic cuts have just been announced in all forms of non-essential spending but John and a lot of other people are thinking, wishfully maybe, of the enormous benefits that a causeway could bring to Vatersay.

'In the old days when we came under Inverness the end of the road was Skye and to the west of Skye there was nothing and that was the way we were treated here, but these islands are more united than ever they were. The Council is now doing something about the islands as a group. I'm sure that one day all these islands will be joined by causeways.'

'A road from Ness to Mingulay?'

'Well, no not Mingulay but certainly a road which would run right down to Vatersay. There's plenty of stone for a causeway in the hill there.'

John has costed it all out in his mind. 'Running ferries between these islands is very expensive and I don't see how the authorities can keep it up in the years to come. I get a subsidy for running this ferry. If you built two jetties for a car ferry to and from Vatersay that would cost you something like £150,000 for a start. You've got £750,000 for a boat which is only going to last you ten years at the most. You've got fuel costs, running costs, surveys. Take all that into account and all the council employees who are on expenses staying away from home because the ferries can't get them back at night and you can see it's got to come.'

At the moment in the Western Isles there are five small ferries constantly on the run, sometimes carrying only a single passenger. It makes sense all right to replace them with causeways, but what makes social sense doesn't necessarily command the millions of pounds that would make the dream come true.

Vatersay is now the only inhabited island in the Western Isles which does not have a car ferry. Old people have left the island to be taken into sheltered housing across the bay on Barra. Young families have left too. The population rose from under 70 in 1971 to about 150 four years ago but now it has dropped back to 80 and, even more discouragingly, the school roll has fallen from 20 to 15 – eight girls and seven boys taught by Mary MacNeil who comes across on the ferry every schoolday from Barra. Although the Western Isles Council has committed itself to building a causeway, the £3 million it would cost is the subject of prolonged haggling between themselves and the Scottish Development Department who are demanding a hydrographic feasibility survey. This will cost £60,000. The council won't commit the money until the SDD gives them a firm promise to build the causeway. It is a typical Hebridean dilemma and while the correspondence goes back and forth Vatersay remains without a car ferry, and the population continues to decline.

On the slip on Vatersay which was only built six years ago Joseph MacDougall is waiting to take me to see one or two old people who may remember their childhood on Mingulay. As most of the islanders left in Edwardian times they would be over eighty now. Like many another islander Barra Joe, as he's nicknamed, worked in the Glasgow shipyards. He was a foreman joiner on the QE2 and his father was one of the ten Vatersay raiders who came here in 1910 from Mingulay. In those days the absentee hand of Lady Gordon Cathcart hung over the whole of the southern isles. Although she visited her properties only once in 54 years, like her father before her, she had very autocratic ideas about the way they should be administered.

When Macculloch came to Vatersay in the 1820s the daily round was pastoral. 'I had', he wrote, 'an opportunity of imagining how life is passed in a remote island, without society or neighbours and where people are born or die without ever troubling themselves to inquire whether the world contains any other countries than Vatersay and Barra. The amusement of the evening consisted in catching scallops for supper, milking the cows and chasing rabbits; and this, I presume, is pretty nearly the round of occupation.'

This idyllic scene was not to last. At the end of the 1830s Barra, South Uist and Benbecula were purchased by Colonel Gordon of Cluny for

£173,000. In one punitive summer this Aberdeenshire laird banished 2,000 souls from his estates to Canada. Like an asset stripper he denuded the land and at one stage, in his efforts to recoup on his investment, offered Barra to the Home Secretary as a Hebridean Alcatraz. In the summer of 1851 a small fleet of transports anchored in Loch Boisdale and an eye witness has left this account of what happened:

> the poor people were commanded to attend a public meeting at Loch Boisdale, where the transports lay and, according to the intimation, any one absenting himself from the meeting was to be fined in the sum of two pounds sterling. At this meeting some of the natives were seized and in spite of their entreaties sent on board the transports. One stout Highlander named Angus Johnston, resisted with such pith that they had to handcuff him before he could be mastered; but in consequence of the priest's interference his manacles were removed and he was marched between four officers on board the emigrant vessel.

In 1912 a Don M'Aulay (could it be Calum and Morag's father?) wrote to a Glasgow solicitor to testify to those wild events which were still a vivid part of his childhood memories:

> both my father and mother were eye-witnesses of people being chased like wild cattle over the hills. People can hardly believe now what took place then, and what my mother who died in my arms at the fall of last year told me, it would be enough to make the devil himself desperate, if I am not using too strong an impression.

Apart from the memories of those who remained behind after the evictions there is a mass of documentary evidence about the despotic activities of Colonel Gordon. A Quebec newspaper described how 1,100 penniless emigrants from Gordon's estate had been begging their way through Upper Canada having been shipped from the Outer Isles like cattle.

To seek a parallel for these events in the nineteenth century you would have to draw on the annals of the slave trade and it was indeed that parallel that the *Quebec Times* drew: 'for cruelty less savage the slave-dealers of the South have been held up to the execration of the world.'

The wretched Gordon of Cluny eventually died and was succeeded by his son John who bequeathed the lands to his wife who then married Sir Reginald Cathcart. Lady Gordon Cathcart, as she styled herself, owned a lot of property on the east coast of Scotland as well but she turned out to be almost as insensitive as her father-in-law when it came to the management of her Hebridean inheritance. Vatersay was eventually bought from Lady Gordon Cathcart by the government for an extortionate £6,250 and its squatters, Joe's father among them, were elevated to the legal status of crofters.

Today, without a causeway and without a car ferry, Vatersay is, one feels, merely marking time. When Joe came back to the island in 1975 he was full of enthusiasm for the future. There were then 130 living on the island. Joe had been an activist in Glasgow at the time of the Upper Clyde Shipbuilders sit-in and he pursued the same policies in Vatersay. He became Chairman of the Co-Operative and turned his mind to ways in which people could be kept on the island.

'I discussed mussel farming and crab processing with the Board – I thought that crab paste being made on Vatersay would give us a better profit than sending crabs to be processed somewhere else. I thought perhaps we could have a net-making factory or a creel-making factory. Now you have to buy your creels in England; why not bring your materials up here and weld them yourself? I suggested a causeway. I suggested you could even put a tidal generator in the middle of it and we could have electricity as well. Everyone laughed at this. Then the Council changed their mind and decided they would have a causeway. It was supposed to come in 1985 but now I hear it's been put off until 1987. I often feel we would have done better if we had a priest living on the island. Not that Father Calum isn't doing his best but he's got three parishes to look after, Vatersay, Castlebay and Borve.'

(In January 1985 the Scottish Office announced financial support for the causeway as part of the EEC's IDP programme for the Western Isles. The project was expected to cost £2.7 million of which £700,000 would have to be found by Comhairle nan Eilean. Even if the Council can find the money the causeway will take at least three years to build.)

Joe makes a coffee. Apart from John his son, he is alone in the house, there is no sign of his wife. 'No, she's working in the hospital, so she's in Barra four or five days a week. We are six of a family. There's four away just now. One's a chiropodist in Glasgow, one's with Morrison's building a bridge on the mainland, the other son is an officer cadet in Denham's, the girl is at college in Stornoway doing a computer course and John here is at secondary school in Castlebay.'

How difficult is it to make a living on Vatersay?

'Well crofting isn't worth it unless you've got ten head of cattle. I've got six just now; I sent three across to the sales this morning and I'm keeping three for breeding. It's just cost me £300 for hay and by the time you buy other feeding stuff you just about break even.'

Undaunted by this chill-sounding future, Joe has just built himself a bungalow. 'You see I was able to do most of it myself. I got a bursary to Inverness Academy when I left school here but that lasted one afternoon and then I became a joiner instead. I got a £9,500 grant and loan for the house. A house like this would cost you £35,000 if you got a contractor to put it up for you. The kit cost me £12,000, then there was £1,500 for tiles so that was quite a saving. The family helped me, we made the blocks ourselves. Not everyone would be able to put up their own house.' There's quite a note of pride in his voice, defiance too. Not all Joe's views are shared by the rest of the island. When the Co-Chomunn's shop opened on Vatersay he would like to have been given the job of running but it went to a man from Barra.

Joe takes me on a tour of the island. He points out the spot where the *Annie Jane* foundered. Vatersay is a curious shape, really two separate islands connected by a low-lying dune, a snare in the old days for sailing ships which frequently mistook the sands for the entrance to Castle Bay. In 1853 a group of Scots and Irish emigrants bound for the New World made their final and fatal landfall on the sands here.

The 1,200-ton ship had been drifting at the mercy of the gales for several days and the captain decided to run her aground on Vatersay beach to save her from a worse fate on the surrounding reefs. Between midnight and one o'clock in the morning she grounded and almost simultaneously a huge wave swept most of the passengers and crew into the water. There were 102 survivors and the story was commemorated on a granite monument close by:

> On 28th Sept. 1853 the ship 'Annie Jane' with emigrants from Liverpool to Quebec was totally wrecked in this bay and three-fourths of the crew and passengers numbering about 350 men, women and children were drowned and their bodies interred here.

Joe remembers a macabre story which was handed down after the event. 'Two shepherds who lived on the island, it was a sheep farm then the whole place, were down on the shore walking among the bodies and one turned to the other and said, "What a pity God has taken all these beautiful young girls," and there was a scraggy old woman lying there among them still alive and she said, "What a good thing for me, you're not God."'

Like Barra, Vatersay is a Catholic island and every Sunday Father Calum comes over on the boat to say mass in the corrugated iron and pine church presented to the island by the Marquess of Bute just before the Great War.

'It belongs', Joe tells me, 'to the people, not the Bishop. I don't think there's another one like it in the diocese.' The church is painted vivid blue – 'It was the only paint we had at the time,' says Joe.

We call at one of the croft houses to talk to Jonathan Maclean who, Joe says, may remember his days on Mingulay. He does.

'Oh yes,' he says, 'I went to school in Mingulay. There would be a hundred people there in those days, a hundred at least maybe more. The men were mostly at the fishing, those that weren't sailing deep sea. They had long lines and herring nets. They used to take the cod and ling to Castlebay and it was sent away from there.'

Jonathan is a Mingulay man, not a man of Vatersay. Indeed none of the few remaining islanders as far as I can gather have roots going further back than Edwardian times on this small and not very productive bit of land. Does it make sense to spend nearly £3 million connecting it to Barra or should it just be evacuated as Mingulay was? It's a point I discuss back on Barra with an official from Stornoway.

'You won't quote me of course.' Few wish to be quoted on so sensitive and emotional an issue. 'My own fear', he says, 'is that unless you give an isolated community all the apparatus of support that they would get if they moved elsewhere there is a perfectly natural tendency for them to move elsewhere. Right, supposing the causeway comes, and it must come if only for political reasons, will that keep the old people there? When they become bedridden or helpless they'll still have to come to Castlebay to be looked after. Are you *really* going to provide jobs on Vatersay? I think not. It will just be a dormitory for people working at Ardveenish or in Northbay or anywhere but Vatersay. You could say Vatersay is just as much an anachronism as Mingulay. It's outlived its usefulness.' You *could* say that but you'd be unwise to say it publicly!

What does young John MacDougall do at the weekend on Vatersay when most of his schoolfriends are on the other side of that tantalising stretch of water in Castlebay? What for that matter does anyone do? Although there is a new £60,000 community hall on Vatersay, what gives a community its purpose and stability is patently lacking.

On Vatersay there appears to be no burning need to remain. It's not often that Fleet Street does the Hebrides a favour but in October 1984 David Black of the *Sunday Times* put the Vatersay dilemma, indeed the whole problem of sustaining remote communities, in a simple sexual perspective. Under the headline 'Awaiting a causeway to romance' he described how the twenty-two bachelors of Vatersay were existing in a celibate state on an island where there was not a single woman of marriageable age. In twenty years there had only been two weddings. Why stay?

I asked one or two young girls in Castlebay how, if a marriage presented itself, they would welcome the prospect of moving to Eriskay, for instance, or Vatersay? One of those girls summed it up succinctly: 'I'm not a heavy drinker and I'm not an alcoholic but what would you do in Eriskay or Vatersay on a Saturday night? There's no bar in either place. Would you want to sit at home and watch all those glamorous bitches in *Dynasty* and then get your kicks out of going to the stack to fetch peats and boiling yourself a cup of Nescafé? You'd need to put me in *chains* to get me to live in Vatersay. And then you wouldn't keep me there.'

The next day we're due to fly out from Barra. On the way to the airstrip we call in to say hello to the Huntingtons. Cuithir House is eighteenth-century, large, the most substantial on the island. Out in the walled kitchen garden there's a wealth of vegetables; in the house one of the finest collections of objets d'art in the Western Isles.

On the kitchen table stands a sculpture by David Wynne; hanging on the walls the original drawings by Barnett Freedman for *Anna Karenina*. In the drawing room a dazzling collection of Meissen and paintings by Leonard Appleby and John Ward. Jack in a former existence was an art dealer in London. Since coming here he's had a spell in the lighthouse at Barra Head. Polly his wife is elegant, she looks as if she might pop out at any moment to fetch something from Harrods or Peter Jones.

'The weather's a bit difficult at times,' she says but they both like the tranquillity, the bird life, the unhurried life style. I am about to ask, impertinently, what on earth made them give up their elegant house down south to migrate to Barra when I recall that Compton Mackenzie, an urbane and urban man if ever there was one, had some of the most productive years of his life in the remoteness of Barra. In Northbay I talked to an old lady well into her eighties who had known the great man well. I asked her when she had first met him?

'Dear knows,' she said, 'I can't remember. My memory is going and I'm half blind. He lived in our house for eleven months while his own was being built. His house was so beautiful and he was so nice about it too, so was Chrissie his wife. It was through Father John Macmillan we met him. He wanted to stay somewhere in Barra. He was writing and he had the gramophone doing his records. He always had visitors. I heard from Lily at Christmas – that's his third wife. Faith was his first wife.'

The house where Compton Mackenzie lived and held court is almost totally obscured from view now by a great mound of shells. It was bought some years ago by Harold Cozens and his wife Brenda from Ullswater. Cozens's main occupation is crushing the cockle shells which form a substantial part of the beach on which Loganair land their planes. There are dark hints that this quarrying will eventually make the beach unsuitable for landing planes altogether; it's altering the drainage they say. But apart from a low defence line of sandbags alongside the road the danger doesn't seem to be all that urgent. There's a lot of noise and dust coming from in front of the house where the shells are being processed to make harling for walls and grit for chickens. And yet in the 1930s it was undoubtedly the hub of the most stimulating coterie the islands have ever seen.

Compton Mackenzie was fascinated by islands. He had already bought the Shiants halfway between Lewis and Skye and when he managed to sell his lease of Jethou in the Channel Islands he acquired this acre of sandy machair close to Traigh Mhor, the great cockle beach, and about 300 yards from the long beach called Traigh Iais which faced the Atlantic. According to legend the site of his future home was where MacNeil of Barra used to sit down and have his lunch when he was out snipe-shooting. So Compton, as the islanders called him, decided to call his three-sided house Suidheachan, the sitting-down place.

He received £3,000 for the lease of Jethou and this is what he decided to spend on Suidheachan. Costs mounted and, perennially short of cash, Mackenzie was faced with the prospect of selling the Shiants to raise more money or eliminating the billiard room, but as that was to house all his books it was the last thing he wished to sacrifice. In the end the money was sorted out and on Silver Jubilee Day 1935 half the island turned up to watch the foundation stone laid and then blessed and sprinkled with holy water by Father Macmillan of Northbay. The *Daily Record* reporting this unique event compared Mackenzie with earlier literary fugitives:

> Mr Mackenzie is a public figure, one of our foremost men of letters, and his way of life is a matter of public interest. We wonder therefore, whether this exile signifies a spiritual adventure, an evasion of life's problems or merely a glorified holiday. Stevenson and Samoa are evoked. Tusitala, as the natives called him, also built himself an island home and became a benignant island chieftain.

Compton Mackenzie revealed some of the attractions of Barra in a broadcast he did for the BBC in 1936 called 'Living off the Map'. The last consideration that moved him to go and live there, he said, was any desire to escape from the world. He liked the laughter of Barra, the native Gaelic wit salting the English and 'the remarkable cosmopolitan outlook of the people due to so many of them having travelled the world over. It is a curious but an extremely pleasant, combination of shyness with good manners and savoir faire.'

Then Mackenzie explained that one of the great virtues of Island life was that the tyranny of time didn't exist. He told the story of Lord Leverhulme explaining to an old Lewis man what he wanted him to achieve in a day's work and of the old man saying: 'But, my lord, you are not giving us any time for contemplation.'

Mackenzie was a great showman and publicist; he was conscious of the public honour he was conveying on the people of Barra by choosing to dwell among them and thus directly make their small community a part of his life and letters. When the time came for him to move into the house the event was the most prestigious flitting ever orchestrated in the west.

He was hoping that the Bishop of Argyll would personally attend on the day in question to celebrate mass in Suidheachan but a cataract operation kept him on the mainland. Compton had to settle for Father Dominic MacKellaig of Craigston and Father John MacQueen, parish priest of Castlebay, who said mass, while P. J. Martin the headmaster of Castlebay school and his pupils provided the choir.

'There were', wrote Compton, 'about 200 crofters with their wives and children present. That they all squeezed themselves in was almost a miracle.'

In the years that followed, *Whisky Galore* and later *Rockets Galore* brought the islands into national prominence and Compton's political and public clout ensured that any grievances which might arise in those parts were taken immediately to the top brass in Edinburgh or Whitehall. Compton knew them all and he introduced many of them to his Barra friends.

The longest campaign that he fought during his Barra period was on behalf of the fishermen of the southern islands. Their traditional method of fishing had been with drift nets which hung in long rows from the surface of the water. They took only mature fish and the herring stocks were never depleted. Then after the Great War ring net boats began to frequent the Minch breaking up the shoals and destroying the spawning beds. The three-mile limit was blatantly ignored to the detriment of local men using drift nets. Such was the greed of the east-coast ring-netters that they very often scooped up two or three times the amount of herring their boats could carry. After taking aboard as much as they could manage without sinking, the rest of the fish would be dumped in the sea to pollute the bottom and destroy the breeding grounds.

John Lorne Campbell, who later bought the island of Canna, was living in Barra at the time devoting himself to a study of Gaelic. He decided that the best way to agitate against illegal trawling was to form a Sea League based on the highly successful anti-laird Land League of the 1880s. Its intention was to press for legislation to close the whole area to trawlers and give 'the same protection for the livelihood of the crofter fisherman as is given to the sporting fishing of the landowners themselves.'

Campbell and Compton fought tirelessly for the Sea League but as Compton finally recorded in 1967: 'of course nothing was done to keep the ring-netters out of the Minch and the drift-net fishing was ruined. However the ring-netters must now face the prospect of devastating competition from new boats employing purse-nets. Their turn has come to petition the authorities with no more likelihood of being helped than the drift-netters of thirty years ago.' And so it has turned out.

The billiard room of Suidheachan in those years was as inflammatory and explosive a spot as any in the Highlands. Compton had insatiable energy and, more important, the ear of those in office. But all that energy was expended with very little result. I wonder what it's like inside now. Harold Cozens and his wife are only too pleased to show me round. The old billiard room and library where Compton used to hold court is now part of the factory.

'That's the only part, that and the far kitchen that's been incorporated into the factory,' Harold explains with a slightly defensive edge in his voice. 'People tend to think the whole thing is factory and when they come up here they get a shock especially when they see the size of the place.'

I stand in the doorway and try to recreate the scene as it might have been in the mid-1930s. At this time Compton was 53. He had been editing the *Gramophone* since 1928. Between 1934 and 1936 he managed to write and publish no fewer than six books as well as being Rector of Glasgow University and Literary Critic of the *Daily Mail*. He dissipated his talents with many another time-consuming enterprise from running the Dickens Fellowship to being President of the Siamese Cat Club. Barra had never seen such industry. Amidst all that, he was able in 1936 to write and revise and send off the typescript to Cassell's of a novel of over 100,000 words in exactly thirty-one days. 'Nellie Boyte typed away all day at my manuscript; Chrissie MacSween sat up playing the gramophone with the huge E.M.G. horn till 3 a.m. I sat on in my chair till 6 a.m., went to bed and slept till 2.30 p.m.'

But Sunday was, as in the rest of the islands, a day of rest and recreation. Every Sunday evening where now the machinery grinds cockle shells there was a gathering round the billiard table. The game was pool and a variant which Compton himself invented. 'At this gathering, sometimes as many as twenty, there were usually the priests, the doctor, the schoolmaster, the Coddie and other Barra personalities with an occasional visitor from the mainland.' Always present at these ceilidhs was the scholarly figure of John Lorne Campbell performing his unique Sabbath feat of concentration. 'He used to sit back on the narrow ledge in front of the bookshelves deep in one of the books without paying the least attention to the performance of his rivals. Then when the time came for him to play his ball the book would be put down on the ledge and his shot played, after which he would return to the book until his turn came again.'

Above all it was intellectual leadership that Compton Mackenzie and his circle gave to the Western Isles; a steady stream of the great and famous flocked to Barra. At the very least they must have given the island something to talk about.

When the composer Dame Ethel Smyth descended on Barra in 1933 she was 75 and strikingly deaf. Father John Macmillan arranged a waulking in the parish hall of Northbay. The Dame watched fascinated as two teams of six women sat on either side of a trestle table and vigorously banged and rolled and pulled a length of tweed to shrink it while an 80-year-old Barra woman sang verse after verse of a traditional waulking song. When it was over Dame Ethel asked if it would be acceptable to offer the ladies a dram. Father John said it would be fine if they had any but there wasn't a bottle in sight. Dame Ethel lifted her skirt, produced a bottle and went round filling the glasses which had appeared like magic. It must have been quite a scene.

'How do you say good health in Gaelic?' she asked Compton. 'Slainte mhath,' he shouted. She couldn't hear. The priest and Compton bellowed the Gaelic at her again.

'Can't hear you,' she said. 'Never mind. Good health to all you nice people and thank you for giving me such a splendid evening.'

After she left she sent Father John a bottle of whisky. 'A noble, glorious woman,' he pronounced.

A week or two later there, descending dramatically from the skies to touch down in Castle Bay, was Malcolm Douglas-Hamilton's flying boat *Cloud of Iona*. On board was Lady Londonderry who had come to consult Father Macmillan about a concert of Gaelic songs she was about to give in Londonderry House.

And so it went on: politicians, socialites, celebrities, journalists, aspirant writers, musicians and painters made Barra the most visited island in the west. And this house, empty now of books and music, was the centre of it all. It could never have been a pretty place. The rooms are box-like and spartan.

'There's another lounge this end the same size as the other one,' says Harold. 'We had to re-window the whole thing and re-spout it; it cost a lot of money!'

The passage we are standing in is ninety feet long but nothing remains to remind you of Mackenzie's expansive and hospitable life style half a century ago. 'The only thing we have of his is an old horn off his gramophone up in the loft. He edited *Gramophone* with his brother-in-law Christopher Stone. In his autobiography he talks about putting a golden sovereign and a Silver Jubilee magazine under the foundation stone and I expect that's still here.'

When Harold and Brenda bought the house the feu charter stipulated that if it burnt down they were required to rebuild it brick for brick as it was. 'So I thought I'll just get a price because I knew Compton paid about £5,500 to build the house. Well that was a few years ago and the estimate to replace it was half a million quid then! It's 6,000 square feet; work that out in terms of London prices and then double it for hauling everything to the island and you'll see what I mean.'

Were they ever conscious of Compton's spirit hanging over the house amid the dust of the machinery?

'Well it's funny you should say that. You know that while he was here he wrote *Whisky Galore* and all that carry on. In fact last spring I was sitting in this room watching the old black-and-white film of *Whisky Galore* and I'm pretty certain he actually sat and wrote the book right in this room. I thought, God I wonder if he's around; it was quite incredible.'

We walk back through the rain to the single-storey airport building. The sea mist has closed right in; the plane is late. Not coming at all? I go outside and cock an ear. Somewhere up there I hear the drone of engines; the sound comes and goes. I know that if the pilot can't find a gap in the clouds he'll turn back to Glasgow. Suddenly the noise turns to a roar; through a gap in the swirling mist the plane appears almost at sea level and coming straight for the beach. There's a rising plume of water as the wheels skim over the sand.

And that's it. Too late to get to Mingulay this year. Better luck in 1984.

13

FORCE SIX MOVING TO EIGHT

MINGULAY

I sat on Skye for most of the summer of 1984; it was the hottest and driest period in living memory. The sun had come out of the clouds on Easter Saturday and with a few striking exceptions it had gone on shining ever since. On practically any day I could have got to Mingulay with no trouble at all but I thought it might be interesting to go when the crofters who owned the island took off their lambs for the autumn sheep sales.

I was in constant touch with Don Rangoon. Every time I rang him he reported fine weather but the day I set off from Skye the wind had been blowing all night. When I arrived at the end of the pier at Uig just before 9.30 Captain Archie MacQueen was not optimistic.

'Force six,' he said, 'probably moving to eight.'

'I was hoping to get to Mingulay,' I said.

'You won't make it', he said, 'if it stays like this. But maybe it'll blow itself out by tomorrow.'

Archie went up to the bridge: the *Hebrides*, with propellors turning the water a milky green, slid stern first away from the pier, turned and headed down Loch Snizort on the two-hour voyage to Lochmaddy. From there I proposed to hitch a lift to Benbecula and catch the afternoon plane to Barra.

Despite a bit of headwind we get to Lochmaddy on schedule. I say goodbye to Archie and on the car deck have a stroke of luck. The first driver I see is a sergeant from the rocket range and he's going to Balivanich. He tells me he slept in the car all night at Uig having driven from the south of England, a round trip of 1,300 miles. We're first off the boat and as we drive down through South Uist in the pouring rain he tells me he gets six weeks' leave a year plus twenty days' travel. His wife stays down in Surrey and he commutes twelve times a year to be with her.

'The wife came up for the Christmas party but she didn't fancy living here; anyway we've got a mortgage of £240 a month down south.' He tells me the quarters are very comfortable. 'There's TV in every bedroom and we have a library of videos. We've got an aqua club, a saddle club, there's badminton and squash.'

Do he and his mates get on well with the locals?

'When we came here there was more mixing but now they seem to keep themselves to themselves. To be quite honest we mixed more with the local people in Malaysia than we did here.'

He has been on Benbecula for 13 months and he tells me that when the army arrived in 1972 they put up a powerful aerial so that the locals got television as well. 'I expect it altered their lives. Some of the young ones come and use the sports facilities on club nights but by and large there's not much to go out for. There's no shops, only two hotels; why go up the road and pay 60p for a whisky when you can get one in the mess for 28p? That's 28p for what we call Teabag.'

'Teabag' turns out to be the blended whisky 'Te Bheag' marketed by the Gaelic-speaking millionaire on Skye, Iain Nobuill. The sergeant is a pleasing and gentle sort of man who obviously regards Benbecula as just another posting, an interlude in his service career. He drops me off at the airport building which is just across the road from the army quarters.

I walk across to the NAAFI and buy a packet of Minstrels. The Comhairle nan Eilean flag is fluttering from the council buildings. In the airport building I chat with an ex-army man who 'stayed on' among the natives, John Bagley who is in charge of the fire appliance. Blowing about on the tarmac is a small private plane on hire to the Fisheries Department. The pilot is making a few swoops on the local lochs with a photographer seeing what's going on among the fish farms. We are joined by a couple of debt collectors from Aberdeen who have been serving writs for non-payment of rent in Eriskay. They are now on their way to Barra to serve more writs.

'What happens if they take to the hills when they see you coming?' I ask.

'We've got a search warrant. We seldom have any trouble; they manage to find the money.'

'And if they don't?'

'Well we seize their goods and they're auctioned off to raise the money.'

It seems a depressing sort of job to have to do; I can think of less chilling ways of earning a living.

'You've got a Greek pilot today,' says John as the Loganair Twin Otter circles and lands. It's only £11.55 for the 20-minute flight to Barra.

'As you can see,' says the pilot as we strap ourselves in, 'it's a very windy day, low cloud, so we shall be at around 300 feet all the way.'

We take off and fly south along the coast of Benbecula, over the rocket range on South Uist, over Daliburgh and North Boisdale, and across the Sound of Barra to the cockle beach of Traigh Mhor. As we come in to land I can see another Twin Otter on the ground. This is the plane Gus Wylie has just arrived in from Glasgow. We touch down in a slight flurry of wet and taxi over the sand. I can see Don Rangoon's Mercedes parked by the little airport building.

Inside the influential and the great are gathered. Father MacLellan is there too; he introduces us to the most powerful man in the Highlands and Islands, Bob Cowan, the Chairman of the Board.

'A big day for Ardveenish,' says Father Calum. 'The Board have been seeing what their money is going on.'

'Not another Breasclete,' I say jokingly.

The Board is rightly prickly about their most conspicuously expensive failure in the west. 'No, I don't think so. Not at all,' says Cowan, his glasses glinting in the sun. 'Anyway, we hope that we might get Breasclete started up sometime in the future.'

Ardveenish is a far more likely project. The big 23,000-square-foot, £2 million factory is being built a mile or so away from the cockle beach. If and when it gets into top gear it will be processing between 30,000 and 50,000 tons of Norway pout, sand eel and blue whiting a year into fishmeal and fish oil.

Lord Gray is with the group too, the former Minister of State for the Highlands and Islands who gave the go-ahead to the scheme the previous August. We have a chat, not about fishmeal, but about the best places to eat in round Inverness which is where he lives.

The pilot comes out of the Loganair office and everyone gets on the plane to fly off to Glasgow. Gus and Don Rangoon and I climb in the Mercedes to drive back to Clachan Beag.

'What do you think then? About Mingulay?'

'Well I'm not sure,' says Don. 'Up to yesterday you would have had no problem; we could have gone out in my own little boat. But we'd never make it in this weather. We'd *make* it all right but it would be very uncomfortable.'

Don Rangoon is the most optimistic of men; if *he's* doubtful have we made another wasted journey?

At the Clachan we turn to CEEFAX on the big TV set in the lounge. Force six it says. For those not up in the Beaufort Scale it goes like this:

3 *Gentle Breeze* Leaves and small twigs in constant motion; extends a light flag.

4 *Moderate Breeze* Raises dust and loose paper; small branches moved.

5 *Fresh Breeze* Small trees in leaf begin to sway; crested wavelets form on inland waters.

6 *Strong Breeze* Large branches in motion; whistling heard in telegraph wires; umbrellas used with difficulty.

And so it goes on and up through moderate gales (7), fresh gales (8), strong gales (9), and up to Force 12 hurricancs.

'We may get an Eight before it blows itself out. You can never tell at this time of the year. You see we're just coming into the equinoctial gale period – that's what you had last year, remember?'

We remember all right and we don't want an inaction replay of that.

'We'll wait and see but don't worry, I'll get you out there. If I could have just an hour or two in the eye of the storm we can be out and back with no trouble at all.'

Since we were last staying at the Clachan Don has built a cocktail lounge and we repair there to drink to a change in the weather. I am delighted to see that my old friend Donald Mackinnon is installed behind the bar. He was the only part of the old fixtures and fittings of the Isle of Barra Hotel which made it tolerable. Now Don Rangoon has lured him to the Clachan. During the day he is in charge of the Barra Council of Social Services and he is a fund of good stories and one-liners.

We are talking about who has the Gaelic and who doesn't and Donald says, wiping a glass, 'Did I ever tell you about the time Father Mackenzie went to Inverness to see if he could get some more money from the Council to repair the roads? In those days it was run by all these lairds and landowners, none of them had a scrap of Gaelic between them, and they were a bit contemptuous of this Gaelic-speaking priest from the islands; they didn't think that anyone who only spoke Gaelic deserved a road. "If you can give me the Gaelic for wireless," said one of them to Father William, "I'll give you some money for your roads!" That didn't put Father down one bit. "If you can give me the English for macaroni," says he, "I agree!"'

There's a laugh round the bar. Nobody in the islands has much time for Inverness and its big city ways.

'You won't believe this,' says Donald, 'but they were talking about Barra once at a Council meeting and one of these anglicised clowns says, "Ah yes, Barrow-in-Furness!"'

We don't believe Donald but it's a good story and there are plenty more.

The door bangs open and a gust of wind blows Archie Maclean into the bar. I'm hoping that he is going to take Gus and myself to Mingulay. Archie and his brother run the Barra Isles Sheep Stock Company which bought the southern islands in 1955 from Lady Grear. Seven crofters are involved and each of them has a seventh share in the profits. In a good year the investment pays off well. There are 800 breeding ewes altogether – 500 on Mingulay, 200 on Barra Head and 100 or so on Pabbay. Lambing time takes its toll: in a bad year the death rate with no shepherds around can be high. All year round silly sheep fall to their death from the crags – on Mingulay the cliffs drop a sheer 700 feet into the foaming sea below. Passing Dutchmen and other light-fingered fishermen come ashore and poach a few sheep for the galley, or so I'm told. But the overheads are low and the ewes with the co-operation of twelve attentive tups reproduce themselves and the flocks grow with no effort on anyone's part. Once a year the shareholders go out to the islands to collect the lambs for shipping to the September auction sale in Oban.

Archie and I repair to a corner of the lounge so that he can tell me exactly when to be ready to leap in the boat for Mingulay. But a bombshell awaits.

'We took the sheep off Mingulay on Monday,' he says drawing on his cigarette and looking me straight in the eye.

'You mean . . .?'

'Yes, we're finished with Mingulay and Barra Head for this year. All we've got to do now is Pabbay.'

Perhaps I could call the book *The Road to Pabbay*? I'll have to think of some other way of ending this journey. This is turning out to be a disappointing night in Barra. Bad weather, now bad news.

'The boat's coming from Oban late on Saturday night so if we're going to send the Pabbay sheep we'll have to get them off by Saturday.'

Archie is more than just a crofter. He studied at the West of Scotland Agricultural College at Auchencruive and then did four years at the Hannah Dairy Research Institute. The only full-time farmer on Barra, he has 200 acres, 200 ewes and 14 breeding cows and their followers. He grows oats and hay for winter feeding and supplements that with concentrates imported from the mainland. Archie sees farming on Barra as viable as farming anywhere else in Scotland. But he is quick to admit that rearing sheep a dozen miles out in the Atlantic and then having to ferry them across to Oban can be expensive.

'It's difficult to work out the cost because Calmac and Corsons the auctioneers work sort of hand in hand and, at the end of the day, when you have your final chitty the thing is broken down to transport, herd and keep, commission and the various expenses – on average, it works out at about £2 a head. Maybe this year we'll get £30 for the average lamb, that's two or three pounds down on last year.'

Archie has built a slaughterhouse with Board help near his croft just outside Castlebay, the first official one the island has had for 20 years or so. He reckons the Barra sheep have a delicate flavour you won't find in lamb reared on grass grown with artificial dressings and fertilisers.

'The benefit farmers have who buy store sheep from the isles is that when they take them down to lush grass in Perthshire or Aberdeen they just come on in leaps and bounds.'

Archie's parents and grandparents on both sides are Barra people. I asked him if he hadn't, with all the experience he'd gained on the mainland, any ambition to stay there?

'I might have had at the time but I had a calling back here to the home ground. I'm certainly not in a majority; very few of the lads I was at school with are here now, not in the crofting line anyway. There's George in the Castlebay Hotel, he's a contemporary of mine, Roddie down in the butcher's shop, but all the rest are at sea or on the rigs.'

Archie was attracted back to Barra because he wanted to prove that despite the poor soil and the unfavourable weather you could farm well on the island. But even he can see that dedication of that intensity doesn't appeal to everyone.

'These boys on the rigs are earning fantastic wages of £200 or £300 a week which in the farming line is unheard of. It's hard here. This has been a wonderful summer but last year I lost five acres of oats, completely washed out. I accept that because I think it's a question of carrying on, doing what your ancestors did before you. It's bred in you.'

While we talk the wind is howling round Clachan Beag. It is unseasonal for August but there's always tomorrow.

Tomorrow begins for me at four o'clock in the morning. I'm woken by the wind battling against the windows. When I go down to get the weather report two of Don Rangoon's guests, a GP and his wife from Sheffield, are peering anxiously out of the window. No sign of the *Claymore*, due in from Lochboisdale at eight.

'She'll be here any minute now,' says Don, lighting another cigarette. 'No problem with the *Claymore*.'

'But what about Mingulay?' I ask.

'Well you'd never land in this. Just look at the entrance to the harbour, you can see the waves out there.'

I certainly can. Rough stuff; not the day for a picnic on Mingulay at all. Don says we must keep our fingers crossed, anything can happen. It's stopped raining, which is a bonus, and fortified with Elizabeth's porridge and bacon and egg and strong hot tea I decide to walk down to the pier.

The *Claymore* arrives half an hour late, a squat side-loading car ferry which will take 5½ hours to make its way south-east to the tip of Coll, round the northern shore of Mull and into Oban Bay – and it won't be very calm.

I peer into the window of the Tourist Information Office and study the notices. The Perth Theatre Company was on tour with *Whisky Galore*, performing in the Castlebay School Hall a fortnight ago. They are subsidised by Dewar's Whisky, the Scottish Arts Council and the HIDB. A strange decision to bring that play of all plays to Barra. If I were acting in it I'd be petrified that my attempt at an island accent would be laughed off the stage.

Somebody had told me in the bar last night that if I wanted to hear about Mingulay the couple to talk to are the Macaulays. 'Donald Macaulay knows it better than anyone; he lives with his sister just past the doctor's,' and sure enough just past the pier and directly opposite Kisimul Castle is what must surely be the most photogenic dwelling in the Hebrides, not at all unlike the boat-shaped bothy that Fulton Mackay inhabited in *Local Hero*.

In front of what obviously was the family's old black house and byre, now artistically crowned with a chimney contrived from an old steamship's periscope-shaped ventilator, there is a more conventional dwelling. In the front garden which looks out to the MacNeil of Barra's castle is a collection of querns removed from Mingulay, a granite cheese press rescued from Barra Head and an elaborately carved ship's bench from the SS *Fair Branch*, a boat wrecked on Sandray in 1882 and owned by the Nautilus Steam Shipping Co. of Sunderland.

I tap discreetly on the open door. A dog appears wagging its tail and behind comes Morag Macaulay who should be in the *Guinness Book of Records*. She has worked continuously for 57 years as cleaner for the Royal Bank of Scotland in Castlebay, their longest-serving employee. Morag lives with her brother Calum, a tall and courtly man with a Roman nose and windswept rheumy eyes. She is white-haired and homely; he is grizzled, long-chinned, two monumental ears supporting a black beret.

'Your father', I say to Donald, 'knew my old and now dead friend Mr MacGregor the author?'

Donald selects a cigarette and lights it. If he has heard the question it makes but little impact. He lights the cigarette and inhales a deep draught.

Donald Macaulay senior had taken Alasdair to Mingulay and Berneray when he was the relieving officer for Barra Head lighthouse. 'Unquestionably', wrote Alasdair, 'one of the most interesting and intellectual men to be found throughout the entire length and breadth of the Western Isles.' 'We liked him,' Morag says drily, 'but he said too much in his book.'

I decide not to pursue the matter. I have been told that Morag possesses a lock of hair belonging to the Duke of Tarentum, Marshal of France, son of the famous Neil MacEachan of Howbeg in South Uist, protector of Bonnie Prince Charlie. It is a house full of memories, the Macaulay's.

Calum removes his cigarette with deliberation from his lips and proceeds to tell me about guillemots eggs. 'Very, very sharp at one end they are,' he says, 'and round at the other. They would put them in dry salt sharp end down because whenever the yellow got to the shell it would rot it and it would take a longer time to get into the sharp end.'

Morag pokes the fire. The dog yawns.

'And where are you staying?', asks Calum.

'At Don Rangoon's.'

'That's where the fillum people stayed,' says Calum, 'the big stars when they were making *Whisky Galore*.' They had come to Castlebay in 1948 and the island had never seen such times.

'Oh we were all in *Whisky Galore*,' says Morag. 'My mother, Calum and myself. In the eightsome reel I was holding Gordon Jackson's hand. And Joan Greenwood was here. I saw her on television the other day. She's got awfully old, the make-up, you know, spoils their faces.'

I said I'd heard stories that even the hens were drunk on Eriskay and every family held open house.

People exaggerate a lot; they were saying they had fur coats milking the cows. Rubbish! Nobody looked at the fur coats it was all the cases of whisky and there's a lot buried yet . . . but you see *they didn't mark it!*'

Donald shakes his head sadly. 'The one with the lead seals would be no good but the "Johnnie Walker" with the cork would be all right.'

No bottles have turned up for years but the stories still circulate, a part of Hebridean folklore now. And they still tell stories of the 'fillum' folk and their strange behaviour.

'There was', says Donald, 'this man who lived with his widowed mother in a thatched house, beautiful it was. And she was about eighty odd years of age and she was sitting on a stone with a big shawl. And this photographer, he was one of the fillums, was taking what they call long shots. And he wanted to get some shots of his own and he had this camera strapped round him. And he said, "Good morning, ma," and she said, "Good morning," and the son was up against the door having a lazy smoke. "Who's the dear old lady?" "My mother." And he got his camera ready and the son was eyeing him up all the time. Now the term they had was "All ready for shooting". "Do you mind if I shoot your mother?" "Shoot my mother you English b———!"' Calum collapses into laughter. 'He knew very well what the fillum man meant but he wasn't letting on!'

The Macaulays were almost hereditary attendant boatmen to the Barra Head lighthouse which was built in 1833 on Berneray. I notice that in Castlebay everyone refers to Berneray as Barra Head, probably to avoid confusion with Berneray, Harris, or Great Bernera in Loch Roag.

'My grandfather went for forty years back and forth to Barra Head,' says Morag, 'then my father went for forty years.' And Mingulay? 'Oh, Mingulay, yes. There were forty families in Mingulay at one time. Mr Finlayson was the teacher then he stayed there for forty years and never left the place.'

One feels that Morag measures life in Biblical decades of four – more to suggest a substantial number than to convey complete accuracy. Like Mr Finlayson, Morag in her 72 years has seldom left the island and never ever been to the mainland. 'No, I'm a bad sailor. It would be desperate going to Mingulay today. You're not going today?'

'Well,' I said, putting a bold face on it, 'if the opportunity presented itself I wouldn't say no.' Morag said that I would have to watch myself. Even when people go for trips there's a lot of them have broken legs but there's a lovely beach there. All the old people from Mingulay had wonderful memories but then they had to; there was no radio or television but they could tell you the weather much better than they tell you today.'

'Did they eat well out there?' I asked Morag.

'Well they had the sea birds, the puffins you know. The older men used to say it took six hours to boil them. Then of course you could put them in a pan and roast them, they're very tasty that way. And they made soup of oatmeal and onion and they had brose with oatmeal and sugar and you could have a whisky with it. We're too well off today, the young ones they won't take this and they won't take that – they're not hungry that's why. But it was different in the old days. They had no peat on Mingulay so they took it from Barra and for their cruisie light they used cuddy oil.'

Morag is not at all sure that the modern amenities of Barra have improved life all that much. 'They have the Puffin Grill now and too many bars. The whist drives I like, we go every week, but I'm sorry for the people who come here for the first time and it's wet weather and there's nowhere for them to go.'

She and Calum belong to the 23-strong Church of Scotland, a small Protestant presence in this flamboyantly Catholic island. 'There's no trouble at all, we mix well together. The Catholic church had a sale of work in July and they made £7,000 and then a month later we had one and made £1,000, they all came, they're good to us.'

The stove is giving off a radiant heat; it is cast iron, the kind of bygone that would excite shrill cries of delight in the King's Road. 'It cost £3,' says Morag, 'that's all it cost.' She gives Djilas the sheepdog a passing pat and the ginger cat leaps on her lap: 'This is Manx, she was born with three and a half legs.'

'They were marvellous people on Mingulay,' Donald says, flicking ash into the fire, 'in a hundred years not one person drowned on the way from Barra to Mingulay!'

We talked of the evacuation and the move to Vatersay and Barra and Donald cast an eye out of the window. 'Well,' he said, 'one thing for sure, the east wind would hold you back today.'

Back at the Clachan Don Rangoon has better news. He's been on the phone and persuaded someone called Donnie Maclean to take us to Mingulay. 'He didn't want to go at all but I told him you were anxious to get there.' That will turn out to be an expensive confidence.

'He said to be down at the pier at 12; so that's you organised.'

Gus goes upstairs to load his cameras and I ask Don about the filming of *Whisky Galore*. 'Morag Macaulay said they all stayed here?'

'Well not all of them, a lot of them put up in the Castlebay Hotel but they couldn't take them all so Mr Mackendrick who was in charge asked us if we would open up the house and we did and they were here all summer coming and going, Basil Radford, James Robertson Justice, all of them.'

'And Compton Mackenzie was part of it?'

'Yes, he played the part of the ship's captain, but he filmed that down in Pinewood I think; a lot of it was done down there. They had a ship up here got up like the *Polly* but it was wrecked in a gale so they made one down in the film studios.'

During the making of *Whisky Galore* Compton and his wife Chrissie came to Barra and stayed with the Coddie, John Macpherson at Northbay. In his autobiography Compton remembered that as his last visit to Barra. 'I cannot', he wrote towards the end of his life, 'bring myself to go back there and look round in vain for so many much loved friends.'

One of those much loved friends was there to welcome him on the occasion of his final flight into Barra on Friday 1 December 1972. Ironically for a man who had made such headlines in his life, there was only one journalist at the graveside and that was Brian Wilson, fledgling editor of the *West Highland Free Press*, then in its seventh struggling month.

Brian had been asked by the Board to go to Barra and write an article for them about the problems facing Vatersay. On the way to Barra he read in the *Glasgow Herald* of Compton Mackenzie's death and his last request that he be buried in Barra. By the time the plane, an old Heron, came in to land on the Traigh Mhor it was blowing a gale and over the weekend the weather got worse and worse.

By Monday the seas were so rough that the ferry didn't sail and the scheduled flight from Glasgow was also cancelled. That left Wilson a lone journalist on Barra. He told me how that stormy Monday went.

'The coffin and and chief mourners were just able to make a landing on a charter flight. In the most ferocious weather conditions about a hundred people had gathered on the beach to meet the plane. Compton Mackenzie had been a popular figure. As Katie Macpherson of BEA told me, "he fitted perfectly well into the classless society of our island". The coffin was transferred to the mini-bus which normally served as an ambulance and the procession then headed straight for Eoligarry cemetery, two miles away. To reach the burial place involved a pretty steep climb.'

When the coffin was being unloaded from the plane the tall figure of Calum Johnston had stepped forward to play the lament. Calum was one of the island's most distinguished tradition-bearers, an old friend of Compton Mackenzie's, and in his 82nd year. 'But for such a poignant occasion', Brian told me, 'he was not prepared to compromise with the weather. He wore the kilt and no coat. Now as the procession climbed the hill and into the teeth of the storm he produced his pipes again and drew from them a mournful wail. The graveside service was conducted by Father Angus MacQueen and lasted less than ten minutes. The mourners headed for their cars but as he reached the bottom of the hill Calum Johnston collapsed. When I arrived back at the warmth of Castlebay Hotel the word had come through that Calum had died before reaching his home in Eoligarry. On Wednesday in weather conditions that came close to being a repetition of those on Monday Calum Johnston was laid to rest in Eoligarry cemetery alongside his old friend. The pipes were played by his nephew, Roderick Campbell.'

It is perhaps ironic too that of the scores of serious books Compton Mackenzie wrote, the one that made his lasting fame on film and television was his lightweight farce about life on Barra – *Whisky Galore.*

By the time Gus and I reached down to the pier things have taken a turn for the better; the sun is shining and the wind seems to be dropping. A bearded figure in a sports jacket and flannels with a plastic bag and a dog on a lead is picking up cigarette packets and crisp packets from the grass beside the slip. An eccentric; certainly not a local.

'You're a very public-spirited man,' I say.

'I can't bear all this rubbish!' The accents are English middle-class, 'Such a lovely island and nobody gives a damn about litter. They just don't seem to care.' He grabs an old pack of Embassy, a lemonade can and a crumpled paper bag. A strange way to spend a holiday. 'Well it's not really a holiday, I'm doing a locum for the GP Dr Bickle. May as well do my bit to see that Barra wins a prize in that contest thing – have you heard about it?'

I had indeed. Earlier that year the British Tourist Authority had chosen Barra as their entry for the Most Beautiful Island in the World competition. The *Glasgow Herald* sent their reporter Anne Johnston to see what chances the island stood and she wasn't impressed. She told her readers about the rubbish she'd seen and the rusting skeletons of old cars, 'hardly a desirable qualification for the most beautiful island in the world'.

Although Barra has a dustcart there's no roadsweeper and maybe that's why in a survey conducted by the Barra Tourist Association they found that 95 per cent of visitors complained about litter and the abandoned wrecks of cars. It's easy if you are motivated by the codes of urban cleanliness to pick up toffee papers but what do you do about your old car when you've cannibalised the usable bits? It becomes a nesting place for hens and cats, somewhere for the children to play, not so much an offence to the eye as part of the domestic scenery. There it lies beside the peatstack, one door gone, no bonnet, with eyeless headlamps gazing out to the hills – annoying no one except 95 per cent of all the passing tourists and the occasional reporter from the big city.

In the nineteenth century there was very little rubbish. Thatched roofs, when they became dank with soot, were forked as fertiliser into the lazybeds; when fishing boats outlived their usefulness the timbers were recycled into a roof and what was too rotten to convert into furniture was burnt. Ropes made of heather or hemp were all bio-degradable and in the fullness of time they vanished back into the ground. Flour sacks could be made into clothes;

nothing was allowed to lie about unused. When coconuts, tree trunks and ship's spars were cast up on a beach they were quickly seized and carried off.

Then came the Galvanised Iron Age, the Brass Bedstead Age and the Plastics Age – indestructible products of the industrial and consumer society. Every tide brings another unwanted cargo of blue fertiliser bags, orange nylon netting, unsinkable polystyrene fish boxes, rubber boots and Fairy Liquid containers. How do you cope with all that? And how do you dispose of a holed fibreglass boat?

The problem of rubbish has been compounded by the built-in obsolescence of practically everything a crofter imports. The detritus grows yearly: old TV sets, the ruins of a plywood caravan wrecked in a winter gale, a blown-down corrugated iron lean-to, a derelict tractor, a defunct Hoovermatic washing machine. From my notebook I find this inventory of 'things' conspicuously surrounding a fairly average crofthouse in Lewis. I list them not necessarily in descending order either of size or interest:

> 5 cwt van (*circa* 1950s); Ford tractor minus one wheel; fragment of pre-Great War reaper; upright piano; 37 blue plastic fishboxes; 7 green lemonade crates; 2 chimney pots; a sizeable pyramid of sand; a pile of cement blocks; 7 lobster creels; assorted timber; 2 bales of barbed wire (rusted); broken garden seat; Hercules bicycle frame; piece of unidentifiable machinery (loom?); a sofa.

The impact of all this was considerable – a rich field of study for the social anthropologist and a challenge to the eye.

Had it all been carted away the landscape, which with the best will in the world one could hardly describe as anything less than bleak, would have lost much of its curiosity. On mature consideration I'll live with the litter and the rusty old cars – at least it makes an arresting focal point for the eye.

The focal point of Castlebay is not new and certainly not offensive. It consists of a great pile of blackened masonry rising from a rock a few hundred yards from the shore. Kisimul was the stronghold of the MacNeils of Barra until they moved ashore in the eighteenth century first to Borve, then to Vaslin and finally to Eoligarry House. Eoligarry is now a pile of rubble but Kisimul, destroyed by fire in the 1790s, has, thanks to American money, been reroofed.

General MacNeil, the 41st chief, sold Barra to Gordon of Cluny in 1858 and when he died in 1863 the line effectively ended. But in 1915 Robert Lister of Canada successfully proved his right to the chiefship in the Court of the Lord Lyon in Edinburgh. An architect by profession, he acquired the estate of Barra and the ruins of the castle in 1937 and by the time he died in 1970 most of the work of restoration was completed. The present chief, Ian R. MacNeil, a lawyer, uses the castle as his holiday home and had just left after a three-week stay.

This American influence in Barra is quite a powerful one. Compton Mackenzie's mother was American; John Lorne Campbell's mother was American too and he reinforced the links by marrying a girl from Pennsylvania, Margaret Fay Shaw, who became a leading authority on Gaelic folklore and song.

During the war the present chief's mum, the widow of an American army officer, wrote from New York to President Roosevelt asking him to send rifles to Barra to arm the people against invasion. An even dafter scheme was the fund which Mr and Mrs MacNeil started in New York to have 500 children evacuated from Glasgow to Barra. It angered Compton Mackenzie, who clearly saw himself as a much more natural and rational chief of Barra than either of the MacNeils. He pointed out that there were already 470 children at the six island schools and an influx of 500 extra non-Gaelic-speaking children, apart from the fact that there was nowhere for them to sleep, would create chaos. He wrote a curt letter to Marie MacNeil:

> your plan would be so utterly disastrous if carried out that I cannot temper my words. I realise how very difficult it is to grasp in America what the conditions are here but having upon my shoulders the defence of Barra against a hostile landing I must beg you to accept my assurance that I shall use every particle of influence I possess to prevent what in the circumstances would be nothing short of a criminal piece of folly.

Suitably chastised the MacNeils piped down for the duration. Waiting for Donnie Maclean to turn up, I saw a boat being readied at the slip by a former Shell tanker skipper, Captain Donald Patrick Sinclair, who looks after the castle in the Chief's absence. He's going to take two visitors out to look at the castle; we join them.

The oak door of the castle is modern and there is a strong smell as we step into the courtyard. 'Rails and other woodwork in the castle are creosoted', says a notice, 'which can easily rub off on clothes.' There's another friendly notice which invites you to introduce yourself if you are a MacNeil: 'don't look for a kilt we're more likely to be in working clothes.'

The MacNeil's private quarters are locked but we peer into the chapel and the dungeon and climb up to the watch tower. There was very little left of Kisimul when the work of reconstruction began and the interior has the same feel as the castle of Eilean Donan in Loch Duich, itself a clever re-creation done in the 1920s. As in Eilean Donan, some of the bygones on display, genuine as they are, have only a tenuous connection with the castle itself. There are some Welsh tin Communion cups dating from the eighteenth century which once did service in the Church of Scotland on Barra, a Victorian spinning wheel, a collection of English pikes and muskets from Culloden and an indifferent painting of Loch Awe done by the 44th Chief in 1910.

Although the strong smell of creosote and the modern asphalting on the roof don't immediately conjure up past glories, we're lucky to have a castle to walk round at all. In the late 1860s Colonel Gordon's factor let the place as a herring-curing station and the chapel in the west corner was broken up and taken away as ballast for boats. 'The native people,' wrote Alexander Carmichael in 1883, 'who still fondly cling to the memory of their once proud chiefs, were grieved at the destruction they were powerless to prevent.'

Unless the native people had very short memories, I find it hard to believe that they had any fond memories of the last chief. They may have had folk memories of happier times in the ancient past but the last MacNeil, General Roderick who succeeded his father in 1822, was a new-style absentee landlord interested solely, judging from his correspondence with the Rev. Angus MacDonald the island's priest (reprinted in *The Book of Barra*, edited by John Lorne Campbell, Routledge, 1936), in getting as much out of the island and its people as he could.

On 30 July 1825 he wrote from 34 Montague Square in London to Father Angus telling him that he thought his parishioners 'from their fickleness, idleness and stiff-necked prejudice' were behaving like 'spoilt children'. The priest was commanded to read from his pulpit on the very first Sunday after receiving it the following ultimatum:

> You will tell the kelpers that they have earned my utmost displeasure. They have not obeyed my orders – nor the order of those by me set over them which I consider as disrespectful to me as it is disgraceful to them.
>
> Say to the fishermen that their audacity and base ingratitude has quite disgusted me. That if they do not within eight and forty hours after this proclamation bend their energies to the daily prosecution of their calling as fishermen, I shall turn every man of them off the Island were they steeped to the ears in debt – tell them also that since they have shown themselves so unworthy of that interest which in my heart I

felt for them, I shall follow out my plans without in the most trifling degree consulting their feelings or prejudice.

Say to those who are about to emigrate that I sincerely wish them well through it and assure those who have signed and repented that their repentance comes too late – So help me God, they shall go, at all events off my property, man, woman and child. Tell the people once and for all, that I shall consider any act of inattention to the orders of my factor Mr Stewart as an impertinence to myself. Nor shall any one who dares even to hesitate to obey him remain on my property should his, or their character [have] been even so good previously.

A week later he was again writing to Father Angus to leave him in no doubt about what would happen if the natives continued in their slothful insubordination:

They are of little or no importance to me whatever may be their value to you and if I don't on my arrival find them heart and hand engaged in fishing, *I pledge you my honour* they shall tramp and the Land shall be this ensuing spring occupied by *strangers*.

MacNeil was as good as his word. His harsh attitude to the people – 500 of them emigrated rather than submit to this ruthless oppression – is tactfully not mentioned in the official history of Kisimul written by the present American chief. He talks only of Gordon of Cluny ('one of the more notorious of Highland landlords') who bought the estates in 1838 from the bankrupted Chief's trustees. But MacNeil himself had created the cowed and impoverished peasantry inherited by Gordon.

It is fashionable these days to see the old clan chiefs as dignified and gentle men overwhelmed by circumstances beyond their control, anxious only to do their best for the children of the clan. General Roderick is a notable exception to any such romantic vision. A bully on a grandiose and psychotic scale, he entertained only contempt for his people. 'I must have fishers and kelpers', he wrote to the priest on another occasion, 'who will cheerfully do my bidding. Every man my good sir has a right to do the best he can for himself in his own affairs – if one set of servants (tenants at will, are nothing else) won't do, the master must try others.' I'm sure Ian R. MacNeil is wise to be reticent about his ancestor – having a monster like that in your clan closet must make family gatherings to celebrate happy days of yore slightly questionable.

Seditious thoughts to entertain as I wander round this enterprising attempt to recreate the past, trying to work out what is original and what is an import of the 1960s. The lintel above the window in the barrack room was brought back from Mingulay when it was evacuated and given to the chief by Morag and Calum Macaulay; the slate on the roof is modern and the beams in the Great Hall are railway sleepers. As castles go it's a bit of a disappointment; it is not easy to imagine that from these walls a trumpet would sound once a day and a clansman would proclaim to the world: 'Hear, o ye people and listen o ye nations. The great MacNeil of Barra having finished his meal the princes of the earth may dine.'

We'd had no lunch at all and by one o'clock were feeling peckish and cheesed off. Where was Donnie Maclean? We went back to the Clachan to see if we could rouse him on the phone. No one was replying. Don Rangoon is getting testy. 'There's two other people I could try, it's a long shot but I'll go and see if I can find them. If we had left at midday we would have been there by now.' Don sets off on foot to the pier.

The problem seems to be that nobody wants to go; those who might have taken us have already gone off to lift their lobster creels and those who are left don't share Don's belief that even if we went we could go ashore. The rocks are very slippery and in high seas you could, as Morag said, easily break a leg.

While Don is rushing round Castlebay looking for a boatman we glumly study the CEEFAX weather report. It's still talking about Force 6 winds although out in the Bay the seas seem to have calmed and the thin gauze of rain masking Vatersay is slowly thinning. Beyond, through the binoculars, I can see the grey misty blur of Macphee's Hill twelve miles away on Mingulay, as indistinct as a mirage and, at this time of the afternoon, about as accessible.

Donald Macaulay had told me the story of Macphee. Evidently long ago there was no news from Mingulay for months on end. Out of curiosity MacNeil despatched a boat to find out what was going on. One of the sailors, a Macphee, scrambed ashore and found that everyone on the island had died, seemingly of the plague. Macphee, a simple-minded man, shouted the news from the shore and that was a great mistake. Fearful of catching the disease, the crew hoisted sail and Macphee was marooned on the island of corpses. He lived on seaware and shellfish and spent most of his time sitting on the 735-foot high summit of his eponymous hill looking hopefully for a boat.

The story, as is the way of all good stories, has a happy ending. After a year and a day Macphee was uplifted from the island and when it was repopulated he was given a good piece of land to compensate him for the callous way he'd been treated.

There's no compensation when Don gets back to the Clachan. 'Can't find a soul. It's too bad, we could have got there with no trouble at all. The wind's dropping every minute.'

'I'll try Donnie Maclean again,' I say and dial but without much hope; he said he would come and didn't, so I can only assume he has lost interest. He answers the phone.

'We waited for you,' I say.

'Couldn't get the car to start. Do you still want to go?'

'Of course I want to go, that's why I'm in Barra.'

'Well I'll come down and we can talk about it,' and Donnie puts the phone down.

'I don't want to *talk* about it,' I tell Don, 'I want to get in the boat and go.'

After a while Donnie and his mate Roddie Macintyre turn up in an old van ready to talk about it. The gist of Donnie's argument is that it's an awful day out there and we wouldn't enjoy it and when we got there it would be far too rough to land. Donnie looks a bit frail, not at all like a man ready to go 24 miles in rough seas to please a patent lunatic.

'We'll land all right,' says Don Rangoon, pulling the rank of all those years on the bridge at sea.

'I tell you what,' I say to Donnie, 'you take me there and if we can't land that's my problem not yours.'

'How much do you want to go?' asks Donnie and the conversation takes a mercenary turn. What he wants to know is how I'm going to twist his arm.

'I need', I say, 'to get to Mingulay today. It's as simple as that.' Donnie looks at Roddie and Roddie raises his eyebrows at Donnie.

'Well,' says Donnie, taking a deep breath, 'it'll cost you.'

Don Rangoon is gazing nervously out of the window whistling through his teeth.

'OK,' I says expansively like the last of the big spenders, 'how much?'

My hands are metaphorically raised high in the air. Donnie, like a high flying poker player makes his outrageous bid.

'A hundred pounds.'

The sum hangs in the air. Don Rangoon breathes in deeply, a measured susurration of disbelief. But Donnie is making me an offer I can't refuse.

'If you want to go that's what it will cost but it's up to you; I'd just as soon not go. You decide.'

'Right. Let's go,' I say.

'Right,' says Roddie.

'Right,' says Donnie, 'give us twenty minutes.'

Don Rangoon decides to come with us. At least when he's an old man he'll be able to say he went on the most reckless and expensive boat trip ever made to Mingulay.

When the three of us get down to the pier Donnie and Roddie are hauling in the anchor of their fibreglass lobster boat which is moored in the bay. Thirty-six feet long, with a deep working well for hauling creels, it has a wheelhouse for'ard and powerful engines. We're off immediately, heading for the thirty-yard wide gap between the east end of Vatersay and the small islet of Uinessan.

'Sorry about the smell,' says Donnie. The fishboxes and the bilge are giving off an oily stink of stale fish. The bows begin to crash into the heavy seas as we gain the open sea outside the bay. It's going to be retching weather.

Donnie tells me he used to sell space for a newspaper in Glasgow; he came back to Barra to go lobster fishing but he's thinking of starting up in business selling equipment to fish farmers. I tell him that with his entrepreneurial instincts he should do well. We banter lightheartedly. He is a bit embarrassed to have Don Rangoon on board. Don knows what the going rate for a trip to Mingulay is and £100 is a slight touch of robbery in the afternoon.

'Did you bring a carry out?', says Donnie to relax the tension.

'For £100 I thought *you'd* bring the carry out,' I say, 'Bollinger preferably!' Donnie, who is looking a little dehydrated, takes a big swig from a litre bottle of Pepsi Cola. Roddie grins. As we break out into the Sound of Sandray the waves get wilder. Gus goes white and thoughtful.

'The only rough bit will be the Sound of Pabbay,' says Don, 'but it won't bother us. I could never have done it in my boat.'

There's rain coming down and spray breaking over the bow; a wet passage. Donnie tells me there's an Englishman called Colin Archer who has bought the old priest's house on Mingulay. 'He was teaching in Strasbourg or somewhere like that. I used to ferry him out when he came here for his holidays. He's working in the Middle East now.'

'With the price Donnie charges for a boat trip,' says Roddie, "he just had to go and work for the Sheikhs." We all laugh. Donnie takes another assuaging swig of the Pepsi.

We pass the thousand-acre island of Sandray on which in the eighteenth century there were nine small farms. In 1911 there were still 41 people on Sandray and 20 left at the beginning of the 1930s when it was finally evacuated. Coming up on the starboard now, Pabbay is smaller and rockier but it too supported in the 1880s 26 people. In 1901 there were only 11 and in 1911 hardly more than a family. This must have been subsistence living at its most primitive, particularly in the winter when for weeks on end it would have been impossible to launch a boat. The coastline of Pabbay, the Priest's Isle, is sandy; it looks a good place to picnic.

To the west there is nothing but 2,000 miles of sea rolling all the way to Labrador and Newfoundland. The seas are still heavy and I begin to wonder, as I see Mingulay drawing closer, whether legs are going to be broken. You could land on the beach in a dinghy but Donnie's boat draws too much water for that. We move south of Mingulay Bay to the slippery and rounded rocks of Hecla Point. At 4.40 p.m. Donnie cuts the engines and we drift closer and closer in.

Mingulay is the biggest of all these southern islands. At its broadest it is 1½ miles wide and 2½ miles from north to south. It is raining gently as our bow nudges against the elephant-grey seaweed-smooth rock face. Jumping is the way to do it but carefully; then cautiously up the slippery surface to the top of the cliffs.

It's been a long journey to the soft green grass of Mingulay and the soft warm August rain.

The first building we see is the old schoolhouse, boarded up and surrounded now by the fank in which a week ago the sheep were penned before being taken off to Barra. Their black droppings litter the ground. On the hill the breeding ewes graze and the sea birds wheel.

The western edge of the island is a stark drop to the sea, a dizzy bird colony almost as dramatic as St Kilda's. The young men of Mingulay used to snare guillemots and razor-bills in nooses held out on the end of bamboo rods. Here and on the neighbouring island of Berneray, which is the true southern limit of the archipelago, they would take the seafowl and salt them with burnt kelp and preserve them in cow's hides against putrefaction.

The schoolhouse, built in the 1880s by the Free Church Ladies' Association, stands overlooking Mingulay Bay and the clachan or village where at one time 150 people lived. A cart road runs down the hill to the ruins below. All the dwellings are now unthatched and the timbers gone, probably taken when the people removed to Vatersay and Barra before the First World War.

I've been on many deserted Hebridean islands but none has so powerful a feeling of humanity about it as Mingulay. The houses are so close one to another that you can almost catch the hum of conversation, see the peat smoke rising, hear the lowing of cattle and the cries of children playing. In the seventy years since the islanders left, the sands have engulfed the walls and risen in dunes where once people slept and told stories and spun wool. It is an idyllic spot with a golden quarter mile of wide beach falling gently to the sea. Above on the hill is the priest's house with its chapel on an upper floor. This is the only house in Mingulay which is now secure against the rain and the wind. There's a pile of plasterboard inside, some of the walls have been stripped, floorboards are up – work in progress. The mantelpieces are stocked with empty bottles of whisky.

But it's the village which gives off a strong almost numinous feel. A few concrete crosses lie broken in what must have been the burial ground; nettles cover door openings; your boots sink into the sand which rises in places almost to the top of the five foot thick walls. Everywhere rabbits are rushing around; no latter-day Macphee would starve here.

The only account I can find of what it would have been like to land in Mingulay on an August day a hundred years ago is a lecture reprinted in the *Helensburgh and Gareloch Times*. It was delivered by a Mrs Murray under the auspices of the Church of Scotland Literary and Scientific Society.

Mrs Murray had been fortunate enough to cruise with her husband in a 45-ton schooner, the *Aglaia*, to the Outer Hebrides. The one person on the island who was not a Catholic was the English schoolmaster, who Mrs Murray reported with unconscious irony, 'is busy with his English standards and methodical training to turn this remote and interesting island into as commonplace a village as any in our own neighbourhood.' She wandered through the village and noted that 'Red Indian wigwams or Hottentot kraals could hardly be more destitute of everything which we are to consider essential to decency and comfort.' This is how she described one of the houses after a closer inspection:

> An old woman at her time-blackened spinning-wheel, sitting on a lump of the naked rock beside the peat fire, which is burning brightly without smoke, in the middle of the floor; two children healthy and brown beside her, playing with a kitten, a hen mother and some chickens foraging for themselves over the clay floor; a small pig scratching his apparently clean little back under the bench of driftwood supported by turf on which we were sitting. A little table but no dresser; one small chair, one three-legged pot and a kettle not to omit the never-failing friend of every old wife in the kingdom, the brown teapot standing by the fire.

What more? A quern or handmill on the table, in daily use still in an island where there is no population to support a miller and where the meal is still prepared by two women grinding it painfully in this way. Three stout kists, the property of the girls of the family who had just returned from the fishing at Peterhead. This is about all.

Most of the houses have separate byres which are cleaned out twice a year but this dwelling was one in which the cows were tied up along with the family in the same end of the cottage in four stalls between the fire and the door. During our visit the cattle were in the fields but there was plenty of evidence to show where they lodged at night.

In spite of this and similar defiances of the laws of sanitation and the fact that a doctor is never to be had at all and also that their food is coarse and poor, the people in Mingulay are healthy, and long-lived.

They had not, according to Mrs Murray, paid a penny of rent to the beneficent Lady Gordon Cathcart for twelve years and they had plenty to spend on tea, whisky and tobacco.

'They must have been tough,' said Don Rangoon, 'to have survived here.'

There is a stillness now, the wind has dropped. Up on the hill you can see the outlines of the old fields where the bere, rye, oats and potatoes were grown. There were ponies too on this bird island but no natural harbour and that must have been one of the determining factors that led to the decision to remove.

We walk up the old grass-grown road back to the point in silence and scramble down the rocks and on to the waiting boat.

Five or six weeks later I get a phone call from the bank. 'We've got a cheque here for a hundred pounds made out to a Mr Maclean. It seems to have been in the water. Is it to go through?'

'Yes,' I say, 'I hired a boat to go to Mingulay.'

'Mandalay? That's a long way away!'

So indeed is Mingulay.

14

CEARTAS – A SPECIAL CASE?

There is nothing more dispiriting than a deserted landscape; Mingulay was a sad climax to my journey through the islands – those ruined houses, the grass-grown cart track down to the silent village, the nettled hillside which had once produced corn for a community of a hundred and more, abandoned for ever.

My jaunt began in August 1983 and ended in September 1984, a long time to cover a distance no further than from Lincoln to London. You could get comfortably from the Butt of Lewis to Barra by car and ferry in less than a day, but then I wasn't in a hurry. I had, after all, been waiting almost 50 years to go to Mingulay and another few months wasn't going to put me up or down.

So I did the journey in stages; a week here and a week there, taking it as it came, gathering impressions. I was of course impressed by the size of the islands in relation to the few people who live there – seven times larger than the Isle of Wight with only about a quarter of the population. And because most of the people are housed in Stornoway, Tarbert, Lochmaddy, Balivanich, Daliburgh, Lochboisdale and Castlebay, the surrounding countryside looks all the more uninhabited. The almost total absence of woodland adds to the air of barren sterility. Some parts seem all peat and bog, others all rock.

One is struck by the small extent to which in the last 4,000 years man's improving hand has been raised to any lasting effect. The monumental profusion of temples, tombs and palaces in Egypt, Greece and Rome in pre-Christian times have no echoes here; no glories of previous civilisations or hints of vanished grandeur. The only historic relic of architectural art in the Western Isles is St Clement's church at Rodel with its superb carved sixteenth-century stonework.

It might well be that the environment was so discouraging, the struggle for survival so unremitting, that there was no instinctive need to leave behind any memorials to the creative spirit. Lichen-covered standing stones, a few piles of rubble marking the site of some uncouth fortification or cairn, is about all the eye falls on in the way of archaeology. The Georgian splendours of Edinburgh are not represented here and even the florid certainties of the Victorian era bequeathed only the ugly pastiche of Lews Castle and a few shooting lodges remarkable solely for their incongruity.

The makeshift hovels of the crofters and cottars which shocked visitors in the nineteenth century were the markers of a society entirely lacking in the pursuit of comfort, aesthetic satisfaction or material self-improvement. The smoke-infested thatched black house which lumped humans and cattle together in conditions of appalling filth was the most primitive and deprived form of dwelling in the whole of Europe.

The genius of the islands certainly didn't manifest itself in the visual arts – no painting, no sculpture, no peasant skills other than the making of tools and implements and the weaving of tweed. The craft shops which litter the islands now with their Celtic jewellery and corn dollies have no more to do with the spirit of the place than a visiting folk group or a passing fish and chip van.

There were on the other hand unique social patterns; co-operative endeavour in the face of a hostile climate and a bleak terrain; fiercely strong ties of kinship, an almost mystical preoccupation with the mythical past and an immensely imaginative oral tradition of story-telling, song, verse and anecdote. People had plenty of time to rehearse their past. Living in close-knit communities they had plenty of time too to study the personality virtues and defects of their neighbours.

The peculiarly Gaelic capacity for observation and introspection is lost on those who have no Gaelic. It is becomingly increasingly lost too as English becomes the preferred language for conversation and the prosecution of day-to-day life even for fluent Gaelic-speakers.

It has been suggested that a conservation strategy should be applied to Gaelic just as it is to the preservation of the osprey. An opportunity to create a Gaelic reserve occurred when Comhairle nan Eilean took over in 1975. Stornoway now has its own Gaelic radio station and its Gaelic publishing house, but the commitment is a half-hearted one; English has penetrated into the islands from the most shallow to the deepest level.

Of the 38 doctors currently practising only three have Gaelic. As one old man said to me, referring to a house visit he had just had from an Asian doctor: 'Even on my deathbed I shall have to describe my state of health in English!' It's a bit crazy when you come to think of it that a speaker of one of the oldest tongues in the western world should be forced to communicate in moments of intimate stress in his second language to a stranger who himself may be using English as a second language. It makes you wonder what has happened to all those high-flown freedoms set out in the United Nations charter – not much freedom of language here.

The desperate enthusiasm for Gaelic and Gaelic culture exhibited by some highly educated incomers can in many ways be counter-productive. There is a deep-seated suspicion of strangers, however well-intentioned they may appear to be, and persons of forceful character bent on doing good can find themselves arousing the darkest kind of resentment. I spent a day with a non-Scottish Celt who had worked in the islands for over 30 years; he had persevered with Gaelic, interested himself in local affairs, stood up for local interests and generally striven with some success to improve the lot of the community. He appeared to me to be a selfless sort of chap. I mentioned him to an islander whose intellect I respect. 'Him!' was the reaction, 'he's the *ultimate* white settler.'

Those non-islanders who make the running publicly, men or women who marry into an island community and bring their own mainland values to bear on local issues, often find themselves confronted with a closing of ranks and a chilling indifference which they may construe as apathy. It is seldom apathy; more an intelligent suspicion of those whose values and ambitions may create unwelcome conflict.

There is also a healthy and often abrasive suspicion of anyone, even a local, who seems to be presenting himself to outsiders as being more knowledgeable about what's going on than anyone else. I was on my way one afternoon to talk to a fisherman whom I had been told was one of the bright hopes of the place. I stopped at a house to find out where he lived. A distinguished-looking man followed a barking sheep dog to the door. Oh yes, he knew where Angus lived and what would I be wanting with Angus? I told him. Angus, said the man with great authority knew *nothing* about these matters, Angus was only a boy, he'd only been at the fishing for a few months. I would be far better off talking to Kenny. Kenny knew all about it; Kenny would put me right. I said that Angus had been suggested to me by a development officer. 'What does *he* know about it?' asked the man. 'He knows nothing about this place.' 'He told me', I said, 'that his mother came from here.' 'Did he?' said the man, 'Is that what he said?' and he looked at me with pity. When I found Angus he told me a great deal about fishing but I still wonder what Kenny would have told me. Something quite different?

'A real chancer!' said one man of another whose analysis of the cultural problems confronting the Western Isles seemed to me to make sense. Not infrequently when I was about to leave somewhere I would be told that I had missed the one man who could unlock all mysteries. 'You mean you haven't contacted Calum? Now that's a pity, Calum would have put you right.' Everyone wanted me to be put right but everyone had their own idea about who was the best person to do it.

I knew from experience that there was more than a chance that Calum would turn out to be a person of advanced age with a relentless memory for stories about fairies and witches and improbable instances of second sight. The inference, when it came out in conversation that I was collecting material for a book, was that it must be a book about the past. People would kindly point out where I could see an old dun or broch or the cave where somebody hid in Jacobite times. Was it imagination or did I get the feeling that there was a yearning for the past; that events then were of more profound importance than they are now; that people were possessed of greater stature, wit, wisdom and *character*?

'You don't get the old characters now,' said a man who himself was patently already a 'character' and afforded by his community the status if not of a *seanachaidh* or bard then certainly a tradition-bearer and keeper of genealogies. Although television has quelled conversation and the quality of social intercourse enshrined in the *ceilidhs* of the past it has not made island life materially easier. Paradoxically, it transmits images from a society where shops and supermarkets are just round the corner and discount stores within the reach of all, to islanders who are hundreds of miles away from the source of these supplies. A crofter's wife on Scalpay might be tempted by some astonishing carpet offer in Aberdeen but getting there could cost her two days' travel and twice her week's housekeeping.

Most of the consumer durables seen nightly on TV exist, if at all, only in Stornoway. Even there the variety of fruit and vegetables, the cuts of meat, the groceries, present only a fraction of the choice available to a city dweller. Living in the islands is abnormally expensive and for anyone used to tubes and trains getting about can be abnormally trying. Boats sometimes don't come, ferries can't make a crossing because of rough weather, planes are diverted. There are often weeks on end when gales and ferocious rain make working the land or launching a boat out of the question.

Even when the weather is good moving from one island to another can present more of a challenge than anything facing you when you arrive.

Doctors, nurses, council officials, advisors and teachers are constantly on the move and a great deal of time is wasted physically getting about – and frequently hanging about. Sometimes a whole morning is spent travelling to achieve just a few minutes' work.

One morning I was catching the ferry from Barra to South Uist. You can see the *Very Likely* coming a long way off with a white wave lathering its bow. As soon as it touched alongside the slip at Eoligarry a young man in oilskins leapt ashore with a black bag and sprinted up to a waiting truck which careered off up the road.

'That's the vet', said Donald Campbell the boatman, 'going to see a bull.' After about 15 minutes the truck roared back, the vet ran down the slip and we were off back on the 30-minute trip to Ludag. David Buckland, like many another member of the professional classes in the Western Isles, is English. 'Like all good *Sasunnachs* I went to Gaelic evening classes but I really do everything in English.' That morning he had left his home at Drimisdale near Loch Druidibeg at 7.45 – 35 miles by car, 12 miles in a boat for one call. The rest of the day would be spent travelling too, visiting sick cows and ailing sheep.

There is never a shortage of adequately qualified applicants when a job for a vet or a surveyor or an architect is advertised; the number of men and women who want a taste of island life is unlimited. 'It calls for a great deal of patience,' a GP from the south told me, 'time is very elastic, you measure things not by the minute but by the hour but you soon adapt to the rhythm of life. No, its not *highly* stressful. Boring? Some people would be bored, I can see that, but then they would have to be totally lacking in inner resources and blind in both eyes – just look at that view!'

I had my ear bent at great length by incomers who have taken raptuously to life in crofting townships and found that it is richly rewarding. An artist who had settled among a group of crofter-fishermen described in rich and comic detail the interaction of his culture with theirs. The man was a natural wit and storyteller and I happened to have my pocket recording machine on while he told me about his hilarious efforts to rent and then buy a house.

A week later he wrote to me. 'I hope I amused you. My story was more-or-less true but it is most emphatically not for publication. Use it, adapt it if you will in parts to amuse your readers, but please do not attribute it to me. I have grown to love and respect my island neighbours and I hope that they have grown to love and respect me. I ask you please not to attribute to me any words of disparagement.' And neither will I.

Mostly incomers talked of the sunsets, the joy of living in an area where acid rain was not being created, where the air was unpolluted, where corncrakes still nested and where there was an endless panorama of sea and cloud. All very romantic but even as I made my journey the islands were facing critical days; bankruptcy was in the air; disillusion too.

The heady early years of Comhairle nan Eilean have been snuffed out by the deepening national recession and the arithmetic of monetarism – communities with little or no economic or commercial contribution to make command very little sympathy in Whitehall. After ten years of effort the Western Isles found itself financially kneecapped, the victim of what they have described as 'benign indifference' on the part of central government. They claim they are 'a special case' entitled to *Ceartas* which might be loosely translated as 'justice'.

Comhairle inherited generations of neglect and under-provision. The two councils which had been charged with responsibility for running the Outer Hebrides up to 1975 had held them in low esteem. The islands were running down, the population was declining and growing older by the year; it was an area of deprivation unparalleled, Comhairle claim, in any other part of the country.

A third of the housing was below acceptable standards, the network of 700 miles of roads was almost entirely single-track; there was only one sheltered housing complex for old people and no provision at all for the mentally handicapped. There were townships with no piped water supply and no access roads; social services were unbelievably inadequate and many children were attending primary schools which had neither running water nor lavatories.

Not unnaturally, one of the first tasks the new Council set itself was to try and bring the standard of living in the islands a little closer to the national norm. In ten years they spent over £81 million. Roads, piers and ferries were improved; a home for the elderly was opened in North Uist, a complex for the mentally handicapped and another home for old people in Stornoway. Over a thousand houses were renovated; 780 council houses were built and 140 sheltered houses. In Barra there was a new secondary community school. Contractors grew rich. But even so the Western Isles remains the only council in Scotland with no nursery school and it spends less per head than any other Scottish council on schools and on leisure, recreation and libraries.

In March 1984 Comhairle was told that they would only get £34,000 extra cash for the forthcoming financial year. 'That is just enough', said Convenor Sandy Matheson, 'to cover two days' unexpected snow. If we were an industry we would have to close at this point.' As the biggest employer in the islands one-third of the Council's revenue goes on wages and an almost equal amount vanishes on interest charges on money borrowed in the big years of spending.

The auguries are not propitious. None of the huge sums spent by the military enriches the community directly; the sporting estates are productive only in menial and undemanding employment. As I write it looks as if future capital expenditure will have to be mothballed. With the lowest rating base in Scotland Comhairle nan Eilean, which receives 85 per cent of its income from the Exchequer is the most vulnerable local authority in Britain. Even with substantial help from the HIDB and the Integrated Development Programme, introduced when the Western Isles was accurately diagnosed as the most deprived area in the United Kingdom, the islands are in crisis.

Because they are so remote from the power bases of Edinburgh and more importantly Westminster – it is as far from London to the Comhairle council chamber in Stornoway as it is to the frontiers of Italy, Czechoslovakia and Austria – the dilemma of the islanders seldom makes the news pages. I am sometimes tempted to believe that readers of quality papers know more about the problems of the people of Bangladesh than the people of Barra.

The attitude of the media tends to be based on the mistaken assumption that intellect diminishes sharply in proportion to your distance from Shepherd's Bush. A few months after I completed my trip I was watching early morning television. A reporter had been sent in the summer to the Outer Hebrides to gather a series of anodyne reports. She was enthusing about the scenery and how nice the crofters were and how she liked the smell of the peat. During the course of her adventures she had interviewed a crofter who suggested that sporting estates like Morsgail would be better divided into 200 acre plots and given to crofters. The male presenter nodded approvingly and said with surprise, much as he might give a pat on the back to a pigmy, 'Such charming people – and they argue so intelligently too!'

On the few occasions when a national television network takes a look at the Western Isles it usually homes in on the quaint and the eccentric or aspects of the scenery which might be of interest to those looking for a peaceful holiday. Indeed were you to live in the Western Isles you might be justified in believing that Caledonian MacBrayne schedules its services more with tourists in mind than residents. In the summer when Barra folk are busy at the fishing and on the land there is a boat from Castlebay to Oban four days a week; in the winter when the islanders have more time for travel the service is cut to three days a week.

In many other ways the needs of the islanders are not always given their due priority by central planners; in a time of recession those on the periphery are the first to be sacrificed. However unquenchable their spirit and however fervent their desire to continue living where their roots are their plight is of minimal political or emotional concern.

It is difficult for someone living in the Western Isles to appreciate that although there may be £40 million available to convert Stornoway into a military base a school has to close in a remote township for lack of money to pay a teacher. Difficult too in a country currently spending £42.5 million a day on national defence to be told that a few hundred pounds is not available to defend a community's right to a nurse. There must be bewilderment too in Benbecula where millions of pounds are spent every year firing missiles when small sums of money cannot be found to surface a road to a clachan where two old people are living.

Whether the culture and heritage of these parts is considered worth preserving or whether yet more islands on the edge of survival should be run down and evacuated in the interest of economy is a question almost entirely of political priorities. It has not passed without comment that huge sums of money have been dispensed in recent years to keep a small and alien British community in the South Atlantic for purely political considerations. Although the Falkland Islands were considered worth fighting for, the presence of a thriving population on the Western Isles is not seen to be equally vital to the national interest.

If their heritage and their way of life is worth preserving, and nobody who has been there in recent years could doubt it, then they are, as they claim, a special case and they are entitled to the sums of money appropriate to keep that way of life at something a little more generous than subsistence level.

It would be sad, though, if such help took the form of keeping the islands on an economic life-support system which would be at risk every time the economy plunged into crisis. Despite all attempts to generate new jobs and productivity, the Western Isles is a very poor financial investment. Deep drilling for oil in western waters is a possibility for the future but even if it is as profitable as some experts predict it may well be that very little of the spin-off will find its way into the islands.

For generations now children have been encouraged by ambitious parents to follow the path that leads to further education and lucrative employment on the mainland. A recent report by the Arkleton Trust, a body which specialises in examining the social and commercial opportunities of remote rural areas, questioned whether such ambitions were not calculated to undermine the stability of the islands. Indigenous resources and the opportunity for local employment were being dangerously neglected in favour of educating children away from their own community and its traditional values. It is a contentious thesis. I found strong evidence that no one with entrepreneurial skill and a workable proposition ever failed to get support from the various bodies empowered to assist economic development. On the other hand the pressures to leave a township are frequently stronger than the attractions of remaining.

Perhaps in the end the future of the Western Isles depends on the survival of Gaelic. Without the language, its rich associations, its reminders of an almost distintegrated past, the anglicisation of Scotland will be complete. Writing in 1968 in his preface to *The Future of the Highlands* (RKP), Ian Grimble likened the fate of the Gael to the Lapps:

> Just as the Lapps retreated north through Scandinavia until they reached the rim of the Arctic and could go no farther, so the Gaels in Scotland have reached the peripheries of the Atlantic and remain there as a protected species, their affairs ordered for them by strangers with scarcely any reference to their wishes or requirements.

Since 1975 the islanders have more say in the way their limited resources are spent than ever before but they still rely on central government to determine their capacity to spend. Possibly the only thing which the people can still determine with no outside interference at all is their personal commitment to the Gaelic language. Comhairle itself spent £383,000 between 1982 and 1984 on fostering Gaelic culture. The Montgomery Report – the Committee of Inquiry into the Functions and Powers of the Islands Council of Scotland – called in 1984 for the government to examine what action would be required in the coming years to maintain and support the Gaelic language and culture.

But propping a decaying fabric up from outside presents a dilemma which was put very concisely by Father Colin MacInnes, who left Barra in 1985 for mission work in Ecuador. During his time on the island he had been instrumental in organising an annual *Feis* or festival of Gaelic to encourage young people to learn about and cherish their inheritance. He was asked how he felt about the future by the *Free Press*.

'Gaelic', he said, 'will die if initiatives are not taken to enable it to survive. We should accept that fact. Do we want Gaelic to die? If we don't we will need to do more about it. If communities, islands, individuals, don't make that commitment, anything that is done nationally or internationally will be completely ineffectual.'

And there is little more to be said.

Just perhaps one more thing, a wry footnote to my expedition in search of Mingulay of the Boat Song. A few weeks after I had come back from Barra the phone rang. It was Sir Hugh Roberton's son Kenneth. 'You won't remember me,' he said, 'it's ages since we met.' I remembered it very well; it was in 1939 in Skye and he had come up from Glasgow to Portree to visit my great aunt. We talked of this and that; he told me that he had inherited his father's musical archive and had indeed edited an anthology about the famous Glasgow choir – *Orpheus With His Lute.*

It wasn't until he rang off that I realised that I had asked him nothing about that famous *Mingulay Boat Song.* So I wrote him a note asking if I could have the Gaelic and English words. A few days later I got his reply: 'As you will see from the enclosed material you are in deep trouble about *Mingulay Boat Song.* On behalf of my father I apologise for bringing this about.'

Kenneth went on to explain that his father had very much liked an air which accompanied some verses by one of the old hunter bards of Lochaber. The song and the words had celebrated a crag near Loch Treig known as Creag Ghuanach. At that time Hugh Roberton was in need of a sea shanty and he took the music, adapted it for the choir, felt that the romantically tri-syllabic Ming-u-lay would sound well and wrote the *Mingulay Boat Song* to be sung in the key of F 'boldly with a big rhythmic sweep.'

'From your long ago journeys on the West Highland Railway', wrote Hugh, 'you will remember Loch Treig I'm sure. I recall it as remote and very beautiful. It is a far cry from Lochaber to Mingulay and I hope you will be able to cobble something without wrecking your book entirely.'

And so my vision of the men of Mingulay straining at the oars and singing into the wind as they pulled past Sandray and Pabbay for their island home was laid to rest. But I forgive Hugh Roberton – if it weren't for him I doubt if I'd have written this book.

> Hill you ho, boys; Let her go, boys;
> Bring her head round, now all together.
> Hill you ho, boys; Let her go, boys;
> Sailing home, home to Ming-u-lay.*

*Words by Hugh Roberton reprinted by permission of the Hugh S. Roberton Trust and Roberton Publications.

FACTS AND MAPS

Some of the following facts reveal the scale of effort, enterprise and financial cost involved in keeping a population of 31,500 in the 10 inhabited islands. I am grateful to Roderick Smith and John Cunningham of the Nicolson Institute who compiled the bulk of the statistics for this book.

Area 716,800 acres (290,202 hectares or 1,119 square miles). Area of principal islands in hectares:

Lewis	163,665
Harris	49,031
North Uist	30,559
Benbecula	7,458
South Uist	29,002
Berneray	1,050
Barra	8,993

Climate Mean summer temperatures range from 12.78°C (55° F) in the north to 13.89°C (57°) in the south.

Mean winter temperatures range from 5°C (41°F) to 5.56°C (42°F).

Rainfall varies from 40 to 60 inches a year rising to 80 inches on the hills of Harris. The long-term average for sunshine in May in Stornoway is 195 hours. Winds frequently reach hurricane force. In exposed parts gusts of 130 m.p.h. have been recorded. At the Butt of Lewis gales are recorded on average for 60 days of the year; the first landfall to the west is Labrador 2,250 miles away.

Population

Lewis	20,743
Harris	2,025
Scalpay	456
Berneray	132
North Uist	1,663
South Uist	2,234
Benbecula	1,857
Eriskay	197
Barra	1,518
Vatersay	80

In this century, St Kilda, Haskeir, Pabbay, Mingulay, Scarp and Taransay have all been evacuated. Taransay was last inhabited in 1974.

Age breakdown

Age Group	0–4	5–15	16–24	25–44	45–65	65+	75+
Britain	6	16.3	14.1	26.3	19.7	17.7	5.7
Western Isles	6.6	18.5	12.3	22.8	18.4	21.5	8.1

Language   79.5 per cent of the population speak Gaelic, an improvement over the last decade of 1.9 per cent in which Gaelic abilities increased amongst school-aged and young adult groups. The areas in which Gaelic speakers have increased numerically since the 1971 census were the civil parishes of Barra, South Uist and Stornoway.

Comhairle nan Eilean employs 2,170 people of whom 518 are in executive positions; 448 are non-manual and 1,204 are manual.

Four department heads speak Gaelic; six do not.

Between 1975 and 1984 the Council spent £81,349,550 on education, roads, transport, water and sewerage, social work, housing and general services. Rateable Value: £4,267,000.

The Western Isles has 426 miles of classified highroad, 299 miles of unclassified roads; 60 cemeteries; 5 baths and pools; 1 central library, 2 branch libraries and 4 mobile libraries; there is one park in Stornoway.

Highlands and Islands Development Board In the 10-year period 1974–83 the Board assisted 830 cases with grant and loan, totalling £23.9 million. This created 2,219 jobs and helped retain a further 1,090 jobs. In 1983 the Board approved £4.5 million in grant and loan assistance for 246 cases.

Unemployment

Western Isles (%)		Scotland (%)	Great Britain (%)
males	24.8	18.5	15.89
females	11.6	11.4	10.29

Education There are 532 teachers – 332 in Lewis, 47 in Harris, 41 in North Uist, 82 in Benbecula, and South Uist and Eriskay and 30 in Barra including Vatersay.
There are 71 schools – 29 in Lewis, 8 in Harris, 8 in North Uist, 10 in Benbecula, South Uist and Eriskay and 5 in Barra and Vatersay.
Pupils in primary school:

Lewis	2,019
Harris	181
North Uist	175
South Uist and Benbecula	564
Barra	185

Pupils in secondary school:

Lewis	1,917
Harris	175
North Uist	149
South Uist and Benbecula	352
Barra	160

Total number at school 6,318.

Health There are 4 hospitals; 2 in Stornoway, 1 in Lochmaddy, 1 in Daliburgh, and in Barra there is a medical unit run jointly by the Health Board and the Social Work Department.

Annual running costs are £2.4 million and a further £266,000 is spent on medicine.

Staff: There are 27 GPs and 11 hospital doctors of whom only 3 can converse with their patients in Gaelic.

There are 3 veterinary practices, one based in Stornoway covering Lewis and Harris, one in North Uist and one in South Uist.

Religion There are 54 clergymen.

Church of Scotland	21
Free Church	17
Free Presbyterian	7
Roman Catholics	8
Episcopal	1

Housing There are 12,663 houses of which 2,440 are council owned. On Benbecula there are a further 258 houses owned by the Ministry of Defence.

2,000 of the houses in the Western Isles are still in a sub-standard condition and 2,000 people are estimated to be on the council house waiting list.

Agriculture The Secretary of State owns 47,000 acres in Harris, Uist and Barra. Much of the rest of the land is privately owned.

Number of crofts: Lewis 3,601; Harris 556; North Uist 465; South Uist 911; Barra 438. Total in the Western Isles: 5,971.

The average age of new tenants obtaining crofts is 41; the average age of people inheriting crofts is 51.

Livestock: Sheep: 310,000. Cattle: 9,500.

Only 14,500 hectares (5 per cent of the total land area) is under cultivation.

Fishing There are 383 full-time fishermen; 86 part-time and 120 workers connected with ancillary services. There are 20 salmon farms employing between 70 and 80 people. Total value of fish caught in the last recorded year was £3,580,000.

Seaweed There are two seaweed drying plants. Keose employs 6 full-time workers and 10 part-time cutters. Lochmaddy employs 20 full-time workers and a number of cutters. Total output of alginate per year is between 4,000 and 5,000 tonnes.

Tweed There are 698 weavers in Lewis and Harris and 2 in the Uists. The 700 looms produce 4.5 million yards a year. Payment to weavers puts £90,000 a week into the Lewis economy.

Tourism There are 34 registered hotels and guesthouses, 43 self-catering units, 4 camp sites and over 100 private individuals doing bed and breakfast.

Crafts There are 36 enterprises involved in the sale of woodcraft, stoneware, knitwear, paintings, macramé, candles, domestic earthenware, handspun wool, ceramic figures, pottery, watercolours, acrylic paintings, table mats, sporrans, paperweights, flower crafts, sealskin items, walking sticks, scarves, hose, mitts, sweaters, slippers, floor rugs, jewellery, hand-painted stones, shell mosaic pictures, perfumes, aftershave, and for all I know tartan plastic gnomes.

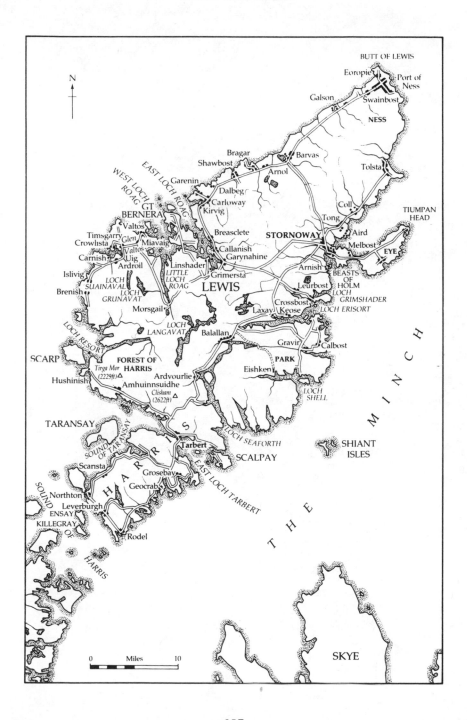

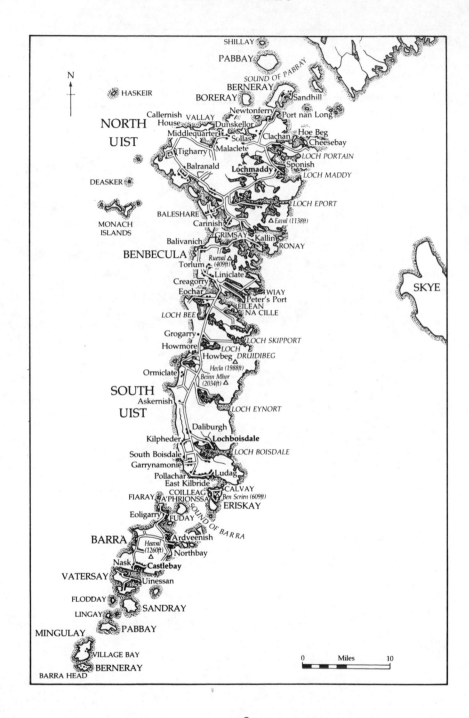

INDEX